STUDY GUIDES

General Editors: John Peck and Martin Coyle

PALGRAVE STUDY GUIDES SERIES LIST

Palgrave Study Guides

A Handbook of Writing for Engineers *Joan van Emden*
Effective Communication for Science and Technology *Joan van Emden*
How to Write Better Essays *Bryan Greetham*
Key Concepts in Politics *Andrew Heywood*
Linguistic Terms and Concepts *Geoffrey Finch*
Literary Terms and Criticism (second edition) *John Peck and
    Martin Coyle*
The Mature Student's Guide to Writing *Jean Rose*
The Postgraduate Research Handbook *Gina Wisker*
Practical Criticism *John Peck and Martin Coyle*
Research Using IT *Hilary Coombes*
The Student's Guide to Writing *John Peck and Martin Coyle*
The Study Skills Handbook *Stella Cottrell*
Studying Economics *Brian Atkinson and Susan Johns*
Studying History (second edition) *Jeremy Black and Donald M. MacRaild*
Studying Mathematics and its Applications *Peter Kahn*
Studying Psychology *Andrew Stevenson*
Teaching Study Skills and Supporting Learning *Stella Cottrell*

How to Begin Studying English Literature (second edition)
    Nicholas Marsh
How to Study a Jane Austen Novel (second edition) *Vivien Jones*
How to Study Chaucer (second edition) *Rob Pope*
How to Study a Charles Dickens Novel *Keith Selby*
How to Study Foreign Languages *Marilyn Lewis*
How to Study an E. M. Forster Novel *Nigel Messenger*
How to Study a Thomas Hardy Novel *John Peck*
How to Study James Joyce *John Blades*
How to Study Linguistics *Geoffrey Finch*
How to Study Modern Drama *Tony Curtis*
How to Study Modern Poetry *Tony Curtis*
How to Study a Novel (second edition) *John Peck*
How to Study a Poet (second edition) *John Peck*
How to Study a Renaissance Play *Chris Coles*
How to Study Romantic Poetry (second edition) *Paul O'Flinn*
How to Study a Shakespeare Play (second edition) *John Peck and
    Martin Coyle*
                            ith Selby and Ron Cowdery

                    m

KEY CONCEPTS IN POLITICS

Andrew Heywood

palgrave

Published by
PALGRAVE
Houndmills, Basingstoke, Hampshire RG21 6XS and
175 Fifth Avenue, New York, N. Y. 10010
Companies and representatives throughout the world

PALGRAVE is the new global academic imprint of
St. Martin's Press LLC Scholarly and Reference Division and
Palgrave Publishers Ltd (formerly Macmillan Press Ltd).

Outside North America
ISBN 0–333–77095–1

Inside North America
ISBN 0–312–23381–7

This book is printed on paper suitable for recycling and
made from fully managed and sustained forest sources.

A catalogue record for this book is available
from the British Library.

Cataloging-in-Publication data is available from the Library of Congress

10   9   8   7   6   5   4   3
09 08 07 06 05 04 03 02

Typeset in great Britain by
Aarontype Ltd, Easton, Bristol

Printed and bound in Great Britain by
Creative Print & Design (Wales), Ebbw Vale

CONTENTS

1 **Uses and Abuses of Political Concepts**   **1**
  Introduction   3
  What is a concept?   4
  Normative and descriptive concepts   5
  Contested concepts   6
  Words and things   7
  How to use this book   8
  Further reading   10

2 **Basic Concepts**   **13**
  Authority   15
  Civil society   17
  Consensus   18
  Government/Governance   19
  Human nature   21
  Ideology   22
  Law   24
  Left/Right   27
  Legitimacy   29
  Order   30
  Policy   31
  Politics   33
  Power   35
  Sovereignty   37
  State   39
  Further reading   42

3 **Ideologies**   **43**
  Anarchism   45
  Christian democracy   47
  Communism   48
  Communitarianism   51
  Conservatism   52
  Ecologism   55

Fascism   56
Feminism   58
Liberalism   60
Libertarianism   62
Marxism   63
Nazism   65
New Left   67
New Right   68
Racialism/Racism   70
Religious fundamentalism   71
Social democracy   73
Socialism   75
Third way   78
Toryism   79
Further reading   80

4 **Approaches**   **83**
Behaviouralism   85
Dialectic   86
Discourse   87
Empiricism   88
Functionalism   89
Historical materialism   90
Idealism   91
Institutionalism   93
Political philosophy   94
Political science   96
Political theory   98
Positivism   100
Postmodernism   101
Rational choice   102
Rationalism   104
Realism   105
Systems theory   107
Utilitarianism   109
Utopianism   110
Further reading   112

5 **Values**   **115**
Accountability   117
Autonomy   118

Citizenship	119
Civil liberty	120
Collectivism	121
Community	122
Consent	123
Constitutionalism	124
Democracy	125
Equality	128
Freedom	129
Human rights	131
Individualism	133
Justice	134
Leadership	136
Meritocracy	138
Neutrality	139
Obligation	140
Property	141
Representation	143
Responsibility	145
Rights	147
Toleration	149
Tradition	150
Welfare	151
Further reading	153
6 Systems	**155**
Absolutism	157
Authoritarianism	158
Capitalism	159
Collectivisation	162
Consociationalism	162
Corporatism	164
Dictatorship	166
Elitism	167
Liberal democracy	169
Militarism	170
Parliamentary government	172
Patriarchy	174
Pluralism	175
Populism	178
Presidential government	179

Republicanism 181
Revolution 182
Totalitarianism 184
Further reading 185

7 Structures **187**
Bicameralism 189
Bill of rights 190
Bureaucracy 191
Cabinet 193
Coalition 194
Committee 195
Constitution 196
Election 199
Executive 201
Gender 204
Hegemony 205
Judiciary 206
Mandate 208
Market 209
Mass media 210
Monarchy 211
Opposition 213
Parliament 214
Political culture 216
Political party 218
President 220
Pressure group 222
Prime minister 224
Race/Ethnicity 226
Referendum 227
Separation of powers 229
Social class 230
Social movement 232
Further reading 234

8 Levels **235**
Centralisation/Decentralisation 237
Devolution 238
Federalism 240
Globalisation 243

Imperialism   245
Intergovernmentalism   246
Internationalism   248
Local government   249
Nation   251
Nation-state   252
Nationalism   254
Patriotism   256
Regionalism   257
Subsidiarity   258
Supranationalism   259
Further reading   261

Glossary of Key Political Thinkers   262

Bibliography   269

Index   276

Part one

USES AND ABUSES OF POLITICAL CONCEPTS

Uses and Abuses of Political Concepts

Introduction

Concepts have a particular importance for students of politics. It is no exaggeration to suggest that political argument often boils down to a struggle over the legitimate meaning of terms. Enemies may argue, fight and even go to war, each claiming to be 'defending freedom', 'upholding democracy' or 'supporting justice'. The problem is that words such as 'freedom', 'democracy' and 'justice' have different meanings to different people, so that the concepts themselves come to seem problematic.

At least three reasons can be suggested to explain the unusual importance of concepts in political analysis. The first is that political analysis typically deals in generalisations. The significance of this can be highlighted by considering differences between politics and history in this respect. Whereas a historian is likely to want to make sense of a particular event (say, the French Revolution, the Russian Revolution or the Eastern European Revolutions of 1989–91), a political analyst is more likely to study such events with a view to making sense of a larger or more general phenomenon, in this case the phenomenon of revolution. For historians a special study of the concept of 'revolution' is of marginal value, because what they are primarily interested in is what is different, even unique, about a particular set of events. For political analysts, on the other hand, a study of the concept of 'revolution' is not only necessary – it is the very process through which political enquiry proceeds.

The second reason is that the language used by students of politics is largely the same as that used by practitioners of politics, and particularly by professional politicians. As the latter are primarily interested in political advocacy rather than political understanding, they have a strong incentive to use language to manipulate and sometimes confuse. This, in turn, forces students of politics to be especially careful in their use of language. They must define terms clearly and refine concepts with precision in order to safeguard them from the misrepresentations often current in everyday political debate.

The final reason is that political concepts are frequently entwined with ideological beliefs. Since the emergence of modern political ideologies in the late eighteenth and early nineteenth centuries, not only has a new language of political discourse emerged, but the terms and concepts of political debate have also been imbued with complex and often conflicting meanings. Political concepts are therefore particularly challenging creatures: they are often ambiguous and not infrequently the subject of rivalry and debate, and they may come 'loaded' with value judgements and ideological implications of which their users may be unaware.

WHAT IS A CONCEPT?

A concept is a general idea about something, usually expressed in a single word or a short phrase. A concept is more than a proper noun or the name of a thing. There is, for example, a difference between talking about a cat (a particular and unique cat) and having a concept of a 'cat' (the idea of a cat). The concept of a cat is not a 'thing' but an 'idea', an idea composed of the various attributes that give a cat its distinctive character: 'a furry mammal', 'small', 'domesticated', 'catches rats and mice' and so on. In the same way the concept of 'presidency' refers not to any specific president, but rather to a set of ideas about the organisation of executive power. Concepts are therefore 'general' in the sense that they can refer to a number of objects, indeed to any object that complies with the general idea itself.

What, then, is the value of concepts? Concept formation is an essential step in the process of reasoning. Concepts are the 'tools' with which we think, criticise, argue, explain and analyse. Merely perceiving the external world does not in itself give us knowledge about it. In order to make sense of the world we must, in a sense, impose meaning upon it, and we do this through the construction of concepts. Quite simply, to treat a cat as a cat, we must first have a concept of what it is. Precisely the same applies to the process of political reasoning: we build up our knowledge of the political world not simply by looking at it, but through developing and refining concepts which will help us make sense of it. Concepts, in

that sense, are the building blocks of human knowledge. Nevertheless, concepts can also be slippery customers, and this is particularly
the case in relation to political concepts. Amongst the problems
posed by political concepts are that they are often value-laden,
that their meanings may be the subject of argument and debate,
and that they are sometimes invested with greater substance and
significance than they actually possess.

NORMATIVE AND DESCRIPTIVE CONCEPTS

Normative concepts are often described as 'values'; they refer to
moral principles or ideals, that which *should, ought* or *must* be brought
about. A wide range of political concepts are value-laden in this
sense – 'liberty', 'rights', 'justice', 'equality', 'tolerance', and so on.
Values or normative concepts therefore advance or prescribe certain
forms of conduct rather than describe events or facts. Consequently,
it is sometimes difficult to disentangle political values from the
moral, philosophical and ideological beliefs of those who advance
them. By contrast, descriptive or positive concepts refer to 'facts'
which supposedly have an objective and demonstrable existence:
they refer to what *is*. Concepts such as 'power', 'authority', 'order'
and 'law' are in this sense descriptive rather than normative. It is
possible to ask whether they exist or do not exist.

The distinction between facts and values is often regarded as a
necessary precondition for clear thinking. Whereas values may be
regarded as a matter of opinion, facts can be proved to be either
true or false. As a result, descriptive concepts are thought to be 'neutral' or value-free: they stand up to the rigour of scientific examination. Indeed, under the influence of positivism, the pressure to
develop a science of politics meant that in the middle decades of the
twentieth century normative concepts were often discarded as
'metaphysical' and therefore nonsense. However, the problem with
political concepts is that facts and values are invariably interlinked,
even apparently descriptive concepts being 'loaded' with a set of
moral and ideological implications. This can be seen, for instance,
in the case of 'authority'. If authority is defined as 'the right to influence the behaviour of others', it is certainly possible to use the concept descriptively to say who possesses authority and who does not,
and to examine the basis upon which it is exercised. However, it is
impossible completely to divorce the concept from value judgements

about when, how and why authority *should* be exercised. In short, no one is neutral about authority. For example, whereas conservatives, who emphasise the need for order to be imposed from above, tend to regard authority as rightful and healthy, anarchists, who believe government and law to be evil, invariably see authority as nakedly oppressive. All political concepts, descriptive as well as normative, need therefore to be understood in the light of the ideological perspectives of those who use them.

One response to the value-laden character of political concepts that has been particularly influential since the late twentieth century has been the movement to insist upon 'political correctness' in the use of language. Political correctness, sometimes simply known as PC, has been advocated by feminists, civil rights activists and representatives of minority groups generally, who wish to purge language of racist, sexist and other derogatory or disparaging implications. It is based upon the belief that language invariably reflects the power structure in society at large, and so discriminates in favour of dominant groups and against subordinate ones. Obvious examples include the use of 'Man' or 'mankind' to refer to the human race, references to ethnic minorities as 'negroes' or 'coloureds', and the description of developing world countries as 'third world' or 'underdeveloped' (although 'developing world' is also attacked for implying that the Western model of development is applicable throughout the world). The goal of political correctness is to develop bias-free terminology that enables political argument to be conducted in non-discriminatory language. The difficulty with this position, however, is that the hope of an unbiased and objective language of political discourse is illusory. At best, 'negative' terms can be replaced by 'positive' ones; for example, the 'disabled' can be referred to as the 'differently abled', and 'negroes' can be described as 'black'. Critics of political correctness argue, moreover, that it imposes an ideological straitjacket upon language that both impoverishes its descriptive power and denies expression to 'incorrect' views.

CONTESTED CONCEPTS

A further problem is that political concepts often become the subject of intellectual and ideological controversy. It is not uncommon, as pointed out above, for political argument to take place between people who claim to uphold the same principle or the same ideal.

Conceptual disagreement is therefore one of the battlegrounds of politics itself. This is reflected in attempts to establish a particular conception of a concept as objectively correct, as in the case of 'true' democracy, 'true' freedom, 'true' justice and so forth. A way out of this dilemma was suggested by W. B. Gallie (1955–6), who suggested that in the case of concepts such as 'power', 'justice' and 'freedom' controversy runs so deep that no neutral or settled definition can ever be developed. These concepts should be recognised, he argued, as 'essentially contested concepts'. In effect, each term encompasses a number of rival concepts, none of which can be accepted as its 'true' meaning. To acknowledge that a concept is 'essentially contested' is not, however, to abandon the attempt to understand it, but rather to recognise that competing versions of the concept may be equally valid.

The notion that most, if not all, concepts are many-faced or 'essentially contested' has nevertheless been subject to criticism, particularly by Terence Ball (1988). Two lines of argument have been advanced. The first notes that many theorists who attempt to apply Gallie's insights (as, for example, Lukes (1974) in relation to 'power') continue to defend their preferred interpretation of a concept against its rivals. This refusal to accept that all versions of the concept are equally valid produces on-going debate and argument which could, at some stage in the future, lead to the emergence of a single, agreed concept. In other words, no concept is 'essentially' contested in the sense that rivalry and disagreement are fundamental to its nature. The second line of argument points out that Gallie's analysis is ahistorical. Certain concepts are now contested which were once the subject of widespread agreement. It is notable, for instance, that the wide-ranging and deep disagreement that currently surrounds 'democracy' only emerged from the late eighteenth century onwards alongside new forms of ideological thinking. As a result, it is perhaps better to treat contested concepts as 'currently' contested (Birch, 1993) or as 'contingently' contested (Ball, 1997).

WORDS AND THINGS

A final problem with concepts is what can be called the fetishism of concepts. This occurs when concepts are treated as though they have a concrete existence separate from and, in some senses, holding sway over, the human beings who use them. In short, words are treated as things, rather than as devices for understanding things. Max Weber (1864–1920) attempted to deal with this problem by classifying particular concepts as 'ideal types'. An ideal type is a mental construct in which an attempt is made to draw out meaning from an otherwise almost infinitely complex reality through the presentation of a logical extreme. Ideal types are thus explanatory tools, not approximations of reality; they neither 'exhaust reality' nor offer an ethical ideal. Concepts such as 'democracy', 'human rights' and capitalism' are thus more rounded and coherent than the unshapely realities they seek to describe. Weber himself treated 'authority' and 'bureaucracy' as ideal types. The importance of recognising particular concepts as ideal types is that it underlines the fact that concepts are only analytical tools. For this reason it is better to think of concepts or ideal types not as being 'true' or 'false', but merely as more or less 'useful'.

Further attempts to emphasise the contingent nature of political concepts have been undertaken by so-called postmodern theorists. They have attacked the 'traditional' search for universal values acceptable to everyone on the grounds that this assumes that there is a moral and rational high point from which all values and claims to knowledge can be judged. The fact that fundamental disagreement persists about the location of this high point suggests that there is a plurality of legitimate ethical and political positions, and that our language and political concepts are valid only in terms of the context in which they are generated and employed. However, perhaps the most radical critique of concepts is developed in the philosophy of Mahayana Buddhism. This distinguishes between 'conventional' truth, which constitutes nothing more than a literary convention in that it is based upon a willingness amongst people to use concepts in a particular way, and 'absolute' truth, which involves the penetration of reality through direct experience and so transcends conceptualisation. In this view, thinking of all kinds amounts to a projection imposed upon reality, and therefore constitutes a form of delusion. If we mistake words for things we are in danger, as the Zen saying puts it, of mistaking the finger pointing at the moon for the moon itself.

How to Use this Book

This book aims to provide students with an introduction to the main concepts encountered in political analysis. Each concept is discussed in two parts. The first part considers definitions: it examines the most important meanings and usages of the concept in question, as well as where and how it has been applied. In the case of contested concepts, or concepts whose meanings change in different contexts, this is indicated by the use of italics. The second part of the discussion, entitled *Significance*, explores the wider importance of the concept in building up political understanding. It examines matters such as the origins and development of the concept, and historical, ideological and other factors that have affected its role and status. By no means, however, is the discussion intended to be exhaustive. Students should be able to acquire from this book a working knowledge of the meanings, usages and applications of concepts, but for more detailed coverage and more thorough explanation they are encouraged to consult the suggestions for further reading that appear at the end of each section.

The concepts are organised in alphabetical order within seven sections – Basic concepts, Ideologies, Approaches, Values, Systems, Structures and Levels. This is intended both to draw attention to the general character and function of a concept and to facilitate comparisons and contrasts between concepts that have similar characters and functions. The general emphasis of each section is as follows:

- **Basic concepts** considers core concepts that deal with the nature of politics and the parameters of political analysis.
- **Ideologies** considers concepts that represent broad traditions of political thought and, often, offer particular perspectives on political understanding.
- **Approaches** considers concepts that deal with how politics is studied and how political understanding is acquired.
- **Values** considers concepts that are normative principles or political ideals; in many cases these are the building-blocks of ideological traditions.
- **Systems** considers concepts that refer to the organisation of political power, or the wider institutional arrangements of government.
- **Structures** considers concepts that stand for particular institutions or governmental bodies; these are often the component features of systems.
- **Levels** considers concepts that relate to the different geographical units of political rule and the levels at which political authority is, or should be, exercised.

Two reservations nevertheless need to be borne in mind about this way of organising political concepts. The first is that, although the categories may be useful in highlighting certain features of a concept, they may also be misleading. In particular, the divisions between the different sections are, at best, permeable. For instance, ideologies are also, in many cases, approaches; levels overlap to some degree with systems; and both systems and structures are invariably entangled with values. The second problem follows naturally from the first. It is that location of particular concepts within the sections is sometimes debatable and may, in the final analysis, be simply arbitrary. 'Communism' can legitimately be viewed as a value, an ideology and a system; 'democracy' is clearly both a value and a system; 'elitism' is here treated as a system, but might equally be regarded as a value or even an ideology. The list could go on. It is important, therefore, that students use the different sections as a (usually) useful guide, and do not take them to be rigid compartments that assign to each concept a one-dimensional character or function. Indeed, where such confusions and complexities exist, they are usually addressed in the discussion of the concept itself.

In order to facilitate cross-referencing and avoid unnecessary repetition, terms that are defined elsewhere in the book are indicated by an asterisk, on the first occasion they appear within the discussion of each concept. They can be located either via the Contents or by a page reference in **bold** in the Index. To ensure a consistent focus upon the meanings and significance of concepts, no information appears in the text on the major political thinkers referred to, except for their dates. However, a Glossary of Political Thinkers is provided at the end of the book that offers a brief introduction to their lives and ideas. Finally, works that are cited in the text are listed in the Bibliography; this does not, however, include works that are only referred to in the Glossary of Political Thinkers.

FURTHER READING

Ball, T., Farr, J. and Hanson, R. L. (eds), *Political Innovation and Conceptual Change* (Cambridge: Cambridge University Press, 1989).

Bellamy, R. (ed.), *Theories and Concepts of Politics: An Introduction* (Manchester and New York: Manchester University Press, 1993).

Birch, A. H., *The Concepts and Theories of Modern Democracy* (London and New York: Routledge, 1993).

Gallie, W. B., 'Essentially Contested Concepts', *Proceedings of the Aristotelian Society*, **56**, 1955/6, pp. 157–97.
Heywood, A., *Political Theory: An Introduction* (London: Macmillan, 1999).
Rorty, R. (ed.), *The Linguistic Turn* (Chicago: University of Chicago Press, 1967).
White, J. B., *When Words Lose Their Meaning* (Chicago: University of Chicago Press, 1984).
Williams, P., *Mahayana Buddhism* (London and New York: Routledge, 1989).

Part two

BASIC CONCEPTS

This section considers core concepts that deal with the nature of politics and the parameters of political analysis.

BASIC CONCEPTS

AUTHORITY

Authority, in its broadest sense, is a form of *power, sometimes thought of as 'legitimate power'. Whereas power is the ability to influence the behaviour of others, authority is the right to do so. Authority is therefore based upon an acknowledged duty to obey rather than any form of coercion or manipulation. In this sense, authority is power cloaked in *legitimacy or rightfulness. However, authority may be used as either a normative or a descriptive term. As a normative term, used by political philosophers, it refers to a 'right to rule' and takes the form of a moral claim. This implies that it is less important that authority *is* obeyed than that it *should be* obeyed. Leaders, for example, could in this sense continue to claim the right to rule, on the basis of election results, constitutional rules, divine right or whatever, even though the majority of the population does not recognise that right.

Political scientists and sociologists, on the other hand, treat authority as a descriptive term. Max Weber (1864–1920) thus defined authority simply as a matter of people's belief about its rightfulness, regardless of where that belief came from and whether or not it is morally justified. Authority, in this sense, is 'legitimate power'. Weber distinguished between three kinds of authority, based upon the different grounds on which obedience can be established. *Traditional authority*, in this sense, is rooted in history and tradition; *charismatic authority* stems from the power of personality; and *legal-rational authority* is grounded in a set of impersonal rules associated with an office rather than the office holder. An alternative distinction can be made between de jure authority and de facto authority. *De jure* authority, or authority in law, operates according to a set of procedures or rules which designate who possesses authority and over what issues. People described as being 'in authority' can be said to possess de jure authority: their 'powers' can be traced back to a particular office. Both traditional and legal-rational authority can therefore be viewed as forms of de jure authority. *De facto* authority, or authority in practice, operates in circumstances in which authority is exercised but cannot be traced back to a set of procedural rules. This includes all forms of charismatic authority, and also what is called expert authority, when a person is recognised as being 'an authority' by virtue of his or her specialist skills or knowledge.

Significance

Authority has been one of the most basic and enduring issues in political analysis. In a sense all studies of *government or the *state are really examinations of the nature and workings of political authority. Indeed, probably no system of rule could survive long without exercising some measure of authority, since to rule through power alone involves such a great expenditure of coercive resources as to be unsustainable. Nevertheless, there are recurrent debates about both the nature of authority and its value. Liberals and socialists tend to view authority as instrumental, believing that it arises 'from below' through the *consent of the governed. From this perspective, authority is rational, purposeful and limited, a view reflected in a preference for legal-rational authority and public *accountability. Conservatives, by contrast, see authority as arising from natural necessity, being exercised 'from above' by virtue of the unequal distribution of experience, social position and wisdom. Those who exercise authority do so for the benefit of others, but this does not set clear limits or checks upon authority, and it may blur the distinction between authority and *authoritarianism.

The justifications for authority include, most basically, that it is essential for the maintenance of *order and is thus the only means of escape from the barbarity and injustice of the 'state of nature', a society without political rule. Authority also establishes common norms and values that bind society together, and thereby gives individuals a social identity and sense of rootedness. Critics of authority, including, particularly, libertarians and anarchists, point out that authority is by definition the enemy of *freedom; that it threatens reason and critical understanding by demanding unquestioning obedience; and that it is psychologically, and perhaps morally, corrupting in that it accustoms people to controlling or dominating others.

CIVIL SOCIETY

Civil society has been defined in a variety of ways. Originally it meant a 'political community', a society governed by law, under the authority of a *state. More commonly, civil society is distinguished from the state, and is used to describe a realm of autonomous groups and associations, such as businesses, *pressure groups, clubs, families and so on. It thus consists of what Edmund Burke (1729–97) called the 'little platoons'. In this sense the division between civil society and the state reflects a 'private/public' divide; civil society encompasses institutions that are 'private' in that they are independent from government and organised by individuals in pursuit of their own ends. G. W. F. Hegel (1770–1831), on the other hand, distinguished civil society not only from the state but also from the family. He viewed civil society as a sphere of 'universal egoism' in which individuals place their own interests before those of others, whereas the state and the family are characterised by 'universal altruism' and 'particular altruism' respectively.

Significance

Civil society is widely used as a descriptive concept to assess the balance between state authority and private bodies and associations. For instance, *totalitarianism is defined by the abolition of civil society, and the growth of private associations and clubs, lobby groups and independent trade unions in post-communist societies is described as the re-emergence of civil society. In most cases, however, civil society is invested with normative and ideological significance. In the conventional, liberal view, civil society is identified as a realm of choice, personal *freedom and individual responsibility. Whereas the state operates through compulsory and coercive authority, civil society allows individuals to shape their own destinies. This explains why a vigorous and healthy civil society is usually regarded as an essential feature of *liberal democracy, and why classical liberals in particular have a moral preference for civil society over the state, reflected in a desire to minimise the scope of public authority and maximise the private sphere. In contrast, the Hegelian use of the term is negative in that it counterposes the egoism of civil society with the altruism that is fostered by the family and within the state. Marxists and socialists generally have viewed civil society unfavourably, associating it in particular with unequal class power and social injustice. Such views would justify either the overthrow of civil society as presently structured, or the contraction of civil society through the expansion of state control and regulation.

CONSENSUS

A consensus is an agreement, but it is an agreement of a particular kind. Consensus implies, first, a broad agreement, the terms of which are accepted by a wide range of individuals or groups. Second, it implies an agreement about fundamental or underlying principles, as opposed to a precise or exact agreement. In other words, a consensus permits disagreement on matters of emphasis or detail. The term 'consensus politics' may be used in two ways. A *procedural* consensus is a willingness to make decisions through consultation and bargaining, either between *political parties or between *government and major interests. A *substantive* consensus is an overlap in the ideological positions of two or more political parties, reflected in agreement about fundamental policy goals (as in the UK's post-1945 social-democratic consensus, and Germany's social-market consensus).

Significance

Consensus is often portrayed as the very stuff of *politics. This is because politics, in one sense at least, is a specifically non-violent means of resolving conflict. Given that the differing interests of individuals and groups are a permanent feature of human life, peaceful co-existence can be achieved only through a process of negotiation, conciliation and compromise; in short, through consensus-building. Procedural consensuses therefore reflect the recognition that the alternative to bargaining and compromise is open conflict and possibly violence. Consensus politics is likely to be a feature of mature pluralist democracies, substantive consensuses often occurring in political systems in which electoral alliances and *coalitions are commonplace. Consensus politics can nevertheless be criticised on the grounds that it fosters unprincipled compromise; that it discourages consideration of bold but controversial policy initiatives; and that it tends to entrench centrist ideological priorities.

GOVERNMENT/GOVERNANCE

In its broadest sense to govern means to rule or control others. Government can therefore be taken to include any mechanism through which ordered rule is maintained, its central features being the ability to make collective decisions and the capacity to enforce them. A form of government can thus be identified in almost all social institutions: families, schools, businesses, trade unions and so on. However, 'government' is more commonly understood to refer to the formal and institutional processes which operate at the national level to maintain order and facilitate collective action. The core functions of government are thus to make law (legislation), implement law (execution) and interpret law (adjudication). In some cases the political *executive alone is referred to as 'the Government', making it equivalent to 'the Administration' in presidential systems. Governmental processes also operate at supranational, regional and local levels.

'Governance' is a broader term than 'government'. It refers, in its widest sense, to the various way through which social life is coordinated. Government can therefore be seen as one of the organisations involved in governance; it is possible, in other words, to have 'governance without government'. The principal modes of governance are *markets, hierarchies and networks. Markets coordinate social life through a price mechanism which is structured by the forces of supply and demand. Hierarchies, which include *bureaucracy and thus traditional forms of government organisation, operate through 'top-down' authority systems. Networks are 'flat' organisational forms that are characterised by informal relationships between essentially equal agents or social agencies.

Significance

Government has traditionally been the principal object of political analysis. Some, indeed, identify *politics with government in treating political activity as the art of government, the exercise of control within society through the making and enforcement of collective decisions. This overriding concern with government has been evident in both *political philosophy and *political science. Political philosophers from Aristotle (384–22 BCE) onwards have evaluated forms of government on normative grounds in the hope of identifying the 'ideal' *constitution. Similarly, social contract theorists focused political analysis on the nature of governmental authority and the basis of citizens' *obligation to government. Political scientists who adopt the once dominant but still influential constitutional–institutional approach to the discipline also accord government central importance. This involves either analysing the legislative, executive and judicial processes of government and examining the relationships between and amongst different levels of government, or comparing systems of government with a view to developing a broader classification or highlighting the distinctive features of each system.

Some political thinkers have nevertheless questioned whether government is centrally important to politics. In the case of *anarchism, government is rejected as fundamentally evil and unnecessary, political activity focusing upon strategies for its abolition. Liberals, who accept that government is vital, place a heavy emphasis upon the need to check or limit government in view of the potential tyranny it embodies. Marxists and feminists, for their part, tend to treat government as a secondary political formation derived from, or operating within, a wider system of, respectively, class politics or sexual politics. Academic political scientists have also in some ways looked beyond government. *Systems theory, for instance, examines not the mechanisms of government, but the structures and processes through which these interact with the larger society, while political sociology interprets the working of government in terms of wider social structures and power systems.

Governance has become an increasingly popular, if imprecise, term since the 1980s. This reflects a series of changes that have taken place within government as well as in the larger society. These include the development of new forms of public management in which government is increasingly confined to 'steering' (that is, setting targets and strategic objectives) as opposed to 'rowing' (that is, administration or service delivery); the blurring of the distinction between government and markets through the growth of public/private partnerships and the introduction of 'internal markets'; the recognition of the importance to policy formulation of so-called policy networks; and the emergence of multi-level governmental systems through the impact of *supranationalism and *devolution or *federalism. However, the term 'governance' still has no settled or agreed definition, and, for some, it conveys an ideological preference for a minimal state or 'less government'.

HUMAN NATURE

Human nature refers to the essential and immutable character of all human beings. It highlights what is innate and 'natural' about human life, as opposed to what human beings have gained from education or through social experience. This does not, however, mean that those who believe that human behaviour is shaped more by society than it is by unchanging and inborn characteristics have abandoned the idea of human nature. Rather, such a view makes clear assumptions about innate human qualities; in this case, the capacity to be shaped or moulded by external factors. Moreover, a concept of human nature does not reduce human life to a one-dimensional caricature. Most political thinkers are aware that human beings are complex, multi-faceted creatures, made up of biological, physical, psychological, intellectual, social and perhaps spiritual elements. The concept of human nature does not conceal or overlook this complexity so much as attempt to impose order upon it by designating certain features as natural or 'essential'. Although this human 'core' will usually be manifest in human behaviour, this is not necessarily the case. Human beings may, for instance, be encouraged to deny their 'true' natures through the influence of a corrupt society.

Significance

Almost all political doctrines and beliefs are based upon some kind of theory of human nature, sometimes explicitly formulated but in many cases simply implied. Assumptions about the content of human nature structure political enquiry in a number of important ways. The most obvious of these is the so-called 'nurture/nature' debate, the question of whether the essential core of human nature is fixed or given, fashioned by 'nature', or whether it is moulded or structured through social experience or 'nurture'. An emphasis upon nature, as adopted, for instance, by most liberals and conservatives, suggests that the individual is the key to the understanding of society: social and political life ultimately reflect characteristics and behavioural patterns that are innate within each human being. This is evident in methodological *individualism. On the other hand, nurture theorists, including most socialists, communists and anarchists, argue that as human nature is 'plastic', the human character and sensibilities can be developed through the reconstruction of society. In this case, society provides the key to the understanding of the individual.

Another important debate about human nature centres upon the relative importance of competition and cooperation. Much of liberal *ideology and many of the ideas of conventional social and *political science reflect assumptions about self-seeking and egotistical human behaviour. If human beings are essentially greedy and competitive, a capitalist economic system is natural and inevitable. However, socialists have traditionally stressed that human beings are naturally sociable, cooperative and gregarious, motivated by altruism and a sense of social responsibility. From this perspective, *capitalism merely serves to corrupt human nature by suppressing our inclination towards collective human endeavour and *equality. Only a limited number of political thinkers have openly rejected the idea of human nature. Jean-Paul Sartre (1905–80), however, argued that 'existence comes before essence', meaning that human beings enjoy the *freedom to define themselves through their own actions and deeds. If this is so, the assertion of any concept of human nature is an affront to that freedom.

IDEOLOGY

Ideology is one of the most contested of political terms. It is now most widely used in a social-scientific sense to refer to a more or less coherent set of ideas that provide the basis for some kind of organised political action. In this sense all ideologies therefore, first, offer an account or critique of the existing order, usually in the form of a 'world view'; second, provide the model of a desired future, a vision of the 'good society'; and, third, outline how political change can and should be brought about (see Figure 2.1). Ideologies thus straddle the conventional boundaries between descriptive and normative thought, and between theory and practice. However, the term was coined by Destutt de Tracy (1754–1836) to

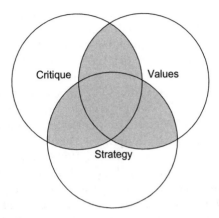

Figure 2.1   Political ideology

describe a new 'science of ideas', literally an idea-ology. Karl Marx (1818–83) used ideology to refer to ideas that serve the interests of the ruling class by concealing the contradictions of class society, thereby promoting false consciousness and political passivity amongst subordinate classes. In this view a clear distinction can be drawn between ideology and science, representing false-hood and truth respectively. Later Marxists adopted a neutral concept of ideology, regarding it as the distinctive ideas of any social class, including the working class. Some liberals, particularly during the Cold War period, have viewed ideology as an officially sanctioned belief system that claims a monopoly of truth, often through a spurious claim to be scientific. Conservative thinkers have sometimes followed Michael Oakeshott (1901–90) in treating ideologies as elaborate systems of thought that orientate politics towards abstract principles and goals and away from practical and historical circumstances.

Significance

The concept of ideology has had a controversial career. For much of its history, ideology has carried starkly pejorative implications, being used as a political weapon to criticise or condemn rival political stances. Indeed, its changing significance and use can be linked to shifting patterns of political antagonism. Marxists, for example, have variously interpreted *liberalism, *conservatism and *fascism as forms of 'bourgeois ideology', committed to the mystification and subordination of the oppressed proletariat. Marxist interest in ideology, often linked to Antonio Gramsci's (1891–1937) theory of ideological *hegemony, grew markedly during the twentieth century as Marxist thinkers sought to explain the failure of Marx's prediction of proletarian revolution. The advent of the Cold War in the 1950s encouraged liberal theorists to identify similarities between fascism and *communism, both being inherently repressive 'official' ideologies which suppressed opposition and demanded regimented obedience. However, the 1950s and 1960s also witnessed growing claims that ideology had become superfluous and redundant, most openly through the 'end of ideology' thesis advanced by Daniel Bell (1960). This view reflected not only the declining importance in the West of ideologies such as communism and fascism, but also the fact that similarities between liberalism, conservatism and *socialism had apparently become more prominent than their differences.

Nevertheless, the proclaimed demise of ideology has simply not materialised. Since the 1960s, ideology has been accorded a more important and secure place in political analysis for a number of reasons. First, the wider use of the social-scientific definition of ideology means that the term no longer carries political baggage and can be applied to all 'isms' or action-orientated political philosophies. Second, a range of new ideological traditions have steadily emerged, including *feminism and *ecologism in the 1960s, the *New Right in the 1970s and *religious fundamentalism in the 1980s. Third, the decline of simplistically behavioural approaches to politics has led to growing interest in ideology both as a means of recognising how far political action is structured by the beliefs and values of political actors, and as a way of acknowledging that political analysis always bears the imprint of values and assumptions that the analyst himself or herself brings to it.

Law

Law is a set of public and enforceable rules that apply throughout a political *community. Law can be distinguished from other social rules on four grounds. First, as law is made by the *government and thus reflects the 'will of the state', it takes precedence over all other norms and social rules. Second, law is compulsory; citizens are not allowed to choose which laws to obey and which to ignore, because law is backed up by a system of coercion and punishment. Third, law consists in published and recognised rules that have been enacted through a formal, usually public, legislative process. Fourth, law is generally recognised as binding upon those to whom it applies; law thus embodies moral claims, implying that legal rules should be obeyed.

Natural law is usually distinguished from positive law. *Natural law* is law that conforms to higher moral or religious principles, meaning that law is a vehicle through which *justice is expressed or guaranteed. Natural law theories can be traced back to Plato (427–347 BCE) and Aristotle (384–22 BCE), and to the idea of God-given 'natural rights' in the early modern period. They became fashionable again in the twentieth century in association with the ideas of *civil liberty and *human rights. *Positive law* is defined by the fact that it is established and enforced. The law is the law because it is obeyed. The 'science of positive law' therefore frees the understanding of law from moral, religious and mystical assumptions, a position developed by John Austin (1790–1859) into the theory of 'legal positivism'. H. L. A. Hart (1961) refined legal positivism by distinguishing between a primary and secondary level of law. The role of primary rules is to regulate social behaviour; these are thought of as the 'content' of the legal system (for instance, criminal law). Secondary rules, on the other hand, are rules which confer powers upon the institutions of government; they lay down how primary rules are made, enforced and adjudicated, and so determine their validity. Another distinction is between public and private law. *Public law* lays down the powers and duties of governmental bodies and establishes the legal relationship between the *state and its citizens. It therefore includes constitutional and administrative law, taxation and welfare law, and is usually taken to encompass criminal law as well. *Private law* apportions *rights and responsibilities amongst private citizens and bodies, and thus establishes the legal relationships within *civil society. It includes the law of contract and property law.

Significance

Law is found in all modern societies, and is usually regarded as the bedrock of civilised existence. Nevertheless, questions about the

actual and desirable relationship between law and *politics –
reflecting on the nature of law, and its function and proper
extent – have provoked deep controversy. Liberal theorists portray
law as an essential guarantee of stability and *order. The role of
law is to protect each member of society from his or her fellow members, thereby preventing their rights from being encroached upon;
as John Locke (1632–1704) put it, 'without law there is no liberty'.
Law should therefore be 'above' politics, in the sense that it applies
equally to all citizens and is impartially administered by the *judiciary. This is reflected in the principle of the rule of law, the idea
that law 'rules' in the sense that it establishes a framework to
which all conduct and behaviour conform, no distinction being
drawn between government officials and private citizens, the rich
and the poor, men and women, and so on. However, in believing
that law's central purpose is to protect liberty, liberals have always
insisted that the proper sphere of law must be limited. The classical interpretation of this position was developed in J. S. Mill's
(1806–73) 'harm principle': the idea that the only legitimate use of
law is to prevent 'harm to others'.

Conservative theorists, in contrast, link law more closely to order,
even to the extent that 'law and order' becomes a single, fused concept. This position draws from a more pessimistic, even Hobbesian,
view of *human nature, and from the belief that social stability
depends upon the existence of shared values and a common culture.
Patrick Devlin (1968) thus argued that society has the right to
enforce 'public morality' through the instrument of law. This position goes clearly beyond Mill's *libertarianism in implying, for
instance, that society has the right to protect itself against 'non-
consensus' practices, such as homosexuality and drug taking. In the
1980s and 1990s the *New Right took up a very similar position in
extolling the virtues of 'traditional morality' and 'family values',
believing also that these should be upheld through the *authority
of law. Alternative and more critical views of law have been
advanced by Marxists, feminists and anarchists. Marxists have traditionally argued that class biases operate within the legal system
that uphold the interests of *property and *capitalism. Feminists
have linked law to *patriarchy and argued that it is one of the principal devices through which women's silence and subordination is
maintained. Anarchists, for their part, portray law as unnecessary
and intrinsically oppressive, and look towards the construction of a
lawless society regulated by reason and human sympathy alone.

LEFT/RIGHT

Left and right are terms that are used as a shorthand method for describing political ideas and beliefs, summarising the ideological positions of politicians, *political parties and movements. They are usually understood as the poles of a political spectrum, enabling people to talk about the 'centre-left', 'far right' and so on. The most common application of the left/right distinction is in the form of a linear political spectrum that travels from left wing to right wing as shown in Figure 2.2.

However, the terms left and right do not have exact meanings. In a narrow sense the political spectrum summarises different attitudes towards the economy and the role of the state: left-wing views support intervention and *collectivism, right-wing ones favour the *market and *individualism. However, this distinction supposedly reflects deeper, if imperfectly defined, ideological or value differences. Ideas such as *freedom, *equality, fraternity, *rights, progress, reform and *internationalism are generally seen to have a left-wing character. Ideas such as *authority, *hierarchy, *order, duty, *tradition, reaction and *nationalism are generally seen to have a right-wing character. In some cases 'the Left' and 'the Right' are used to refer to collections of people, groups and parties that are bound together by broadly similar ideological stances.

Significance

The origin of the terms left and right dates back to the French Revolution and the seating arrangements adopted by aristocrats and radicals at the first meeting of the Estates General in 1789. The left/right divide was therefore originally a stark choice between revolution and reaction. The wider use of the terms demonstrates their general value in locating political and ideological positions. However, the terms are simplistic and generalised, and must always be used with caution. Problems with the conventional left/right divide include the fact that it appears to offer no place for

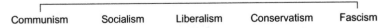

| Communism | Socialism | Liberalism | Conservatism | Fascism |

Figure 2.2   Linear spectrum

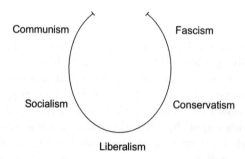

Figure 2.3 Horseshoe spectrum

*anarchism, which may be both ultra left-wing and ultra right-wing; that it ignores the fact that communism and fascism to some extent resemble one another by virtue of a shared tendency towards *totalitarianism; and that it attempts to reduce politics to a single dimension – the market–state divide – and thereby ignores other political distinctions such as the libertarian–authoritarian divide and the autocratic–democratic divide. For these reasons various horseshoe-shaped and two-dimensional spectrums have been developed to offer a more complete picture of ideological positions (see Figures 2.3 and 2.4). Finally, some argue that the emergence of new political issues such as *feminism, *ecologism and animal rights, which simply do not fit in to the conventional spectrum, and the development of *'third way' politics have rendered the ideas of left and right largely redundant.

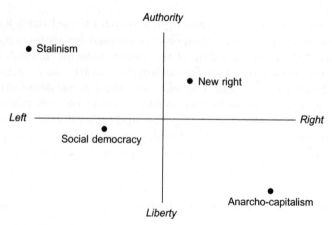

Figure 2.4 Two-dimensional spectrum

LEGITIMACY

Legitimacy (from the Latin *legitimare*, meaning 'to declare lawful') broadly means rightfulness. Legitimacy confers upon an order or command an authoritative or binding character, thus transforming *power into *authority. It differs from legality in that the latter does not necessarily guarantee that *government is respected or that citizens acknowledge a duty of obedience. However, the term legitimacy is used differently in *political philosophy and *political science. Political philosophers generally treat legitimacy as a moral or rational principle, as the grounds upon which governments may demand obedience from their citizens. The *claim* to legitimacy is thus more important than the *fact* of obedience. Political scientists, on the other hand, usually view legitimacy in sociological terms, that is, as a willingness to comply with a system of rule regardless of how this is achieved. Following Max Weber (1864–1920), this position takes legitimacy to mean a *belief* in legitimacy; in other words, a belief in the 'right to rule'.

Significance

The issue of legitimacy is linked to the oldest and one of the most fundamental of political debates: the problem of political *obligation. In examining whether citizens have a duty to respect the *state and obey its *laws, social contract theorists such as Hobbes (1588–1679) and Locke (1632–1704) were considering the question: when, and on what basis, may government exercise legitimate authority over society? In modern political debate, however, legitimacy addresses not the question of why people *should* obey the state, in an abstract sense, but the question of why they *do* obey a particular state or system of rule. The classic contribution to the understanding of legitimacy as a sociological phenomenon was provided by Weber, who identified three types of political legitimacy based, respectively, upon history and customs (traditional authority), the power of personality (charismatic authority) and a framework of formal, legal rules (legal-rational authority). In Weber's view, modern societies are increasingly characterised by the exercise of legal-rational authority and a form of legitimacy that arises from respect for formal and usually legal rules.

An alternative to the Weberian approach to legitimacy has been developed by neo-Marxist theorists, who focus upon the mechanisms through which capitalist societies constrain class antagonisms, that is, by manufacturing *consent via the extension of *democracy and social reform. Legitimacy is thus linked to the maintenance of ideological *hegemony. In this light neo-Marxists such as Jürgen Habermas (1973) have identified 'legitimation crises' in capitalist societies that make it difficult for them to maintain political stability through consent alone. At the heart of these 'crisis tendencies' lies the alleged contradiction between the logic of capitalist accumulation on the one hand, and the popular pressures which democratic politics unleashes on the other.

ORDER

Order, in everyday language, refers to regular and tidy patterns, as when soldiers are said to stand 'in order' or the universe is described as being 'ordered'. In social life, order describes regular, stable and predictable forms of behaviour, for which reason social order suggests continuity, even permanence. Social disorder, by contrast, implies chaotic, random and violent behaviour, that is by its very nature unstable and continually changing. As a political principle, therefore, order is associated with personal security, both physical security, freedom from intimidation and violence and the fear of such, and psychological security, the comfort and stability which only regular and familiar circumstances engender. However, order may be conceived of as either a political or a natural phenomenon. *Political order* stands for social control which is imposed 'from above' through a system of *law and *government. Order in this sense is linked to the ideas of discipline, regulation and *authority. *Natural order*, on the other hand, arises 'from below' through the voluntary and spontaneous actions of individuals and groups. In this sense, order is linked to ideas such as social harmony and equilibrium.

Significance

A fear of disorder and social instability has been one of the most fundamental and abiding concerns of Western *political philosophy.

Order has, moreover, attracted almost unqualified approval from political theorists, at least in so far as none of them is prepared to defend disorder. However, there are deep differences about the most appropriate solutions to the problem of order. The public/natural order divide has profound implications for *government and reflects differing views of *human nature. At one extreme Thomas Hobbes (1588–1679) argued that absolute government is the only means of maintaining order because the principal human inclination is a 'perpetual and restless desire for power, that ceaseth only in death'. At the other extreme, Peter Kropotkin (1842–1921) supported *anarchism on the grounds that order can be established by 'liberty and fraternal care', and that crime is merely the result of 'idleness, law and authority'.

In modern politics the conservative view of order links it closely to law, often viewing 'law and order' as a single, fused concept. Domestic order is therefore best maintained through a fear of punishment, based upon the strict enforcement of law and stiff penalties, and also respect for traditional values, seen as the moral bedrock of society. Modern liberals and socialists, in contrast, have traditionally argued that a reliance upon fear and respect is inadequate because disorder is largely a consequence of poverty and social deprivation. From this perspective, order is best maintained through social reform designed, for example, to improve housing conditions, reduce unemployment and counter urban decay.

POLICY

A policy, in a general sense, is a plan of action adopted by, for example, an individual, group, business or *government. To designate something as a policy implies that a formal decision has been made, giving official sanction to a particular course of action. Public policy can therefore be seen as the formal or stated decisions of government bodies. However, policy is better understood as the linkage between intentions, actions and results. At the level of intentions, policy is reflected in the stance of government – what government says that it will do. At the level of actions, policy is reflected in the behaviour of government – what government actually does. At the level of results, policy is reflected in the consequences of government action – the impact of government upon the larger society.

Significance

In a sense, policy is the aspect of government which concerns most people. As the 'outputs' of the political process, it reflects the impact government has upon society; that is, its ability to make things better or make things worse. During the 1960s and 1970s, policy analysis emerged as a distinctive area of study. It set out to examine both how policy is made (the 'how' of policy-making), and the impact of policy for the larger society (the 'what' of policy-making). Policy is usually seen to be 'made' though four distinct stages: initiation, formulation, implementation and evaluation. Policy initiation sets the political agenda by defining certain problems as 'issues', as matters that engage the interest of government usually because they are the subject of public debate or disagreement. Policy formulation is often seen as the crucial stage in the policy process, because it develops a political issue into a firm policy proposal through a process of debate, analysis and review. Policy implementation comprises the actions though which policy is put into effect, sometimes in ways that differ from the original intentions of policy-makers. Policy evaluation is a review of the impact of public policy, which produces a policy feedback process by stimulating further policy initiation and shaping the formulation process.

Another aspect of policy analysis focuses upon how decisions are made. *Rational choice theorists, influenced by *utilitarianism, assume that political actors are rationally self-interested creatures, who select whatever means are most likely to secure their desired ends. This emphasis upon rationality has, however, been criticised by supporters of 'bounded rationality', who acknowledge that decision-making is essentially an act of compromising between differently valued and imprecisely calculated outcomes (Simon, 1983). The principal alternative to rational decision-making, incrementalism, has been described as the 'science of muddling through' (Lindblom, 1959). It views policy-making as a continuous, exploratory process; lacking overriding goals and clear-cut ends, policy-makers tend to operate within the existing pattern or framework, adjusting their position in the light of feedback in the form of information about the impact of earlier decisions. Bureaucratic organisation models of decision-making shift attention away from the motives of political actors to the impact that the structure of the policy-making process has upon the resulting decisions. This either draws attention to the impact upon decisions of the values, assumptions and regular patterns of behaviour that are found in any large organisation, or the impact upon decisions of bargaining between personnel and agencies each pursuing different perceived interests. Finally, there are decision-making models that place emphasis upon the role of beliefs and *ideology. These recognise that beliefs are the 'glue' of politics, binding together people on the basis of shared values and preferences. In the hands of Marxists and feminists, such ideas have led to the conclusion that the policy process is biased, respectively, in favour of *capitalism or in favour of men.

POLITICS

Politics, in its broadest sense, is the activity through which people make, preserve and amend the general rules under which they live. Although politics is also an academic subject (sometimes indicated by the use of 'Politics' with a capital P), it is then clearly the study of this activity. Politics is thus inextricably linked to the phenomena of conflict and cooperation. On the one hand, the existence of rival opinions, different wants, competing needs and opposing interests guarantees disagreement about the rules under which people live. On the other hand, people recognise that, in order to influence these rules or ensure that they are upheld, they must work together with others – hence Hannah Arendt's (1906–75) definition of political power as 'acting in concert'. This is why the heart of politics is often portrayed as a process of conflict resolution, in which rival views or competing interests are reconciled with one another. However, politics in this broad sense is better thought of as a search for conflict resolution than as its achievement, as not all conflicts are, or can be, resolved. From this perspective, politics arises from the facts of diversity (we are not all alike) and scarcity (there is never enough to go round).

However, four quite different notions of politics can be identified. First, it is associated specifically with the art of *government and the activities of the *state. This is perhaps the classical definition of politics, developed from the original meaning of the term in Ancient Greece (politics is derived from *polis*, literally meaning city-state). In this view politics is an essentially state-bound activity, meaning that most people, most institutions and most social activities can be regarded as being 'outside' politics. Second, politics is viewed as a

specifically 'public' activity in that it is associated with the conduct
and management of the community's affairs rather than with the
'private' concerns of the individual. Such a view can be traced
back to Aristotle's (384–22 BCE) belief that it is only within a political community that human beings can live 'the good life'. Third,
politics is seen as a particular means of resolving conflict, that is,
by compromise, conciliation and negotiation, rather than through
force and naked *power. This is what is implied when politics is portrayed as 'the art of the possible', and it suggests a distinction between 'political' solutions to problems involving peaceful
debate and arbitration, and 'military' solutions. Fourth, politics is
associated with the production, distribution and use of resources in
the course of social existence. In this view politics is about power:
the ability to achieve a desired outcome, through whatever means.
Advocates of this view include feminists and Marxists.

Significance

The 'what is politics?' debate highlights quite different approaches
to political analysis and exposes some of the deepest and most
intractable conflicts in political thought. In the first place it determines the very subject matter and parameters of the discipline itself.
The traditional view that politics boils down to 'what concerns the
state' has been reflected in the tendency for academic study to focus
upon the personnel and machinery of government. To study politics
is in essence to study government or, more broadly, to study what
David Easton (1981) called the 'authoritative allocation of values'.
However, if the stuff of politics is power and the distribution of
resources, politics is seen to take place in, for instance, the family,
the workplace, and schools and universities, and the focus of political analysis shifts from the state to society.

Moreover, different views of politics embody different conceptions of social order. Definitions of politics that relate it to the art of
government, public affairs or peaceful compromise are based upon
an essentially *consensus model of society, which portrays government as basically benign and emphasises the common interests of
the community. However, views of politics that emphasise the distribution of power and resources tend to based upon conflict models
of society that stress structural inequalities and injustices. Karl
Marx (1818–83) thus referred to political power as 'merely the

organised power of one class for oppressing another', while the feminist author Kate Millett (1970) defined politics as 'power-structured relationships, arrangements whereby one group of persons is controlled by another'. Finally, there is disagreement about the moral character of political activity and about whether it can, or should, be brought to an end. On the one hand, to link politics to government is to regard it as, at worst, a necessary evil, and to associate politics with community activity and non-violent forms of conflict resolution is to portray it as positively worthwhile, even ennobling. On the other hand, those who link politics to oppression and subjugation often do so to expose structures of inequality and injustice in society, which, once overthrown, will result in the end of politics itself.

POWER

Power can be broadly defined as the ability to achieve a desired outcome, sometimes referred to in terms of the 'power *to*' do something. This notion of power includes everything from the ability to keep oneself alive to the ability of government to promote economic growth. In political analysis, however, power is usually thought of as a relationship; that is, as the ability to influence the behaviour of others in a manner not of their choosing. It is referred to in terms of having 'power *over*' others. Power thus exists when A gets B to do something that B would not otherwise have done. Power is often distinguished from *authority on the grounds that the former is based upon the 'ability' to influence others, whereas the latter involves the 'right' to do so. Power may, more narrowly, be associated with the ability to punish and reward, bringing it close to force or manipulation, in contrast to 'influence', which also encompasses rational persuasion.

However, power can be exerted in various ways. This has resulted in the emergence of different conceptions of power, sometimes viewed as different dimensions or 'faces' of power. First, power is understood as decision-making: conscious judgements that in some way shape actions or influence decisions. This notion is analogous to the idea of physical or mechanical power, in that it implies that power involves being 'pulled' or 'pushed' against one's will. Keith Boulding (1989) has distinguished between three ways of influencing decisions: the use of force or intimidation ('the stick');

productive exchanges involving mutual gain ('the deal'); and the creation of obligations, loyalty and commitment ('the kiss'). Second, power may take the form of agenda setting: the ability to prevent decisions being made, that is, in effect, non-decision-making. This involves the ability to prevent issues or proposals being aired; E. E. Schattschneider (1960) summed this up in his famous assertion that 'organisation is the mobilisation of bias'. Third, power can take the form of thought control: the ability to influence another by shaping what he or she thinks, wants or needs. This is sometimes portrayed by Lukes (1974) as the 'radical' face of power because it exposes processes of cultural and psychological control in society and, more generally, highlights the impact of *ideology.

Significance

There is a sense in which all *politics is about power. The practice of politics is often portrayed as little more than the exercise of power, and the academic subject as, in essence, the study of power. Without doubt, students of politics are students of power: they seek to know who has it, how it is used and on what basis it is exercised. However, disagreements about the nature of power run deep and have significant implications for political analysis. Although it would be wrong to suggest that different 'faces' of power necessarily result in different models of the distribution of power in society, power as decision-making is commonly linked to *pluralism (because it tends to highlight the influence of a number of political actors), while power as agenda setting is often associated with *elitism (because it exposes the capacity of vested interests to organise issues out of politics), and power as thought control is commonly linked to *Marxism (because it draws attention to forms of ideological indoctrination that mask the reality of class rule).

The concept of power is accorded particular significance by analysts who subscribe to what is called 'power politics'. Power politics is an approach to politics based upon the assumption that the pursuit of power is the principal human goal. The term is generally used descriptively and is closely linked to *realism. This is a tradition that can be traced back to Thomas Hobbes (1588–1679) and his assertion that the basic human urge is to seek 'power after power'. The theory of power politics portrays politics as nothing more than an arena of struggle or competition between differently interested actors. At the national level on-going struggle between individuals and groups is usually used to justify strong government, the virtue of *government being that, as the supreme power, it alone is capable of establishing order. At the international level the power politics approach emphasises the inherent instability of a world riven by competing national interests and links the hope of peace to the establishment of a balance of power.

SOVEREIGNTY

Sovereignty, in its simplest sense, is the principle of absolute and unlimited *power. However, a distinction is commonly made between legal sovereignty and political sovereignty. *Legal sovereignty* refers to supreme legal *authority; that is, an unchallengeable right to demand compliance, as defined by *law. *Political sovereignty*, in contrast, refers to unlimited political power; that is, the ability to command obedience, which is typically ensured by a monopoly of coercive force. The term sovereignty is used in two distinct though related senses, usually understood as external sovereignty and internal sovereignty. *External sovereignty* relates to a *state's place in the international order and its capacity to act as an independent and autonomous entity. This is what is meant by terms such as 'national sovereignty' and 'sovereign state'. *Internal sovereignty* is the notion of a supreme power/authority within the state, located in the body that makes decisions that are binding on all citizens, groups and institutions within the state's territorial boundaries. This is how the term is used in cases such as 'parliamentary sovereignty' and 'popular sovereignty'.

Significance

The concept of sovereignty emerged in the sixteenth and seventeenth centuries, as a result of the development in Europe of the modern state. As the authority of transnational institutions, such as the Catholic Church and the Holy Roman Empire faded, centralising monarchs in England, France, Spain and elsewhere were able to claim to exercise supreme power, and they did this in a new language of sovereignty. In the writings of Jean Bodin (1530–96) and

Thomas Hobbes (1588–1679), sovereignty was used as a justification for monarchical *absolutism. For Bodin, law amounted to little more than the command of the sovereign, and subjects were required simply to obey. However, whereas Bodin accepted that the sovereign monarch was constrained by the will of God or natural law, Hobbes defined sovereignty as a monopoly of coercive power and advocated that it be vested in the hands of a single, unchallengeable rule. The basic justification for internal sovereignty as developed by Bodin and Hobbes is that the existence of a single focus of allegiance and a supreme source of law within a state is the only sure guarantee of order and stability. Hobbes in particular offered citizens a stark choice between absolutism and anarchy.

Other versions of internal sovereignty, such as a Rousseau's (1712–78) notion of popular sovereignty, expressed in the idea of the 'general will', and John Austin's (1790–1859) doctrine of parliamentary sovereignty, viewed as the 'Monarch in Parliament', linked sovereignty, respectively, to *democracy and *constitutionalism. What all such thinkers, however, had in common is that they believed that sovereignty could be, and should be, located in a determinate body. In an age of pluralistic and democratic government this 'traditional' doctrine of sovereignty has come in for growing criticism. Its opponents argue either that it is intrinsically linked to its absolutist past, and if so is frankly undesirable, or that it is no longer applicable to modern systems of government which operate according to networks of checks and balances. It has been suggested, for instance, that liberal democratic principles are the very antithesis of sovereignty in that they argue for a distribution of power amongst a number of institutions, none of which can meaningfully claim to be sovereign. This is particularly evident in the case of *federalism, which is based upon the paradoxical notion of shared sovereignty.

While questions about internal sovereignty have in a democratic age appeared increasingly outdated, the issue of external sovereignty has become absolutely vital. Indeed, some of the deepest divisions in modern politics, from the Arab–Israeli conflict to tensions in former Yugoslavia, involve disputed claims to such sovereignty. Historically, the notion of external sovereignty has been closely linked to the struggle for popular government, the two ideas fusing to create the modern notion of 'national sovereignty'. External sovereignty has thus come to embody the principles of national independence and self-government. Only if a *nation is sovereign are its people capable of fashioning their own destiny according to their particular needs and interests. To ask a nation to surrender its sovereignty is tantamount to asking its people to give up their *freedom. This is why external or national sovereignty is so keenly felt and, when it is threatened, so fiercely defended. The potent appeal of political *nationalism is the best evidence of this. However, external sovereignty has been criticised on both moral and theoretical grounds. Moral concerns about external sovereignty arise from its capacity to block interference in the affairs of other states, even when they are violating the natural rights of their citizens. Theoretical problems stem from the fact that the notion of an independent or sovereign state may no longer be meaningful in an increasingly interdependent world. *Globalisation, for instance, may mean that political sovereignty is impossible while legal sovereignty has been reduced to a diplomatic nicety.

STATE

The state can most simply be defined as a political association that establishes sovereign jurisdiction within defined territorial borders and exercises *authority through a set of permanent institutions. It is possible to identify five key features of the state. First, the state exercises *sovereignty – it exercises absolute and unrestricted *power in that it stands above all other associations and groups in society; Thomas Hobbes (1588–1679), for this reason, portrayed the state as a 'leviathan', a gigantic monster. Second, state institutions are recognisably 'public', in contrast to the 'private' institutions of *civil society – state bodies are responsible for making and enforcing collective decisions in society and are funded at the public's expense. Third, the state is an exercise in legitimation – its decisions are usually (although not necessarily) accepted as binding on its citizens because, it is claimed, it reflects the permanent interests of society. Fourth, the state is an instrument in domination – it possesses the coercive power to ensure that its *laws are obeyed and that transgressors are punished; as Max Weber (1864–1920) put it, the state has a monopoly of the means of 'legitimate violence'. Fifth, the state is a territorial association – it exercises jurisdiction within geographically defined borders and in international politics is treated (at least in theory) as an autonomous entity.

States nevertheless come in different shapes and sizes. *Minimal states* or 'nightwatchman' states, advocated by classical liberals and the New Right, are merely protective bodies whose sole function is to provide a framework of peace and social order within which citizens can conduct their lives as they think best. *Developmental states*, found in Japan and the 'tiger' economies of East and Southeast Asia, operate through a close relationship between the state and major economic interests, notably big business, and aim to develop strategies for national prosperity in a context of transnational competition. *Social-democratic states*, the ideal of both modern liberals and democratic socialists, intervene widely in economic and social life in order to promote growth and maintain full employment, reduce poverty and bring about a more equitable distribution of social rewards. *Collectivised states*, found in orthodox communist countries, abolished private enterprise altogether and set up centrally planned economies administered by a network of economic ministries and planning committees. *Totalitarian states*, as constructed in Hitler's Germany and Stalin's USSR (although modern regimes such as Saddam Hussain's Iraq arguably have similar characteristics), penetrate every aspect of human existence through a combination of comprehensive surveillance and terroristic policing, and a pervasive system of ideological manipulation and control.

A distinction should be drawn between the state and the *government, two terms that are often used interchangeably. The state is more extensive than government. The state is an inclusive association that encompasses all the institutions of the public realm and embraces all the members of the community (in their capacity as citizens), meaning that government is merely part of the state. In this sense government is the means through which the authority of the state is brought into operation; it is 'the brains' of the state. Nevertheless, the state is a continuing, even permanent, entity, while government is temporary. Within an enduring state system, governments may come and go, and systems of government may be reformed and remodelled. Moreover, the state exercises impersonal authority, in the sense that the personnel of state bodies is recruited and trained in a bureaucratic manner and is (usually) expected to be politically neutral, enabling state bodies to resist the ideological enthusiasms of the government of the day. Finally, the state, in theory at least, represents the public interest or the common good. Government, on the other hand, represents the partisan sympathies of those who happen to be in power at any particular time.

Significance

The state has always been central to political analysis, to such an extent that *politics is often understood as the study of the state. This is evident in two key debates. The first and most fundamental of these focuses upon the need for the state and the basis of political *obligation. The classic justification for the state is provided by social contract theory, which constructs a picture of what life would be like in a stateless society, a so-called 'state of nature'. In the view of thinkers such as Hobbes and Locke (1632–1704), as the state of nature would be characterised by an unending civil war of each against all, people would be prepared to enter into an agreement – a social contract – through which they would sacrifice a portion of their liberty in order to create a sovereign body without which orderly and stable existence would be impossible. In the final analysis, then, individuals should obey the state because it is the only safeguard they have against disorder and chaos. The rival view, advanced by *anarchism, is based upon markedly more optimistic assumptions about *human nature, and places a heavier emphasis upon natural order and spontaneous cooperation amongst individuals. Anarchists have also looked to a range of social institutions, such as common ownership or the market mechanism, to underpin social stability in the absence of a state.

The second area of debate concerns the nature of state power. Much of *political theory deals specifically with rival theories of the state. The major positions in this debate can be summarised as follows. Liberals view the state as a neutral arbiter amongst competing interests and groups in society, a vital guarantee of social order; the state is at worst a 'necessary evil'. Marxists have portrayed the state as an instrument of class oppression, a 'bourgeois' state, or, allowing for its 'relative autonomy' from the ruling class, have emphasised that its role is to maintain stability within a system of unequal class power. Democratic socialists often regard the state as an embodiment of the common good, highlighting its capacity to rectify the injustices of the class system. Conservatives have generally linked the state to the need for authority and discipline to protect society from incipient disorder, hence their traditional preference for a strong state. The New Right has highlighted the

non-legitimate character of the state by drawing attention to
the extent to which it articulates its own interests separate from
those of the larger society and often to the detriment of the economic
performance. Feminists have viewed the state as an instrument of
male power, the 'patriarchal' state serving to exclude women
from, or subordinate them within, the 'public' or political sphere
of life. Finally, anarchists argue that the state is nothing less than
legalised oppression operating in the interests of the powerful, propertied and privileged.

The late twentieth century nevertheless witnessed a general 'hol-
lowing out' of the state, leading, some argue, to its growing irrelevance in the modern world. Chief amongst these developments have
been: *globalisation and the incorporation of national economies
into a global one that cannot be controlled by any state; privatisation and the growing preference for market organisation over state
management; and localism, the unleashing of centrifugal pressures
through a strengthening of regional and community politics and the
rise of particularist *nationalisms.

FURTHER READING

Beetham, D., The Legitimation of Power (London: Macmillan, 1991).
Berry, C., Human Nature (London: Macmillan, 1986).
Dunleavy, P. and O'Leary, B., Theories of the State: The Politics of Liberal
    Democracy (London: Macmillan, 1987).
Flatham, R., The Practice of Political Authority (Chicago: Chicago University
    Press, 1980).
Freeden, M., Ideologies and Political Theory: A Conceptual Approach (Oxford:
    Clarendon, 1996).
Green, L., The Authority of the State (Oxford: Clarendon, 1988).
Hart, H. L. A., The Concept of Law (Oxford: Oxford University Press, 1961).
Heywood, A., Political Ideologies: An Introduction (London: Macmillan,
    1998).
Leftwich, A. (ed.), What is Politics? The Activity and its Study (Oxford and
    New York: Blackwell, 1984).
Lukes, S. (ed.), Power (Oxford: Basil Blackwell, 1986).
McLellan, D., Ideology (Milton Keynes: Open University Press, 1986).
Parsons, W., Public Policy: Introduction to the Theory and Practice of Policy
    Analysis (Aldershot: Edward Elgar, 1995).
Raz, J., The Authority of Law (Oxford: Clarendon, 1986).

Part three

IDEOLOGIES

This section examines concepts that represent broad traditions of political thought and, often, offer different perspectives on political understanding.

IDEOLOGIES

ANARCHISM

Anarchism is an *ideology that is defined by the central belief that political *authority in all its form, and especially in the form of the *state, is both evil and unnecessary (anarchy literally means 'without rule'). Anarchists believe that the state is evil because, as a repository of sovereign, compulsory and coercive authority, it is an offence against the principles of *freedom and *equality, the core value of anarchism being unrestricted personal *autonomy. The state and the accompanying institutions of *government and *law are therefore rejected as corrupt and corrupting. However, the belief that the state is unnecessary is no less important to anarchism. Anarchists reject 'political' *order but have considerable faith in 'natural' order and spontaneous social harmony, ultimately underpinned by optimistic assumptions about *human nature. Government, in other words, is not the solution to the problem of order, but its cause.

Nevertheless, the anarchist preference for a stateless society in which free individuals manage their own affairs through voluntary agreement and cooperation has been developed on the basis of two rival traditions: socialist *communitarianism and liberal *individualism. Anarchism can thus be thought of as a point of intersection between *socialism and *liberalism: a form of both 'ultra-socialism' and 'ultra-liberalism'. This is reflected in two rival anarchist traditions, collectivist anarchism and individualist anarchism. *Collectivist anarchism*, or classical anarchism, is rooted in the idea of social solidarity or what Peter Kropotkin (1842–1921) called 'mutual aid', the belief that the natural and proper relationship amongst people is one of sympathy, affection and harmony. Collectivist anarchists have typically stressed the importance of social equality and common ownership, supporting Pierre-Joseph Proudhon's (1809–65) famous assertion that 'Property is theft', most radically expressed in the form of anarcho-communism. *Individualist anarchism* is based upon the idea of the sovereign individual, the belief that individual conscience and the pursuit of self-interest should not be constrained by any collective body or public authority. Individualist anarchism overlaps with *libertarianism and is usually linked to a strong belief in the market as a self-regulating mechanism, most obviously manifest in the form of anarcho-capitalism.

Significance

Anarchism is unusual amongst political ideologies in that it has never succeeded in winning power, at least at a national level. As no society or *nation has been re-modelled according to anarchist principles, it is tempting to regard anarchism as an ideology of lesser significance. As a political movement, anarchism has suffered from three major drawbacks. First, its goal, the overthrow of the state and all forms of political authority, is often considered to be simply unrealistic. The most common criticism of anarchism is that it is an example of *utopianism in its negative sense, in that it places excessive faith in 'human goodness' or in the capacity of social institutions, such as the market or social ownership, to maintain order and stability. Second, in viewing government as corrupt and corrupting, anarchists have rejected the conventional means of political activism, such as forming *political parties, standing for *election and seeking public office, and have had to rely instead upon the capacity of the masses to engage in spontaneous rebellion. Third, anarchism does not constitute a single, coherent set of political ideas: apart from anti-statism, anarchists disagree profoundly about the nature of an anarchic society and particularly about property rights and economic organisation.

However, the significance of anarchism is perhaps less that it has provided an ideological basis for acquiring and retaining political *power, and more that it has challenged, and thereby fertilised, other political creeds. Anarchists have highlighted the coercive and destructive nature of political power, and in so doing have countered statist tendencies within other ideologies, notably liberalism, socialism and *conservatism. In this sense anarchism has had growing influence upon modern political thought. Both the *New Left and *New Right, for instance, have exhibited libertarian tendencies, which bear the imprint of anarchist ideas. Indeed, the continuing importance of anarchism is perhaps merely concealed by its increasingly diverse character. In addition to, and in some ways in place of, established political and class struggles, anarchists have come to address issues such as ecology, transport, urban development, consumerism, new technology and sexual relations. To argue that anarchism is irrelevant because it has long since lost the potential to become a mass movement maybe misses the point. As the world becomes increasingly complex and fragmented, it may be that it is mass politics itself that is dead.

CHRISTIAN DEMOCRACY

Christian democracy is a political and ideological movement which advances a moderate and welfarist brand of *conservatism. The origins of Christian democracy lie in Catholic social theory, which, in contrast to Protestantism's stress upon *individualism, emphasises the importance of social groups, and especially the family, and highlights a harmony of interests amongst these groups. Although Christian democracy is ideologically vague and has adapted itself to different national cultures and political circumstances, two major themes have been recurrent. The first is a concern about the effects of unregulated market capitalism, reflected in a willingness to embrace Keynesian (see *social democracy) and welfarist policies. The second is a fear of state control, reflected in a hostility to *socialism in general and to *communism in particular. The most influential of Christian democrat ideas, particularly associated with the German Christian Democratic Union (CDU), is the notion of the social market. A social market is an economy that is structured by market principles and largely free from government control, operating in the context of a society in which cohesion is maintained through a comprehensive welfare system and effective public services. The market is thus not so much an end in itself as a means of generating wealth in order to achieve broader social goals.

Significance

Christian democracy has been an important political movement in many parts of Europe in the post-Second World War period. Its success has been associated in particular with the influence of Christian democratic parties in France during the Fourth

Republic, Italy, Germany, Austria, Belgium and the Netherlands, and, to a lesser extent, in Latin America and post-communist Eastern Europe. The success of these parties stems partly from their centre–right political stance, which parallels that of paternalistic conservatism and consolidates middle-class support, but it is also due to the fact that 'Christian' has served as a rallying cry against communism, while 'democracy' indicates a concern with the common good rather than with elite or aristocratic interests (thereby breaking with pre-war conservative parties). It is notable, for instance, that Christian democratic parties generally resisted the *New Right enthusiasms that characterised conservatism in the UK and the USA in the 1980s and 1990s. The chief threats to Christian democracy have come from the declining importance of religion as a source of political motivation, from the receding threat of communism since the Eastern European Revolutions of 1989–91, and from the ideological ambiguities and uncertainties of Christian democracy itself. Since it both praises and warns against government intervention, it sometimes appears to be little more than a vehicle for winning or retaining government power.

Communism

The term communism has been used in three different, if related, ways: as a political principle, as a social model or regime-type based upon this principle, and as an ideological movement whose central purpose is to establish such a society or regime. As a political principle, communism stands for the communal organisation of social existence and, in particular, the common or collective ownership of wealth. In the *Communist Manifesto* ([1848] 1967), Karl Marx (1818–83) thus summed up the theory of communism as the 'abolition of private property'. There are two versions of communism as a social model or regime-type. The first of these is a model of a future society described in the writings of Marx and Engels (1820–95). Marx predicted that after the overthrow of *capitalism there would be a transitionary 'socialist' stage of development, characterised by the 'revolutionary dictatorship of the proletariat', which would, as class antagonisms abated, eventually lead to full communism.

Although Marx refused to describe in detail this communist society, he envisaged that it would have the following features:

- it would be based upon the common ownership of wealth and would thus be classless;
- it would be stateless in the sense that once the class system had been abolished the *state would gradually 'wither away';
- it would be geared not towards commodity production and the market, but to production-for-use and the satisfaction of human needs;
- it would lead to the further development of the 'forces of production' as technology is liberated from the constraints of class-based production;
- by fostering unalienated labour, it would release creative energies and allow for the full development of human potential.

The second version of communism as a social model is based upon the regimes that communist parties established when they gained power in the twentieth century, for example in the USSR and Eastern Europe and in China, Cuba, Vietnam and elsewhere. Communism in this sense came to mean 'actually existing socialism', sometimes seen as 'orthodox communism'. Orthodox communism amounted to a form of state *socialism in which political control was vested in the hands of a monopolistic and hierarchical communist party and the economy was organised on the basis of state *collectivisation and central planning.

As an ideological movement, communism is intrinsically linked to *Marxism: the terms are either used interchangeably, or communism is viewed as operationalised Marxism, Marxism being the theory and communism the practice. However, communism in this sense is better linked to so-called orthodox Marxism, sometimes portrayed as 'dialectical materialism', because it was as much influenced by the ideas of Leninism and Stalinism as it was by the classical ideas of Marx. Just as Soviet communism became the dominant model of communist rule in the twentieth century, Marxism–Leninism became the ruling *ideology of the communist world. Although communist ideology was reinterpreted in different societies and by different leaders, it was characterised by a number of recurrent themes. The most important of these were a sometimes crude belief in the primacy of economics over other historical factors, strong support for revolution rather than reform, the identification of the proletariat as the revolutionary class, a belief in the communist party as the 'vanguard of the working class', support for socialist or proletarian *internationalism, and a belief in comprehensive collectivisation.

Significance

Communism as the principle of common ownership long pre-dates Marx and can be found in the writings of Plato (427–347 BCE) and Thomas More (1478–1535); however, its modern significance is almost entirely associated with the theory and practice of Marxism. As an ideological movement, communism was one of the most powerful political forces of the twentieth century, although its influence was largely confined to the 1917–91 period. However, during this period, communism presented the chief alternative to capitalism: it provided the basis for political and social reconstruction in what became known as the communist East, and constituted the principal oppositional force in many parts of the capitalist West. The ideological potency of communism stemmed from its stress upon social equality and the common good, and its promise to bring to an end what Marx called 'the exploitation of the many by the few'. Its political success was closely linked to its capacity to mobilise oppressed or disadvantaged classes in support of revolutionary leaders who were well organised and followed clear political strategies. Communism in power proved to be a formidable force: the construction of one-party states not only weakened 'class enemies' and opposition groups, but also allowed communist parties to operate as 'ruling' parties in the sense that they dominated all aspects of government, the military, the economy and the ideological apparatus. In practice, twentieth-century communism was largely a vehicle for modernisation that was most successful in economically backward societies where its success was ultimately judged in terms of its capacity to deliver social development.

Critics of communism have usually lighted upon the more unattractive aspects of orthodox communism, sometimes tracing these back to the classical ideas of Marx. In this light, communism is seen to be intrinsically dictatorial, if not implicitly totalitarian. The oppressive face of communism stems from the fact that it combines the ideas of concentrated political power and centralised state control (despite Marx's doctrine of 'withering away'), creating an all-powerful party-state apparatus, typically dominated by a charismatic leader. The dramatic collapse of communism in the Eastern European Revolutions of 1989–91 and the radical reforms that have occurred where communist parties have clung on to power indicate a number of structural weaknesses within orthodox communism. The most important of these are the (arguably) inherent inefficiency of planning systems and the inability of communist states to match the economic prosperity enjoyed in capitalist ones (and in particular, the failure to produce Western-style consumer goods); the tendency towards sclerosis in a political system that was dominated by entrenched party and bureaucratic interests; and the fact that communist political systems lacked the mechanisms through which elite groups could monitor and respond to popular pressures.

COMMUNITARIANISM

Communitarianism is the belief that the self or person is constituted through the *community, in the sense that individuals are shaped by the communities to which they belong and thus owe them a debt of respect and consideration – there are no 'unencumbered selves'. Communitarianism is not an *ideology in its own right, but is, rather, a theoretical position that has been adopted by a variety of ideological traditions. Left-wing forms of communitarianism link the idea of community to the notions of unrestricted *freedom and social *equality (for example, *anarchism and utopian *socialism). Centrist forms of communitarianism hold that community is grounded in an acknowledgement of reciprocal rights and responsibilities (for example, *social democracy and Tory paternalism). Right-wing forms of communitarianism hold that community requires respect for *authority and established values (for example, neo-conservatism and, in its extreme form, *fascism). In the 1980s and 1990s, communitarianism has developed into a school of thought that articulates a particular political philosophy. In this form, associated with theorists such as Alasdair MacIntyre (1981) and Michael Sandel (1982), it advances a specific critique of *liberalism, which highlights the damage done to the public culture of liberal societies by their emphasis upon individual rights and liberties over the needs of the community. So-called 'high' and 'low' forms of communitarianism are sometimes identified. The former engages primarily in philosophical debate, while the latter, whose best known figure is Amitai Etzioni (1995), is more concerned with issues of public policy.

Significance

Communitarianism has its origins in the nineteenth-century socialist *utopianism of thinkers such as Robert Owen (1771–1858) and Peter Kropotkin (1842–1921). Indeed, a concern with community can be seen as one of the enduring themes in modern political thought, expressed variously in the socialist stress upon fraternity and cooperation, the Marxist belief in a classless communist society, the conservative view of society as an organic whole, and even the fascist commitment to an indivisible national community.

However, modern communitarianism emerged as a late twentieth-century reaction against the imbalances in modern society and political thought that have occurred through the spread of liberal *individualism. Communitarians warn that, unconstrained by social duty and a moral responsibility, individuals have been allowed or encouraged to take account only of their own interests and their own rights. In this moral vacuum, society, quite literally, disintegrates. The communitarian project thus attempts to restore to society its moral voice and, in a tradition dating back to Aristotle (384–22 BCE), to construct a 'politics of the common good'. As a critique of *laissez-faire* *capitalism, communitarianism has had a growing influence upon modern liberalism and social democracy.

However, critics of communitarianism allege that it has both conservative and authoritarian implications. Communitarianism has a conservative disposition in that it amounts to a defence of existing social structures and moral codes. Feminists, for example, have criticised communitarianism for attempting to bolster traditional sex roles under the guise of defending the family. The authoritarian features of communitarianism stem from its tendency to emphasise the duties and responsibilities of the individual over his or her rights and entitlements.

CONSERVATISM

Conservatism, as a political attitude, is defined by the desire to conserve and is reflected in a resistance to, or at least suspicion of, change. However, although the desire to resist change may be the recurrent theme within conservatism, what distinguishes conservatism as an *ideology from rival political creeds is the distinctive way in which this position is upheld. The central themes of conservative ideology are *tradition, human imperfection, organic society, *authority and *property. For a conservative, tradition reflects the accumulated wisdom of the past, and institutions and practices that have been 'tested by time'; it should be preserved for the benefit of the living and for generations yet to come. Conservatives view *human nature pessimistically in at least three senses. First, human beings are limited, dependent and security-seeking creatures; second, they are morally corrupt, tainted by selfishness, greed and a thirst for power; third, human rationality is unable to cope with the infinite complexity of the world (hence conservatives' faith in pragmatism and their preference for describing their beliefs as an 'attitude of mind' rather than an ideology). The belief that society should be viewed as an organic whole implies that institutions and values have arisen through natural necessity and should be preserved to safeguard the fragile 'fabric of society'. Conservatives view authority as the basis for social cohesion, arguing that it gives people a sense of who they are and what is expected of them, and reflects the hierarchical nature of all social institutions. Conservatives value property because it gives people security and a measure of independence from government, and also encourages them to respect the law and the property of others.

However, there are significant divisions within conservative thought. *Authoritarian conservatism* is starkly autocratic and reactionary, stressing that government 'from above' is the only means of establishing *order, and thus contrasts with the more modest and pragmatic Anglo-American conservatism that stems from the writing of Edmund Burke (1729–97). *Paternalistic conservatism* draws upon a combination of prudence and principle in arguing both that 'reform from above' is preferable to 'revolution from below', and that the wealthy have an obligation to look after the less well-off, duty being the price of privilege. Such ideas were most influentially expressed by Benjamin Disraeli (1804–81). This tradition is most fully developed in the form of One Nation conservatism, which advocates a 'middle way' approach to state–market relations and gives qualified support to economic management and welfarism. *Libertarian conservatism* advocates the greatest possible economic liberty and the least possible government regulation of social life, echoing *laissez-faire* liberalism, but harnesses this to a belief in a more traditional, conservative social philosophy that stresses the importance of authority and

duty. This tradition provided the basis for *New Right theories
and values.

Significance

Conservative ideas and doctrines first emerged in the late eighteenth century and the early nineteenth century. They arose as a
reaction against the growing pace of economic and social change,
which was in many ways symbolised by the French Revolution
(1789). In trying to resist the pressures unleashed by the growth of
*liberalism, *socialism and *nationalism, conservatism stood in
defence of an increasingly embattled traditional social order.
Authoritarian conservatism took root in continental Europe but
was increasingly marginalised by the advance of *constitutionalism
and *democracy, and eventually collapsed with the fall of *fascism,
with which it had often collaborated. The Disraelian form of conservatism ultimately proved to be more successful. Using Burke's
notion of 'change in order to conserve', it allowed conservatism to
adapt values such as tradition, hierarchy and authority to the emerging conditions of mass politics, thereby broadening its social and
electoral base. Conservatism's remarkable resilience stems from its
ideological caution and political flexibility, enabling it, at different
times, to embrace welfarist and interventionist policies as manifestations of the One Nation ideal, and to advocate 'rolling back the
state' as recommended by the New Right.

Conservative thought, however, has always been open to the
charge that it amounts to nothing more than ruling-class ideology.
In proclaiming the need to resist change, it legitimises the status quo
and defends the interests of dominant or elite groups. Other critics
allege that divisions between traditional conservatism and the New
Right run so deep that the conservative tradition has become
entirely incoherent. In their defence, conservatives argue that they
merely advance certain enduring, if at times unpalatable, truths
about human nature and the societies we live in. That human
beings are morally and intellectually imperfect, and seek the security that only tradition, authority and a shared culture can offer,
merely underlines the wisdom of 'travelling light' in ideological
terms. Experience and history, conservatives warn, will always provide a sounder basis for political action than will abstract principles
such as *freedom, *equality and *justice.

ECOLOGISM

The central feature of ecologism is the belief that nature is an inter-connected whole, embracing humans and non-humans as well as the inanimate world (the term 'ecology' means the study of organisms 'at home' or 'in their habitats'). A distinction is often drawn between ecologism and environmentalism. Environmentalism refers to a moderate or reformist approach to the environment that responds to ecological crises but without fundamentally questioning conventional assumptions about the natural world. It thus includes the activities of most environmental *pressure groups and is a stance that may be adopted by a range of *political parties. Ecologism, in contrast, is an *ideology in its own right, in that it adopts an ecocentric or biocentric perspective that accords priority to nature or the planet, and thus differs from the anthropocentric or human-centred perspectives of conventional ideological traditions. Nevertheless, two strains of ecologism are normally identified. 'Deep ecology' completely rejects any lingering belief that the human species is in some way superior to, or more important than, any other species – or, indeed, nature itself. 'Shallow ecology', on the other hand, accepts the lessons of ecology but harnesses them to human needs and ends. In other words, it preaches that if we can serve and cherish the natural world, it will, in turn, continue to sustain human life.

A variety of hybrid forms of ecologism have emerged. *Eco-socialism*, usually influenced by modern *Marxism, explains environmental destruction in terms of *capitalism's rapacious quest for profit. *Eco-anarchism* draws parallels between natural equilibrium in nature and in human communities, using the idea of 'social ecology'. *Eco-feminism* portrays *patriarchy as the chief source of environmental destruction, and usually believes that women are naturally ecological. *Reactionary ecologism* links the conservation of nature to the defence of the traditional social order, and was most radically expressed in the 'blood and soil' ideas of *Nazism. However, 'deep' ecology rejects all conventional political creeds. It tends to regard both capitalism and *socialism as examples of the 'super-ideology' of industrialism, characterised by large-scale production, the accumulation of capital and relentless growth. It supports biocentric *equality, holding that the *rights of animals have the same moral status as those of humans, and portrays nature as an ethical community within which human beings are merely 'plain citizens'.

Significance

Ecological or green political ideas can be traced back to the nine-teenth-century backlash against the spread of industrialisation and urbanisation. Modern ecologism emerged during the 1960s along with renewed concern about the damage done to the environment by pollution, resource depletion, over-population and so on. Such concerns have been articulated politically by a growing number of green parties which now operate in most developed societies and, at least in the case of the Greens in Germany, have shared government power, and through the influence of a powerful environmentalist lobby whose philosophy is 'think globally, act locally'. Although, in origin at least, green parties styled themselves as 'anti-party parties' and adopted radical ecological perspectives, environmental *pressure groups generally practise 'shallow' ecologism.

However, the spread of ecologism has been hampered by a number of factors. These include the limited attraction of its anti-growth, or at least sustainable growth, economic model, and the fact that its critique of industrial society is sometimes advanced from a pastoral and anti-technology perspective that is out of step with the modern world. Some, as a result, dismiss ecologism as simply an urban fad, a form of post-industrial romanticism. Ecologism, nevertheless, has at least two major strengths. First, it draws attention to an imbalance in the relationship between humans and the natural world that is manifest in a growing catalogue of threats to the well-being of both. Second, ecologism has gone further than any other ideological tradition in questioning and transcending the limited focus of Western political thought. In keeping with *globalisation, it is the nearest thing that political theory has to a world philosophy.

FASCISM

Fascism is a political *ideology whose core theme is the idea of an organically unified national community, embodied in a belief in 'strength through unity'. The individual, in a literal sense, is nothing; individual identity must be entirely absorbed into the community or social group. The fascist ideal is that of the 'new man', a hero, motivated by duty, honour and self-sacrifice, prepared to dedicate his life to the glory of his *nation or *race, and to give unquestioning obedience to a supreme leader. In many respects, fascism constitutes a revolt against the ideas and values that dominated Western political thought from the French Revolution onwards; in the words of the Italian fascist slogan: '1789 is Dead'. Values such as *rationalism, progress, *freedom and *equality were thus overturned in the name of struggle, *leadership, *power, heroism and war. In this sense, fascism has an 'anti-character'. It is defined largely by what it opposes: it is anti-rational, anti-liberal, anti-conservative, anti-capitalist, anti-bourgeois, anti-communist and so on. Fascism represents the darker side of the Western political tradition, the central values of which it transformed rather than abandoned. For fascists, freedom means complete submission, democracy is equated with dictatorship, progress implies constant struggle and war, and creation is fused with destruction.

Fascism has nevertheless been a complex historical phenomenon, and it is difficult to identify its core principles or a 'fascist minimum'. For instance, although most commentators treat Mussolini's fascist *dictatorship in Italy and Hitler's Nazi dictatorship in Germany as the two principal manifestations of fascism, others regard fascism and *Nazism as distinct ideological traditions. Italian fascism was essentially an extreme form of statism that was based upon unquestioning respect and absolute loyalty towards a 'totalitarian' state. As the fascist philosopher Giovanni Gentile (1875–1944) put it, 'everything for the state; nothing against the state; nothing outside the state'. German Nazism, on the other hand, was constructed largely on the basis of *racialism. Its two core theories were Aryanism (the belief that the German people constitute a 'master race' and are destined for world domination) and a virulent form of anti-Semitism that portrayed the Jews as inherently evil and aimed at their eradication. *Neo-fascism* or 'democratic fascism' claims to have distanced itself from principles such as charismatic leadership, *totalitarianism and overt racialism. It is a form of fascism that is often linked to anti-immigration campaigns and is associated with the growth of insular, ethnically or racially based forms of *nationalism that have sprung up as a reaction against *globalisation and *supranationalism.

Significance

Although the major ideas and doctrines of fascism can be traced back to the nineteenth century, they were fused together and shaped by the First World War and its aftermath, in particular by a potent mixture of war and *revolution. Fascism emerged most dramatically in Italy and Germany, manifest respectively in the Mussolini regime (1922–43) and the Hitler regime (1933–45). Some historians regard fascism as a specifically inter-war phenomenon, linked to a historically unique set of circumstances. These circumstances included: the First World War's legacy of disruption, lingering militarism and frustrated nationalism; the fact that in many parts of Europe democratic values had yet to replace older, autocratic ones; the threat to the lower middle classes of the growing might of big business and organised labour; the fears generated amongst propertied classes generally and elite groups in particular by the Bolshevik Revolution in Russia; and the economic insecurity of the 1920s which deepened with the full-scale world economic crisis of the early 1930s. According to this view, fascism died in 1945 with the final collapse of the Hitler and Mussolini regimes, and it has been suppressed ever since by a combination of political stability and economic security. The late twentieth century nevertheless witnessed a renewal of fascism in the form of neo-fascism. Neo-fascism has been particularly influential in Eastern Europe, where it has sought to revive national rivalries and racial hatreds, and has taken advantage of the political instability that resulted from the collapse of *communism. However, it is questionable whether fascism can meaningfully adopt a 'democratic' face, since this implies an accommodation with principles such as *pluralism, *toleration and *individualism.

FEMINISM

Feminism is a political movement and *ideology that aims to advance the social role of women. Feminists have highlighted what they see as the political relationship between the sexes: the supremacy of men and the subjection of women in most, if not all, societies. Feminist ideology is therefore characterised by two basic beliefs. First, women and men are treated differently because of their sex; and second, this unequal treatment can and should be overturned. Although most feminists therefore embrace the goal of sexual *equality, it is misleading to define feminism in terms of this goal as some feminists distinguish between liberation and equality, arguing that the latter implies that women should be 'like men'.

The central concept in feminist analysis is *patriarchy, which draws attention to the totality of oppression and exploitation to which women are subject. This, in turn, highlights the political importance of *gender, understood to refer to socially imposed rather than biological differences between women and men. Most feminists view gender as a political construct, usually based upon stereotypes of 'feminine' and 'masculine' behaviour and social roles.

Feminist theory and practice is highly diverse, however. Distinctive liberal, socialist/Marxist and radical forms of feminism are conventionally identified. *Liberal feminism* reflects a commitment to *individualism and formal equality, and is characterised by the quest for equal *rights and opportunities in 'public' and political life. *Socialist feminism*, largely derived from *Marxism, highlights links between female subordination and the capitalist mode of production, drawing attention to the economic significance of women being confined to the family or domestic life. *Radical feminism* goes beyond the perspectives of established political traditions in portraying gender divisions as the most fundamental and politically significant cleavages in society, and in calling for the radical, even revolutionary, restructuring of personal, domestic and family life. Radical feminists proclaim that 'the personal is the political'. However, the breakdown of feminism into three traditions – liberal, socialist and radical – has become increasingly redundant since the 1970s as feminism has become yet more sophisticated and diverse. Amongst its more recent forms have been black feminism, psychoanalytic feminism, eco-feminism and postmodern feminism.

Significance

The so-called 'first wave' of feminism was closely associated with the women's suffrage movement, which emerged in the 1840s and 1850s. The achievement of female suffrage in most Western countries in the early twentieth century meant that the campaign for legal and civil rights assumed a lower profile and deprived the women's movement of a unifying focus. The 'second wave' of feminism arose during the 1960s and expressed, in addition to the established concern with equal rights, the more radical and revolutionary demands of the growing Women's Liberation Movement. Since the early 1970s, feminism has undergone a process of de-radicalisation, leading some to proclaim the emergence of post-feminism. This was undoubtedly linked to a growing back-lash against feminism, associated with the rise of the *New Right, but it also reflected the emergence of more individualised and con-ventionalised forms of feminism, characterised by an unwillingness any longer to view women as 'victims'.

The major strength of feminist ideology is that it has exposed and challenged the gender biases that pervade society and which have been ignored by conventional political thought. As such, feminism has gained growing respectability as a distinctive school of political thought. It has shed new light upon established concepts such as *power, domination and equality, but also introduced a new sensi-tivity and language into *politics related to ideas such as connec-tion, voice and difference. Feminism has nevertheless been criticised on the grounds that its internal divisions are now so sharp that feminist theory has lost all coherence and unity. Post-modern feminists, for example, even question whether 'woman' is a meaningful category. Others suggest that feminism has become dis-engaged from a society that is increasingly post-feminist, in that, largely thanks to the women's movement, the domestic, profes-sional and public roles of women, at least in developed societies, have undergone a major transformation.

LIBERALISM

Liberalism is a political *ideology whose central theme is a commit-ment to the individual and to the construction of a society in which individuals can satisfy their interests or achieve fulfilment. The core values of liberalism are *individualism, *rationalism, *freedom, *justice and *toleration. The liberal belief that human beings are, first and foremost, individuals, endowed with reason, implies that each individual should enjoy the maximum possible freedom consis-tent with a like freedom for all. However, although individuals are 'born equal' in the sense that they are of equal moral worth and should enjoy formal *equality and equal opportunities, liberals generally stress that they should be rewarded according to their differing levels of talent or willingness to work, and therefore favour the principle of *meritocracy. A liberal society is charac-terised by diversity and *pluralism and is organised politically around the twin values of *consent and *constitutionalism, com-bined to form the structures of *liberal democracy.

rooted in, respectively, the idea of individual *rights and *laissez-faire* (literally 'leave to do', meaning unconstrained by *government) economic doctrines. Libertarian theories of rights generally stress that the individual is the owner of his or her person and thus that people have an absolute entitlement to the *property that their labour produces. Libertarian economic theories emphasise the self-regulating nature of the market mechanism and portray government intervention as always unnecessary and counter-productive. Although all libertarians reject government's attempts to redistribute wealth and deliver social *justice, a division can nevertheless be drawn between those libertarians who subscribe to anarcho-capitalism and view the state as an unnecessary evil, and those who recognise the need for a minimal state, sometimes styling themselves as 'minarchists'.

Significance

Libertarianism has influenced a number of ideological forms. Libertarianism clearly overlaps with classical *liberalism (although the latter refuses to give priority to liberty over *order); it constitutes one of the major traditions from which the *New Right draws; and in the form of socialist libertarianism, it has encouraged a preference for self-management rather than state control. In embodying an extreme faith in the individual and in freedom, libertarianism provides a constant reminder of the oppressive potential that resides within all the actions of government. However, criticisms of libertarianism fall into two general categories. One sees the rejection of any form of welfare or redistribution as an example of capitalist *ideology, linked to the interests of business and private wealth. The other highlights the imbalance in libertarian philosophy that allows it to stress rights but ignore responsibilities, and which values individual effort and ability but fails to take account of the extent to which these are a product of the social environment.

MARXISM

Marxism is an ideological system within *socialism that developed out of, and drew inspiration from, the writings of Karl Marx (1818–83). However, Marxism as a codified body of thought came into existence only after Marx's death. It was the product of the attempt, notably by Friedrich Engels (1820–95), Karl Kautsky (1854–1938) and Georgie Plekhanov (1856–1918), to condense Marx's ideas and theories into a systematic and comprehensive world view that suited the needs of the growing socialist movement. The core of Marxism is a philosophy of history that outlines why *capitalism is doomed and why *socialism and eventually *communism are destined to replace it. This philosophy is based upon *historical materialism, the belief that economic factors are the ultimately determining force in human history, developed into what Marx and Engels classified as 'scientific socialism'. In Marx's view, history is driven forward through a dialectical process in which internal contradictions within each mode of production, or economic system, are reflected in class antagonism. Capitalism, then, is only the most technologically advanced of class societies, and is itself destined to be overthrown in a proletarian *revolution which will culminate in the establishment of a classless, communist society.

However, there are a number of rival versions of Marxism, the most obvious ones being classical Marxism, orthodox Marxism and modern Marxism. *Classical Marxism* is the Marxism of Marx and Engels (although Engels' *Anti-Dühring*, written in 1876, is sometimes seen as the first work of Marxist orthodoxy, since it emphasises the need for adherence to an authoritative interpretation of Marx's work). *Orthodox Marxism* is often portrayed as 'dialectical materialism' (a term coined by Plekhanov and not used by Marx), and later formed the basis of Soviet communism. This 'vulgar' Marxism placed a heavier stress upon mechanistic theories and historical inevitability than did Marx's own writings. However, further complications stem from the breadth and complexity of Marx's own writings and the difficulty of establishing the 'Marxism of Marx'. Some see Marx as a humanist socialist, while others proclaim him to be an economic determinist. Moreover, distinctions have also been drawn between his early and later writings, sometimes presented as a distinction between the 'young' Marx and the 'mature' Marx. The 'young' Marx developed a form of socialist humanism that stressed the link between communism and human fulfilment through unalienated labour; the 'mature' Marx gave much greater attention to economic analysis and appeared to subscribe to a belief in historical inevitably. *Modern Marxism* (sometimes called Western or neo-Marxism) has tried to provide an alternative to the mechanistic and determinist ideas of orthodox Marxism by looking to

Hegelian philosophy (see *dialectic), *anarchism, *liberalism, *feminism and even *rational choice theory, and has been concerned to explain the failure of Marx's predictions, looking, in particular, to the analysis of *ideology and the *state.

Significance

Marxism's political impact has largely been related to its ability to inspire and guide the twentieth-century communist movement. The intellectual attraction of Marxism has been that it embodies a remarkable breadth of vision, offering to understand and explain virtually all aspects of social and political existence, and uncovering the significance of processes that conventional theories ignore. Politically, it has attacked exploitation and oppression, and had a particularly strong appeal to disadvantaged groups and peoples. However, Marxism's star dimmed markedly in the late twentieth century. To some extent this occurred as the tyrannical and dictatorial features of communist regimes themselves were traced back to Marx's ideas and assumptions. Marxist theories were, for instance, seen as implicitly monistic in that rival belief systems are dismissed as ideological. The crisis of Marxism, however, intensified as the result of the collapse of communism in the Eastern European Revolutions of 1989–91. This suggested that if the social and political forms that Marxism had inspired (however unfaithful they may have been to Marx's original ideas) no longer exist, Marxism as a world-historical force is dead. The alternative interpretation is that the collapse of communism provides an opportunity for Marxism, now divorced from Leninism and Stalinism, to be rediscovered as a form of humanist socialism, particularly associated with the ideas of the 'young' Marx.

NAZISM

Nazism, or national socialism, is an ideological tradition within *fascism that is fashioned out of a combination of racial *nationalism, anti-Semitism and social Darwinism. The core of Nazi *ideology is a set of racial theories, encouraging some to define Nazism as 'fascism plus *racialism'. German Nazism, the original and archetypal form of Nazism, portrayed the German people as supremely gifted and organically unified, their creativity resting upon their blood purity. For the Nazis this was reflected in Aryanism, the belief that the Aryans or Germans are a 'master race' and are ultimately destined for world domination. The Jews, in contrast, were seen as fundamentally evil and destructive; in *Mein Kampf* ([1925] 1969), Hitler portrayed the Jews as a universal scapegoat for all Germany's misfortunes. Nazism thus portrayed the world in pseudo-religious and pseudo-scientific terms as a struggle for dominance between the Germans and the Jews, representing respectively the forces of 'good' and 'evil'. The logic of Hitler's worldview was that this racial struggle could only end either in the final victory of the Jews and the destruction of Germany, or in Aryan world conquest and the elimination of the Jewish race. Forms of Nazism that have sprung up outside of Germany since 1945, sometimes termed neo-Nazism, have retained the cult of Hitler but have often reassigned Hitler's racial categories. The Aryans are defined more broadly as the Nordic peoples – pale-skinned, people of north European stock – or simply as the 'whites'. Their enemies are not only the Jews but any convenient racial minority, but most commonly the 'blacks'.

Significance

Nazism had profound and tragic consequences for world history in the twentieth century. The Hitler regime, which was established in 1933, embarked upon a programme of re-militarisation and expansionism which resulted in the Second World War, and in 1941 the Nazis instigated what they called the 'final solution', the attempt to exterminate European Jewry in an unparalleled process of mass murder. This resulted in the death of some six million people. Historians have nevertheless debated how far such events can be explained in terms of the ideological goals of Nazism. One school of thought insists that the entire regime was geared to the fulfilment of Hitler's world-view as outlined in *Mein Kampf*, while another suggests that genocidal slaughter and world war, while consistent with Hitler's goals, were in fact the outcome of tactical blunders and the institutional chaos of a Nazi regime that was structured by bureaucratic rivalries and Hitler's laziness. Germany's susceptibility to Nazism in the 1930s is usually linked to a combination of frustrated nationalism, defeat in the First World War and the terms of the

Treaty of Versailles, and to the deep instabilities of the Weimar republic, exacerbated by the world economic crisis. If Nazism is a specifically German phenomenon, it is associated with chauvinist and anti-Semitic currents that ran through traditional German nationalism and flourished in the peculiar historical circumstances of the inter-war period. However, as a general ideology of race hatred, Nazism, or neo-Nazism, may remain a constant threat as a means of articulating the anger and resentment of socially insecure groups which have become disengaged from conventional politics.

NEW LEFT

The New Left is a broad term that refers to a collection of thinkers and intellectual movements that sought to revitalise socialist thought by developing a radical critique of advanced industrial society. The New Left rejected both 'old' left alternatives: Soviet-style state *socialism and de-radicalised Western *social democracy. Influenced by the humanist writings of the 'young' Marx, *anarchism and radical forms of phenomenology and existentialism, New Left theories were often diffuse. Common themes nevertheless included a rejection of conventional society ('the system') as oppressive; a commitment to personal *autonomy and self-fulfilment in the form of liberation; disillusionment with the role of the working class as the revolutionary agent; and a preference for *decentralisation and participatory *democracy. The term New Left was also used in the 1990s in reference to the quite different and less radical ideas of 'new' social democracy.

Significance

New Left ideas and theories emerged in the late 1950s and reached their high point of prominence in the 1960s and early 1970s. Politically, they amounted to an attack upon conventionalised forms of socialism that appeared no longer able to offer a systematic critique of existing society, or to provide worthwhile alternatives to *capitalism. Socially, they drew inspiration from the phenomenon of post-materialism, the tendency of rising affluence to shift economic priorities away from material concerns to 'quality of life' issues. Although the New Left never had, or claimed to offer, a coherent or unified philosophical position, it provided a broad ideological framework which in the 1960s supported student radicalism, anti-Vietnam war protest and the rise of new *social movements such as *feminism and *ecologism. The strength of New Left was that it developed an unashamed *utopianism that inspired disadvantaged groups and the young in particular, and that it was radically critical of all aspects of conventional life, including family structures and sexuality, consumerism, economic organisation and environmental destruction. However, the New Left can be criticised because of its diffuse and sometimes contradictory nature, and because it addressed the concerns of a radicalised youth more effectively than it did the larger concerns of society.

NEW RIGHT

The New Right is an ideological tradition within *conservatism that advances a blend of market *individualism and social or state *authoritarianism. These different tendencies are usually termed neo-liberalism and neo-conservatism. Neo-liberalism is an updated version of classical *liberalism and particularly classical political economy. Its central pillars are the *market and the individual. The principal neo-liberal goal is to 'roll back the frontiers of the state', in the belief that unregulated market capitalism will deliver efficiency, growth and widespread prosperity. In this view the 'dead hand' of the *state saps initiative and discourages enterprise; *government, however well intentioned, invariably has a damaging effect upon human affairs. This is reflected in a preference for privatisation, economic deregulation, low taxes and anti-welfarism. Such ideas are underpinned by a form of rugged individualism, expressed in Thatcher's famous assertion that 'there is no such thing as society, only individuals and their families'. The 'nanny state' is seen to breed a culture of dependency and to undermine *freedom, which is understood as freedom of choice in the marketplace. Instead, faith is placed in self-help, individual responsibility and entrepreneurialism.

Neo-conservatism reasserts nineteenth-century conservative social principles. The conservative New Right wishes, above all, to restore *authority and return to traditional values, notably those linked to the family, religion and the *nation. Authority is seen as guaranteeing social stability, on the basis that it generates discipline and respect, while shared values and a common culture are believed to foster social cohesion and make civilised existence possible. Neo-conservatism therefore attacks permissiveness, the cult of the self and 'doing one's own thing', thought of as the values of the 1960s. Another aspect of neo-conservatism is the tendency to view the emergence of multi-cultural and multi-religious societies with concern, on the basis that they are conflict-ridden and inherently unstable. This position tends to be linked to an insular form of *nationalism that is sceptical about both immigration and the growing influence of supranational bodies.

Significance

The New Right amounts to a kind of counter-revolution against both the post-war drift towards state intervention and the spread of liberal and progressive social values. New Right ideas can be traced back to the 1970s and the conjunction between the apparent failure of Keynesian *social democracy, signalled by the end of the post-1945 economic boom, and growing concern about social breakdown and the decline of authority. Such ideas had their greatest impact in the UK and the USA, where they were articulated in the 1980s in the form of Thatcherism and Reganism, respectively. However, New Right theories and values have spread well beyond conservatism and have, in particular, been instrumental in converting modern-liberal and social-democratic parties to the cause of the market. The New Right may therefore have succeeded in overthrowing a 'pro-state' tendency that had characterised government throughout much of the twentieth century, especially after 1945, and in establishing an alternative 'pro-market' tendency.

However, there is evidence that, since its high point in the 1980s, the New Right has been in retreat. This stems from two major problems. The first is that New Right ideas are incoherent and, to some extent, contradictory. Neo-liberalism upholds values such as freedom, choice, *rights and competition, while neo-conservatism champions authority, discipline, respect and duty. The danger therefore is that, to the extent that neo-liberals are successful in unleashing the dynamism of unregulated *capitalism, they threaten the established values and traditional institutions which neo-conservatives hold dear. Secondly, the long-term viability of free-market economics has been called into question. 'Rolling back the state' in economic life may sharpen incentives, intensify competition and promote entrepreneurialism, but sooner or later its disadvantages become apparent, notably in the form of short-termism, low investment, widening inequality and the growth of social exclusion.

RACIALISM/RACISM

Racialism is, broadly, the belief that political or social conclusions can be drawn from the idea that humankind is divided into biologically distinct *races. Racialist theories are thus based upon two assumptions. The first is that there are fundamental genetic, or species-type, differences amongst the peoples of the world – racial differences are meaningful. The second is that these genetic divisions are reflected in cultural, intellectual and/or moral differences, making them politically or socially significant. Political racialism is manifest in calls for racial segregation (for instance, apartheid) and in doctrines of 'blood' superiority or inferiority (for instance, Aryanism or anti-Semitism).

'Racialism' and 'racism' are commonly used interchangeably, but the latter is better used to refer to prejudice or hostility towards a people because of their racial origin, whether or not this is linked to a developed racial theory. 'Institutionalised' racism is racial prejudice that is entrenched in the norms and values of an organisation or social system, and so is not dependent upon conscious acts of discrimination or hostility. Nevertheless, the term is highly contentious and has been used, amongst other things, to refer to unwitting prejudice, insensitivity to the values and culture of minority groups, racist stereotyping, racism as a deliberate act of policy, and racial oppression as an ideological system (as in *Nazism).

Significance

Racial theories of politics first emerged in the nineteenth century in the work of theorists such as Count Gobineau (1816–82) and H. S. Chamberlain (1855–1929). They developed through the combined impact of European *imperialism and growing interest in biological theories associated with Darwinism. By the late nineteenth century, the idea that there were racial differences between the 'white', 'black' and 'yellow' peoples of the world was widely accepted in

European society, extending beyond the political *right and including many liberals and even socialists. Overt political racialism has been most clearly associated with *fascism in general and Nazism in particular. However, covert or implicit forms of racialism have operated more widely in campaigns against immigration by far-right groups and parties such as the French National Front and the British National Party. Anti-immigration racialism is based ideologically upon conservative *nationalism, in that it highlights the danger to social cohesion and national unity that is posed by multi-culturalism. The attraction of racialism is that it offers a simple, firm and apparently scientific explanation for social divisions and national differences. However, racialism has little or no empirical basis, and it invariably serves as a thinly veiled justification for bigotry and oppression. Its political success is largely associated with its capacity to generate simple explanations and solutions, and its capacity to harness personal and social insecurities to political ends.

RELIGIOUS FUNDAMENTALISM

Fundamentalism (from the Latin *fundamentum*, meaning 'base') is a style of ideological thought in which certain principles are recognised as essential 'truths' that have unchallengeable and overriding *authority, regardless of their content. Substantive fundamentalisms therefore have little or nothing in common except that their supporters tend to evince an earnestness or fervour born out of doctrinal certainty. Fundamentalism in this sense can be found in a variety of political creeds. For example, *Marxism and *communism are sometimes viewed as forms of fundamentalist *socialism (as opposed to the revisionist socialism endorsed by *social democracy), on the grounds of their absolute and unequivocal rejection of *capitalism. Even liberal scepticism can be said to incorporate the fundamental belief that all theories should be doubted (apart from this one). Although the term is often used pejoratively to imply inflexibility, dogmatism and authoritarianism (and may therefore be avoided by fundamentalists themselves), fundamentalism may suggest selflessness and a devotion to principle.

Religious fundamentalism is characterised by a rejection of the distinction between religion and *politics – 'politics is religion'. This implies that religious principles are not restricted to personal or 'private' life, but are also seen as the organising principles of 'public' existence, including *law, social conduct and the economy as well as politics. The fundamentalist impulse therefore contrasts sharply with secularism, the belief that religion should not intrude into secular (worldly) affairs, reflected in the separation of church from *state. Although some forms of religious fundamentalism co-exist with *pluralism (for example, Christian fundamentalism in the USA and Jewish fundamentalism in Israel) because their goals are limited and specific, other forms of religious fundamentalism are revolutionary (for example, Islamic fundamentalism in Iran, Pakistan and Sudan) in that they aim to construct a theocracy in which the state is reconstructed on the basis of religious principles, and political position is linked to one's place within a religious hierarchy. In some cases, but not necessarily, religious fundamentalism is defined by a belief in the literal truth of sacred texts.

Significance

Religious fundamentalism has been a growing political force since the 1970s. Its most important form has been Islamic fundamentalism, most closely associated with the 'Islamic revolution' in Iran since 1979 but also evident throughout the Middle East and in parts of north Africa and Asia. However, forms of Christian fundamentalism (USA), Jewish fundamentalism (Israel), Hindu fundamentalism and Sikh fundamentalism (India), and even Buddhist fundamentalism (Sri Lanka) have also emerged. It is difficult to generalise about the causes of this fundamentalist upsurge because in different parts of the world it has taken different doctrinal forms and displayed different ideological features. What is clear, however, is that fundamentalism arises in deeply troubled societies, particularly societies afflicted by an actual or perceived crisis of identity. Amongst the factors that contributed to such crises in the late twentieth century were secularisation and the apparent weakening of society's 'moral fabric'; the search in post-colonial states for a non-Western and perhaps anti-Western political identity; the declining status of revolutionary socialism; and the tendency of *globalisation to weaken 'civic' *nationalism and stimulate the emergence of forms of 'ethnic' nationalism. There is, nevertheless, considerable debate about the long-term significance of religious fundamentalism. One view is that fundamentalist religion is merely a symptom of the difficult adjustments that modernisation brings about, but it is ultimately doomed because it is out of step with the secularism and liberal values that are implicit in the modernisation process. The rival view holds that secularism and liberal culture are in crisis and that fundamentalism exposes their failure to address deeper human needs and their inability to establish authoritative values that give social order a moral foundation.

The great strength of fundamentalism is its capacity to generate political activism and mobilise the faithful. Fundamentalism operates on both psychological and social levels. Psychologically, its appeal is based upon its capacity to offer certainty in an uncertain world. Being religious, it addresses some of the deepest and most perplexing problems confronting humankind; being fundamentalist, it provides solutions that are straightforward, practical and, above all, absolute. Socially, although its appeal has extended to the educated and professional classes, religious fundamentalism has been particularly successful in addressing the aspirations of the economically and politically marginalised.

The main criticisms of religious fundamentalism are that it breeds, or legitimises, political extremism and that it is implicitly oppressive, even totalitarian. While the popular image of fundamentalists as bombers and terrorists is unbalanced and misleading, it is impossible to deny that some forms of religious fundamentalism have expressed themselves through militancy and violence. The most common fundamentalist justification for such acts is that, as they are intended to eradicate evil, they fulfil the will of God. The association between fundamentalism and oppression derives from its insistence upon a single, unquestionable truth and a single, unchallengeable source of political authority. This creates profound tension between religious fundamentalism and core features of the Western political tradition such as pluralism and *liberal democracy.

SOCIAL DEMOCRACY

Social democracy is an ideological position, usually, but not necessarily, associated with democratic *socialism, which endorses a reformed or 'humanised' capitalist system (although the term was originally used by Marxists to distinguish between the narrow goal of political democracy and the more radical task of collectivising, or democratising, productive wealth). Social democracy therefore stands for a balance between the *market and the *state, a balance between the individual and the community. At the heart of the social democratic position is an attempt to establish a compromise between, on the one hand, an acceptance of *capitalism as the only reliable mechanism for generating wealth, and, on the other, a desire to distribute social rewards in accordance with moral, rather than market, principles. The chief characteristic of social democracy is thus a belief in reform within capitalism, underpinned by a general concern for the underdog in society, the weak and vulnerable.

However, social democracy can take a variety of forms. In its classical form, associated with ethical socialism, it embodies an underlying commitment to *equality and the politics of social *justice. Nevertheless, social democracy may also be informed by modern liberal ideas, such as positive *freedom and even by a paternalistic conservative emphasis upon social duty, as in the case of the One Nation tradition. In terms of public policy the three traditional pillars of social democracy have been the mixed economy (and therefore selective nationalisation), economic management (usually in the form of Keynesianism, the use of fiscal policies to achieve the goal of full employment, as recommended by J. M. Keynes, 1883–1946), and the welfare state (serving as a redistributive mechanism). Modernised or 'new' social democracy is usually associated with a fuller acceptance of market economics, and with sympathy for communitarian ideas such as mutual obligations and responsibility, breaking, or at least weakening, the traditional link between social democracy and egalitarianism.

Significance

Social democratic ideas and policies had their greatest impact in the early post-1945 period. Advanced by socialist and sometimes liberal and conservative parties, they resulted in the extension of economic and social intervention in most Western states. Social democracy has therefore often been credited with having contained the vagaries of capitalism and delivering wider prosperity and general social stability. However, the 'forward march' of social democracy went hand-in-hand with the 'long boom' of the post-war period, and, when this came to an end with the recessions of the 1970s and 1980s, the underlying contradiction of social democracy (between maintaining capitalism and promoting equality) came to the surface. This has resulted in a widespread abandonment of traditional social democratic positions and the adoption of more market-orientated values and policies. However, just as the flaws of the social democratic pro-state position created opportunities for the *New Right in the 1980s, growing doubts about the New Right's pro-market position may open up fresh opportunities for modernised or 'new' social democracy.

The attraction of social democracy is that it has kept alive the humanist tradition within socialist thought in particular. Its attempt to achieve a balance between efficiency and equality has been, after all, the centre ground to which *politics in most developed societies has tended to gravitate, regardless of whether socialist, liberal or conservative governments are in power. From the Marxist perspective, however, social democracy amounts to a betrayal of socialist principles, and attempts to prop up a defective capitalist system in the name of socialist ideals. Nevertheless, social democracy's central weakness is its lack of firm theoretical roots. Although social democrats have an enduring commitment to equality and social justice, the kind and extent of equality they support, and the specific meanings they have given to social justice, have constantly been revised. For instance, to the extent that social democracy has been recast in terms of the politics of *community, it can be said to have assumed an essentially conservative character. Instead of being a vehicle for social transformation, it has developed into a defence of duty and responsibility, and so serves to uphold established institutions and ways of life.

SOCIALISM

Socialism is an *ideology that is defined by its opposition to *capitalism and its attempt to provide a more humane and socially worthwhile alternative. The core of socialism is a vision of human beings as social creatures united by their common humanity; as the poet John Donne put it, 'No man is an Island entire of itself; every man is a piece of the Continent, a part of the main.' This highlights the degree to which individual identity is fashioned by social interaction and the membership of social groups and collective bodies. Socialists therefore prefer cooperation to competition, and favour *collectivism over *individualism. The central, and some would say defining, value of socialism is *equality, socialism sometimes being portrayed as a form of egalitarianism. Socialists believe that a measure of social equality is the essential guarantee of social stability and cohesion, and that it promotes *freedom in the sense that it satisfies material needs and provides the basis for personal development. The socialist movement has traditionally articulated the interests of the industrial working class, seen as systematically oppressed or structurally disadvantaged within the capitalist system. The goal of socialism is thus to reduce or abolish class divisions.

Socialism, however, contains a bewildering variety of divisions and rival traditions. *Ethical socialism*, or utopian socialism, advances an essentially moral critique of capitalism. In short, socialism is portrayed as morally superior to capitalism because human beings are ethical creatures, bound to one another by the ties of love, sympathy and compassion. *Scientific socialism* undertakes a scientific analysis of historical and social development which, in the form of *Marxism, does not suggest that socialism *should* replace capitalism, but predicts that it inevitably *would* replace capitalism.

A second distinction is about the 'means' of achieving socialism, namely the difference between *revolution and reform. *Revolutionary socialism*, most clearly reflected in the communist tradition, holds that socialism can only be introduced only by the revolutionary overthrow of the existing political and social system, usually based upon the belief that existing state structures are irredeemably linked to capitalism and the interests of the ruling class. *Reformist socialism* (sometimes termed evolutionary, parliamentary or democratic socialism), on the other hand, believes in 'socialism through the ballot box', and thus accepts basic liberal democratic principles such as *consent, *constitutionalism and party competition. Finally, there are profound divisions over the 'end' of socialism, that is, the nature of the socialist project. *Fundamentalist socialism* aims to abolish and replace the capitalist system, viewing socialism as qualitatively different from capitalism. Fundamentalist socialists, such as Marxists and communists, generally equate socialism with common ownership of some form. *Revisionist socialism* aims not to abolish capitalism but to reform it, looking to reach an accommodation between the efficiency of the market and the enduring moral vision of socialism. This is most clearly expressed in *social democracy.

Significance

Socialism arose as a reaction against the social and economic conditions generated in Europe by the growth of industrial capitalism. The birth of socialist ideas was closely linked to the development of a new but growing class of industrial workers, who suffered the poverty and degradation that are so often a feature of early industrialisation. For over two hundred years socialism has constituted the principal oppositional force within capitalist societies, and has articulated the interests of oppressed and disadvantaged peoples in many parts of the world. The principal impact of socialism has been in the form of the twentieth-century communist and social-democratic movements. However, in the late twentieth century socialism suffered a number of spectacular reverses, leading some to proclaim the 'death of socialism'. The most spectacular of these reverses was the collapse of communism in the Eastern European Revolutions of 1989–91. Partly in response to this, and partly as a result of *globalisation and changing social structures, parliamentary socialist parties in many parts of the world re-examined, and sometimes rejected, traditional socialist principles.

The moral strength of socialism derives not from its concern with what people are like, but with what they have the capacity to become. This has led socialists to develop utopian visions of a better society in which human beings can achieve genuine emancipation and fulfilment as members of a community. In that sense, despite its late-twentieth-century setbacks, socialism is destined to survive if only because it serves as a reminder that human development can extend beyond market *individualism. Critics of socialism nevertheless advance one of two lines of argument. The first is that socialism is irrevocably tainted by its association with statism. The emphasis upon collectivism leads to an endorsement of the *state as the embodiment of the public interest. Both communism and social democracy are in that sense 'top-down' versions of socialism, meaning that socialism amounts to an extension of state control and a restriction of *freedom. The second line of argument highlights the incoherence and confusion inherent in modern socialist theory. In this view socialism was only ever meaningful as a critique of, or alternative to, capitalism. The acceptance by socialists of market principles therefore demonstrates either that socialism itself is flawed or that their analysis is no longer rooted in genuinely socialist ideas and theories.

THIRD WAY

The 'third way' is a slogan that encapsulates the idea of an alternative to both *capitalism and *socialism. It draws attention to an ideological position that has attracted political thinkers from various traditions. The term originated within Italian *fascism and was first publicly used by Mussolini (who claimed to have coined it). The fascist 'third way' took the form of *corporatism, a politico-economic system in which major economic interests are bound together under the auspices of the *state. The organic unity of fascist corporatism was supposedly superior to the rampant *individualism of profit-orientated capitalism and the stultifying state control of communism. In the post-1945 period a very different 'third way' was developed in relation to Keynesian *social democracy, found in its most developed form in Sweden. The Swedish economic model attempted to combine elements of both socialism and capitalism. Productive wealth was largely concentrated in private hands, but social *justice was maintained through a comprehensive welfare system funded by a steeply progressive tax regime. More recently, the idea of the 'third way' has resurfaced in association with 'new' social democratic or post-socialist thought. Widely associated with the Blair government and 'new' Labour in the UK, but also influenced by the Clinton administration in the USA, this 'third way' is defined as an alternative to 'top-down' state intervention (and therefore traditional social democracy) and free-market capitalism (and therefore Thatcherism or Reganism). The ideological character of this post-social democratic 'third way' is, however, unclear. In most forms it involves a general acceptance of the *market and of globalised capitalism, qualified by a communitarian emphasis upon social duty and the reciprocal nature of *rights and responsibilities.

Significance

The recurrence of the idea of a 'third way' highlights deep, but perhaps incoherent, dissatisfaction with the two dominant twentieth-century models of economic organisation: market capitalism and state socialism. Proponents of 'third way' politics in effect attempt to develop a non-socialist critique of an unregulated market economy. Although the philosophical and ideological basis of this critique changes, the major reservations about capitalism remain remarkably similar: a concern about the random and often immoral implications of market competition. The flaw of capitalism, from this point of view, is that it is a constant threat to social cohesion and stability. At the same time, however, 'third way' thinkers reject socialism because of its association with state control and because they believe that *collectivisation and planning fail to provide a viable alternative to the capitalist market. Two key criticisms are advanced of 'third way' politics. The first is that the idea of the 'third way' is merely a populist slogan devoid of political or economic content. The second is that 'third way' theories are inherently contradictory because, whilst criticising competition and market individualism, they are not capable of looking beyond a capitalist model of economic organisation.

TORYISM

'Tory' was used in eighteenth-century Britain to refer to a parliamentary faction that (as opposed to the Whigs) supported monarchical *power and the Church of England and represented the landed gentry; in the USA it implied loyalty to the British crown. Although in the mid-nineteenth century the British Conservative Party emerged out of the Tories, and in the UK 'Tory' is still widely (but unhelpfully) used as a synonym for Conservative, Toryism is best understood as a distinctive ideological stance within broader *conservatism. Its characteristic features are a belief in hierarchy, *tradition, duty and an organic society. While 'high' Toryism articulates a neo-feudal belief in a ruling class and a pre-democratic faith in established institutions, the Tory tradition is also hospitable to welfarist and reformist ideas, providing these serve the cause of social and institutional continuity. One Nation conservatism can thus be seen as a form of 'welfare Toryism' or 'Tory democracy'. Tory democracy is an idea developed in the late nineteenth century by Randolph Churchill, who proclaimed that the way to generate wider popular support for traditional institutions was through advancing the cause of social reform.

Significance

Toryism amounts to the vestiges of the feudal political tradition, the remnants of the ideological stance of the landed aristocracy. Tory ideas survived because they were absorbed into conservative *ideology, their attraction being both that they served the interests of new capitalist elites and, because they are not expressed in terms of abstract principles, they proved to be ideologically flexible and adaptable. However, the match between Toryism and conservatism has always been imperfect, as the latter has accommodated, to a greater or lesser extent, capitalist values such as *individualism, self-striving and competition. The rise of the New Right in the 1970s pushed Toryism, and its associated One Nation ideals, to the margins of conservative politics. The attraction of Toryism is that it advances a vision of a stable, if hierarchical, social order, in which the strong take some responsibility for the weak and vulnerable. The disadvantages of Toryism are that it legitimises the class system and articulates values that are entirely out of step with a modern, meritocratic society.

FURTHER READING

Barry, N. P., The New Right (London: Croom Helm, 1987).

Bobbio, N., Left and Right (Cambridge: Polity Press, 1996).

Bryson., V., Feminist Political Theory: An Introduction (London: Macmillan, 1995).

Clarke, P., Liberals and Social Democrats (Cambridge: Cambridge University Press, 1978).

Eatwell, R. and O'Sullivan, N. (eds), The Nature of the Right: European and American Politics and Political Thought since 1789 (London: Pinter, 1989).

Giddens., A., The Third Way: The Renewal of Social Democracy (Cambridge: Polity Press, 1998).

Gray, J., Liberalism (Buckingham: Open University Press, 1995).

Griffin, R. (ed.), Fascism (Oxford and New York: Oxford University Press, 1995).

Heywood., A., Political Ideologies: An Introduction (London: Macmillan, 1998).

Kenny, M., The First New Left: British Intellectuals after Stalin (London: Lawrence and Wishart, 1995).

Kolakowski, L., Main Currents of Marxism, 3 vols (Oxford: Oxford University Press, 1978).

Marty, M. E. and Appleby, R. S. (eds), Fundamentalisms and the State: Re-making Polities, Economies, and Militance (Chicago and London: University of Chicago Press, 1993).

Matchan, T. R. (ed.), The Libertarian Reader (Totowa, NJ: Rowan and Littlefield, 1982).

Miller, D., Anarchism (London: Dent, 1984).

Scruton, R., The Meaning of Conservatism (London: Macmillan, 1984).

Smith, M. J., *Ecologism* (Buckingham: Open University Press, 1998).
Tam, H., *Communitarianism: A New Agenda for Politics and Citizenship* (London: Macmillan, 1998).
Vincent, A., *Modern Political Ideologies* (Oxford: Blackwell, 1995).
Wright, A., *Socialisms: Theories and Practices* (Oxford and New York: Oxford University Press, 1987).

Part four

APPROACHES

This section examines concepts that deal with how politics is studied and how political understanding is acquired.

Approaches

Behaviouralism

Behaviouralism is the belief that social theories should be constructed only on the basis of observable behaviour (as opposed to behaviourism, which is the school of psychology that holds that human behaviour can ultimately be explained in terms of conditioned reactions or reflexes). The behavioural approach to political analysis developed out of *positivism, adopting its assertion that scientific knowledge can be developed only on the basis of explanatory theories that are verifiable or falsifiable. Behavioural analysis typically involves the collection of quantifiable data through research surveys, statistical analysis and the construction of empirical theories that have predictive capacity.

Significance

The so-called 'behavioural revolution' of the 1950s made behaviouralism the dominant force in US political science and a powerful influence elsewhere, notably in the UK. The attraction of behaviouralism was that it allowed political analysis to break away from its concern with *constitutions and normative theory, and gave the study of *politics, perhaps for the first time, reliable scientific credentials. This fuelled the belief, expressed by political analysts such as David Easton (1979), that politics could adopt the methodology of the natural sciences through the use of quantitative research methods in areas such as voting behaviour and the behaviour of legislators, lobbyists and municipal politicians. Behaviouralism, however, came under growing pressure from the 1960s onwards. In the first place, it significantly constrained the scope of political analysis, preventing it going beyond what was directly observable. Although behavioural analysis produced, and continues to produce, invaluable insights in fields such as voting studies, a narrow obsession with quantifiable data threatens to reduce the discipline of politics to little else.

Moreover, the scientific credentials of behaviouralism were called into question, in that its claim to be objective, reliable and 'value-free' is compromised by a range of unstated biases. For instance, if *democracy is redefined in terms of observable behaviour, it means what goes on in so-called democratic political systems in the developed West, and is disengaged from ideas such as popular participation and public accountability. Behaviouralism has, finally, been criticised for treating human behaviour as predictable and determined by the interaction of objective factors, when in fact it is shaped by a variable mix of psychological, social, cultural and historical circumstances. The now more common stance of post-behaviouralism differs from behaviouralism in that it goes further in recognising the role of theory in imposing meaning on data and acknowledges the degree to which theoretical perspectives may impinge upon seemingly objective observations.

DIALECTIC

A dialectic is a process of development brought about by conflict between two opposing forces. Plato's (427–347 BCE) method of developing a philosophical argument by means of a dialogue between Socrates and a protagonist is thus referred to as dialectical. G. W. F. Hegel (1770–1831) explained the process of reasoning and both human and natural history in terms of a theory of the dialectic. According to this, both thought and reality develop towards a determinant end-point through conflict between a 'thesis' and the negation it embodies, the 'antithesis', producing a higher stage of development, the 'synthesis', which, in turn, serves as a new 'thesis'. By contrast with Hegel's *idealism, Karl Marx (1818–83) gave the dialectic a materialist interpretation in identifying the driving force of history as internal contradictions within class society that are manifest in the form of class conflict.

Significance

The strength of the dialectical method is that it draws attention to tensions or contradictions within belief systems and social structures, often providing important insights into the nature of change. In addition, in emphasising relationships and interdependence, dialectics can feature as part of a holistic perspective and be used to analyse ecological processes. Nevertheless, dialectical thinking plays little part in conventional social and political analysis. Its main drawbacks are that, in always linking change to internal contradictions, it over-emphasises conflict in society and elsewhere, and, as in the writings of Hegel and, later, Friedrich Engels (1820–95), the dialectic has been elaborated into a metaphysical system supposedly operating in nature as well as human society. 'Dialectical materialism' (a term coined by the Russian Marxist Georgi Plekhanov (1856–1918), not Marx), refers to a crude and deterministic form of *Marxism that dominated intellectual life in orthodox communist states.

DISCOURSE

Discourse, in everyday language, refers to verbal communication, talk or conversation. However, discourse has been adopted as an analytical concept or theoretical approach by a variety of academic disciplines, including linguistics, literature, philosophy and, most enthusiastically, cultural studies. In its technical sense a discourse is a specialist system of knowledge embodied in a particular language, a kind of mind-set that structures understanding and behaviour (examples could range from legal jargon and religious rituals to ideological traditions). Discourse theory thus uncovers meaning in objects and practices by recognising their discursive character and analysing the part they play in particular discourses and within a wider framework of meaning. Following Michel Foucault (1926–84), an emphasis upon discourse, or what he called 'discursive formation', reflects the belief that knowledge is deeply enmeshed in power, truth always being a social construct.

Significance

Political and social theorists sympathetic to *postmodernism have been attracted to discourse theory for a number of reasons. These include that it recognises that meaning is not implicit in social objects and practices but is historically and politically constructed, and that it can uncover social antagonisms and struggles for *hege-mony that conventional theory ignores.

Criticisms of discourse theory are either philosophical or substan-tive. Philosophically, an emphasis upon discourse may reduce everything to thought or language and deny that there is a reality independent of our ideas or conceptions. It may also imply that everything is relative because truth or falsity can be asserted only in relation to particular discourses. Substantive criticisms include that discourse theory limits or discourages the analysis of political and social institutions, and that, insofar as discourse displaces the concept of *ideology, it shifts the attention of political analysis away from issues of truth and falsity.

EMPIRICISM

Empiricism is the doctrine that sense-experience is the only basis of knowledge, and that therefore all hypotheses and *theories should be tested by a process of observation and experiment. This was evi-dent in John Locke's (1632–1704) belief that the mind is a *tabula rasa* (blank tablet) on which information is imprinted by the senses in the form of sense-data. For David Hume (1711–76), empiricism also implied a deep scepticism which, in its extreme form, should lead us to doubt the existence of objects independent of our percep-tion of them – for instance, does a tree exist if no-one can see it, touch it and so on? In the twentieth century, empiricism has been closely associated with pragmatism, as an epistemological theory. Philosophical pragmatism is the belief that the only way of estab-lishing truth is through practical application, by establishing 'what works out most effectively'. All forms of empiricism draw a clear distinction between 'facts', propositions that have been veri-fied by experience, observation and experiment, and 'values', which as subjective beliefs or opinions are always to be distrusted.

Significance

An empirical tradition can be traced back to the earliest days of political thought. It can be seen in Aristotle's (384–22 BCE) attempt to classify *constitutions, in Machiavelli's (1469–1527) realistic account of statecraft, and in Montesquieu's (1689–1775) sociological theory of *government and *law. In many ways such writings constitute the basis of what is now called comparative government, and gave rise to an essentially institutional approach to the discipline. The empirical approach to political analysis is characterised by the attempt to offer a dispassionate and impartial account of political reality. It is 'descriptive' in that it seeks to analyse and explain, whereas the normative approach is 'prescriptive' in the sense that it makes judgements and offers recommendations. Empiricism thus provided the basis for *positivism and, later, *behaviouralism. However, the high point of philosophical empiricism was reached in the early twentieth century and it has subsequently been subjected to considerable attack. Strict empiricism has been criticised because it is linked to a simplistic model of science that has been badly damaged by advances in the philosophy of science. It also fails to recognise the extent to which human perception and sense-experience are structured by concepts and theories, and is of limited value in dealing with matters that are ethical or normative in character.

FUNCTIONALISM

Functionalism is the doctrine that social institutions and practices can be understood in terms of the functions they carry out in sustaining the larger social system. As functions are the actions or impacts that one thing has on other things, functionalism suggests that social and political phenomena should be understood in terms of their consequences rather than their causes. In the functionalist view the whole is more than merely a collection of its parts, in the sense that the various parts are structured according to the 'needs' of the whole. A variety of political theories have adopted a functionalist methodology. These include the tendency of *historical materialism to interpret the *state, *law and *ideology in terms of their function in sustaining the class system, and the general *systems theory approach to political analysis.

Significance

While a willingness to use aspects of a functional approach to understand political processes has a long heritage, functionalism has never enjoyed the academic status in political analysis that it did in sociology in the 1950s and 1960s, when it was accepted, in the United States in particular, as the dominant theoretical perspective. Nevertheless, an important application of functionalist thinking has been in the traditional conservative notion of an organic society. This is based upon an organic analogy that draws parallels between society and living entities. In this view, society and social institutions arise out of natural necessity, and each part of society – family, church, business, *government and so on – plays a particular role in sustaining the whole and maintaining the 'health' of society. Functionalism's impact upon academic political analysis was greatest in the early post-1945 period, when it was linked to the application of the systems model of political interaction, and was widely used in analysing institutional relationships and performance.

However, the star of functionalism has faded since the 1960s, in political analysis as in sociology. Functionalism has been criticised in two main ways. First, it has been accused of reductionism in that it appears to deprive the *state and political institutions of meaning in their own right and interprets them only in terms of their role in relation to the whole political system. Second, functionalism is implicitly, and sometimes explicitly, conservative. If what is important about institutions is their function in maintaining society, all existing institutions must play a worthwhile role in this respect and the value of maintaining the existing social order is taken for granted. For example, the very survival of the *monarchy becomes its defence – it has survived because of its capacity to generate social cohesion, national unity or whatever, and it should therefore be preserved for the benefit of present society and future generations.

HISTORICAL MATERIALISM

Historical materialism is the theory of history developed by Karl Marx (1818–83), described by his friend and collaborator Friedrich Engels (1820–95) as 'the materialist conception of history'. It highlights the importance of economic life and the conditions under which people produce and reproduce their means of subsistence. This is reflected, simplistically, in the belief that the economic 'base', consisting essentially of the 'mode of production', or economic system, conditions or determines the ideological and political 'superstructure', which encompasses all other institutions including *politics, *law, religion, art and so on. Another formulation of this is Marx's assertion that 'social being determines consciousness'. Historical materialism therefore explains social, historical and cultural development in terms of material and class factors. Considerable debate has nevertheless surrounded the precise nature of the 'base/superstructure' relationship. Marx's early writings are dialectical in the sense that they acknowledge a two-way relationship between human beings and the material world, an idea that Engels tried to acknowledge in describing economic factors as 'the *ultimately* determining element in history'. Historical materialism should be distinguished from 'dialectical materialism', which dominated intellectual life in the Soviet Union and had an overtly mechanistic and determinist character.

Significance

Historical materialism has had considerable significance as the philosophical cornerstone of *Marxism and therefore as the basis of social and political analysis for generations of Marxist thinkers. Its attraction as a means of enquiry has undoubtedly been that it promises to explain virtually all aspects of social and political existence and uncovers the significance of processes that conventional theory ignores. In particular, it establishes what Lenin (1870–1924) referred to as 'the primacy of economics' and allows all other aspects of life to be interpreted in material or class terms. However, historical materialism can be criticised in a number of ways. These include that it is based upon questionable philosophical assumptions about the impact material production and social existence has upon consciousness, and that there are technical difficulties about the precise meaning of and relationship between the 'base' and the 'superstructure'. Moreover, as neo-Marxists accept, it overstates the importance of economics and threatens to turn into a form of materialist reductionism. The final problem is that if the 'base' *determines* the 'superstructure', historical materialism is determinist, and if it does not the theory has no predictive value.

IDEALISM

Idealism is understood in one of two senses, metaphysical and political. *Metaphysical idealism* is the belief that, in the final analysis, only ideas exist. The structure of reality is thus understood in terms of consciousness, as in the work of Plato (427–347 BCE), Kant (1724–1804) and Hegel (1770–1831). Kant's 'transcendental idealism' holds that meaning is not inherent in the external world but is imposed by the knowing subject. Idealism in this sense contrasts with philosophical materialism (as opposed to *historical materialism), the belief that nothing exists except matter, and *empiricism, the theory that knowledge is derived from experience or observation of the external world. *Political idealism* refers to theories or practices that are characterised by an unbending commitment to stipulated ideals or principles (the term is sometimes used pejoratively to suggest a belief in an impossible goal). As a theoretical school of international politics, idealism views international relations from the perspective of values and norms, such as *justice, peace and international law. It thus contrasts with *realism in that it is concerned less with empirical analysis (with how international actors behave) than with normative judgements (with how they *should* behave). Political idealism may be seen as a species of *utopianism.

Significance

Metaphysical idealism underpinned much of the political philosophy of the classical, medieval and early modern periods. Its strength was that, in holding that values such as justice, natural law and reason are implicit in the structure of reality itself, it gave thinkers a firm and universalist perspective from which to judge existing arrangements and engage in political advocacy. However, the status of metaphysical individualism was gradually eroded by the emergence of empirical and scientific approaches to political theorising. Political idealism has been criticised on the grounds that it encourages political energies to be expended on goals that may be unrealistic or unachievable; that it fails to recognise the extent to which political action is determined by practical considerations such as the pursuit of power or the satisfaction of material interests; and that, anyway, political ideals may be contested and lack universal authority. For example, realist theorists in international politics have long ridiculed the idealist's faith in collective security and international harmony. Nevertheless, as examples such as Mahatma Gandhi and Martin Luther King demonstrate, idealism has an undoubted and enduring capacity to inspire commitment and stimulate political activism. Similarly, to downgrade the importance of ideals and principles in political analysis may simply be to legitimise power-seeking and unprincipled behaviour. Thus, disenchantment with the amoral power politics of the superpower era has led in international politics to the emergence of neo-idealism, a perspective that emphasises the practical value of morality and, in particular, of respect for *human rights and national interdependence.

INSTITUTIONALISM

An institution is an enduring and stable set of arrangements that regulates individual and/or group behaviour on the basis of established rules and procedures. Political institutions have a formal and often legal character, employ explicit and usually enforceable rules and decision-making procedures, and are typically part of the machinery of the *state. For this reason political institutions have been defined as 'the rules of the game'. Examples of political institutions include *constitutions, *elections, *parliaments, *bureaucracies, *judiciaries, party systems and so on. Institutionalism, as an approach to political analysis, is the attempt to make sense of political realities by studying the causes and consequences of political institutions. It thus views institutions as political actors in their own right, independent from and capable of influencing wider social, economic and cultural forces.

Traditional institutionalism took political institutions to be the key political actors in that it encouraged reflection upon *politics to focus upon descriptions of institutional behaviour, the analysis of formal or legal rules, or a comparative or historical examination of institutional structures. The idea of *new institutionalism* or neo-institutionalism has been increasingly fashionable since the 1980s. Although it does not have a clear or developed meaning, it tends to be characterised by a recognition of the importance of informal as well as formal institutions and looks beyond traditional institutionalism by accepting that formal-legal approaches to political understanding have only a limited value. As such, it reflects a shift in perspective away from *government and towards *governance. The principal forms which new institutionalism has taken are historical institutionalism, rational-choice institutionalism and sociological institutionalism.

Significance

Institutionalism was the dominant tradition of political analysis until the 1950s. In a sense it can be traced back to the classical political theory of Plato (427–347 BCE) and Aristotle (384–22 BCE), and was developed by Machiavelli (1469–1527), Hobbes (1588–1679), Locke (1632–1704) and Rousseau (1712–78), in that such thinkers not only grappled with political ideals such as *justice, *order and *freedom, but also examined the political institutions most likely to secure these political goods. In the nineteenth and early twentieth centuries this developed into a constitutional–institutional approach to political analysis that emphasised, for instance, differences between codified and uncodified constitutions, parliamentary and presidential systems, and federal and unitary systems. However, the institutional approach became distinctively less fashionable in the 1950s and 1960s in the light of the rise of *behaviouralism, *systems theory and subsequently growing interest in *Marxism.

The main criticisms of institutionalism are that it is guilty of the sin of what David Easton (1981) called 'hyperfactualism', a reverence for facts and a disregard for theory; that it ignores non-institutional influences upon *policy and the distribution of *power; and that it is an entirely state-centred approach to politics that ignores the degree to which the state is linked to and shaped by society. Nevertheless, institutionalism continued to be a significant school of political analysis and, since the 1970s, has been revived through growing interest in constitutional reform, public administration and policy analysis. While an exclusive focus upon institutions may reduce political analysis to dull legalism, to neglect political institutions on the grounds that they may merely be a reflection of, for instance, the utility-maximising behaviour of their members (as *rational choice theory suggests), the distribution of power amongst groups (*pluralism or *elitism), or the basic economic structure of society (*Marxism), is to ignore the fact that state structures and the organisation of government matter.

POLITICAL PHILOSOPHY

Philosophy, in general terms, is the search for wisdom and understanding using the techniques of critical reasoning. However, philosophy has also been seen more specifically as a second-order discipline, in contrast to first-order disciplines which deal with empirical subjects. In other words, philosophy is not so much concerned with revealing truth in the manner of science, as with asking secondary questions about how knowledge is acquired and about how understanding is expressed; it has thus been dubbed the science of questions. Philosophy has traditionally addressed questions related to the ultimate nature of reality (metaphysics), the grounds of knowledge (epistemology) and the basis of moral conduct (ethics).

Political philosophy is often viewed as a subfield of ethics or moral philosophy, in that it is preoccupied with essentially prescriptive or normative questions, reflecting a concern with what *should, ought* or *must* be brought about, rather than what *is*. Its central questions have included 'why should I obey the state?', 'who should rule?', 'how should rewards be distributed?' and 'what should be the limits of individual freedom?' Academic political philosophy addresses itself to two main tasks. First, it is concerned with the critical evaluation of political beliefs, paying attention to both inductive and deductive forms of reasoning. Second, it attempts to clarify and refine the concepts employed in political discourse. What this means is that, although political philosophy may be carried out critically and scrupulously, it cannot be objective in that it is inevitably concerned with justifying certain political viewpoints at the expense of others and with upholding a particular understanding of a concept rather than alternative ones. Political philosophy is therefore clearly distinct from *political science. Although political philosophy is often used interchangeably with *political theory, the former deals strictly with matters of evaluation and advocacy, while the latter is broader, in that it also includes explanation and analysis and thus cuts across the normative/empirical divide.

Significance

Political philosophy constitutes what is called the 'traditional' approach to politics. It dates back to Ancient Greece and the work of the founding fathers of political analysis, Plato (427–347 BCE) and Aristotle (384–22 BCE). Their ideas resurfaced in the writings of medieval thinkers such as Augustine (354–430) and Aquinas (1224–74). In the early modern period, political philosophy was closely associated with the social contract theories of Hobbes (1588–1679), Locke (1632–1704) and Rousseau (1712–78), while in the nineteenth century it was advanced through J. S. Mill's (1806–73) work on *freedom and Marx's (1818–83) materialist conception of history. However, the status of political philosophy was gradually weakened from the late nineteenth century onwards by the rise of the empirical and scientific traditions, which led by the 1950s and 1960s to a frontal assault on the very basis of normative theorising. Political philosophy was declared to be dead, on the grounds that its central principles, such as *justice, *rights, liberty and *equality, are meaningless because they are not empirically ver-ifiable entities. However, there has been a significant revival in poli-tical philosophy since the 1970s and the tendency is now for political philosophy and political science to be seen less as distinct modes of political enquiry, and still less as rivals. Instead they have come to be accepted simply as contrasting ways of disclosing political knowl-edge. This has occurred through disillusionment with *behavioural-ism and the recognition that values, hidden or otherwise, underpin all forms of political enquiry, and as a result of the emergence of new areas of philosophical debate, linked, for instance, to *feminism and to rivalry between *liberalism and *communitarianism.

POLITICAL SCIENCE

Science (from the Latin *scientia*, meaning knowledge) is a field of study that aims to develop reliable explanations of phenomena through repeatable experiments, observations and deductions. The 'scientific method', by which hypotheses are verified (proved true) by testing them against the available evidence, is therefore seen as a means of disclosing value-free and objective truth. Karl Popper (1902–94), however, suggested that science can only falsify hypotheses, since 'facts' can always be disproved by later experi-ments. Scientism is the belief that the scientific method is the only source of reliable knowledge, and so should be applied to fields such as philosophy, history and *politics, as well as the natural sciences. Doctrines such as *Marxism, *utilitarianism and *racial-ism are scientistic in this sense.

Political science can either be understood generally or more spe-cifically. In general terms political science is an academic discipline which undertakes systematically to describe, analyse and explain the workings of *government and the relationships between politi-cal and non-political institutions and processes. The traditional subject matter of political science, so defined, is the *state, although this has broadened during the twentieth century to include social, economic and other processes that influence the allocation of values and general resources. In this view political science encompasses both descriptive and normative theory: the task of describing and analysing the operations of government institutions has often been linked to evaluative judgements about which ones work best. More narrowly defined, political science sets out to study the traditional subject matter of *politics using only the methods of the natural sciences. From this perspective, political science refers to a strictly empirical and value-free approach to political understanding that was the product of *positivism and reached its highest stage of development in the form of *behaviouralism. This implies a sharp distinction between political science and *political philosophy, reflecting the distinction between empirical and normative analysis. It may also, in its scientistic form, imply that the philosophical or normative approach to political understanding is, in the final analysis, worthless.

Significance

Although it is widely accepted that the study of politics should be scientific in the broad sense of being rigorous and critical, the claim that it should be scientific in the stricter sense, that it can and should use the methodology of the natural sciences, is much more controversial. The attraction of a science of politics is clear. Most importantly, it promises an impartial and reliable means of distinguishing truth from falsehood, thereby giving us access to objective knowledge about the political world. The key to achieving this is to distinguish between 'facts' (empirical evidence) and 'values' (normative or ethical beliefs). Facts are objective in the sense that they can be demonstrated reliably and consistently; they can be proved. Values, in contrast, are inherently subjective, a matter of opinion.

However, any attempt to construct a science of politics confronts three difficulties. First, there is the problem of data. Human beings are not tadpoles that can be taken into a laboratory or cells that can be observed under a microscope. We cannot get 'inside' a human being, or carry out repeatable experiments on human behaviour. What we can learn about individual behaviour is therefore limited and superficial. In the absence of exact data we have no reliable means of testing our hypotheses. Second, there are difficulties that stem from the existence of human values. The idea that models and theories of politics are entirely value-free is difficult to sustain when examined closely. Facts and values are so closely intertwined that it is often impossible to prise them apart. This is because theories are inevitably constructed on the basis of assumptions about *human nature, society and the role of the state that have hidden political and ideological implications. Third, there is the myth of neutrality in the social sciences. Whereas natural scientists may be able to approach their studies in an objective and impartial manner, holding no presuppositions about what they are going to discover, this is difficult and perhaps impossible to achieve in politics. However politics is defined, it addresses questions relating to the structure and functioning of the society in which we live and have grown up. Family background, social experience, economic position, personal sympathies and so on thus build into each and every one of us a set of pre-conditions about politics and the world around us. Scientific objectivity, in the sense of absolute impartiality or *neutrality, must therefore always remain an unachievable goal in political analysis.

POLITICAL THEORY

A theory is anything from a plan to a piece of abstract knowledge. In academic discourse, however, a theory is an explanatory proposition, an idea or set of ideas that in some way seeks to impose order or meaning upon phenomena. As such, all enquiry proceeds through the construction of theories, sometimes thought of as hypotheses, explanatory propositions waiting to be tested. *Political science, no less than the natural sciences and other social sciences, therefore has an important theoretical component. For example, theories such as that *social class is the principal determinant of voting behaviour and that *revolutions occur at times of rising expectations, are essential if sense is to be made of empirical evidence. This is what is called empirical political theory.

Political theory is, however, usually regarded as a distinctive approach to the subject, even though, particularly in the USA, it is seen as a subfield of political science. Political theory involves the analytical study of ideas and doctrines that have been central to political thought. Traditionally, this has taken the form of a history of political thought, focusing upon a collection of 'major' thinkers – for instance, from Plato to Marx – and a canon of 'classic' texts. As it studies the ends and means of political action, political theory is concerned with ethical or normative questions, related to issues such as *justice, *freedom, *equality and so on. This traditional approach has about it the character of literary analysis: it is primarily interested in examining what major thinkers said, how they developed or justified their views and the intellectual context in which they worked. An alternative approach has been called formal political theory. This draws upon the example of economic theory in building up models based upon procedural rules, as in the case of *rational choice theory. Although political theory and *political philosophy clearly overlap, and the two terms are sometimes used interchangeably, a distinction can be drawn on the grounds that political theory may content itself with explanation and analysis, while political philosophy is inevitably involved at some level with evaluation and advocacy.

Significance

Political theory, as an approach to *politics that embraces normative and philosophical analysis, can be seen as the longest and most clearly established tradition of political analysis. However, the status of political theory was seriously damaged in the twentieth century by the rise of *positivism and its attack upon the very normative concepts that had been its chief subject matter. Although the notion that political theory was abandoned in the 1950s and 1960s is an exaggeration, the onset of the 'behavioural revolution' and the passion for all things scientific persuaded many political analysts to turn their backs upon the entire tradition of normative thought. Since the 1960s, however, political theory has re-emerged with new vitality, and the previously sharp distinction between political science and political theory has faded. This occurred through the emergence of a new generation of political theorists, notably John Rawls (1971) and Robert Nozick (1974), but also through growing criticism of *behaviouralism and the re-emergence of ideological divisions, brought about, for instance, through anti-Vietnam war protest, the rise of *feminism and the emergence of the *New Right and *New Left.

However, revived political theory differs in a number of respects from its earlier manifestations. One feature of modern political theory is that it places greater emphasis upon the role of history and culture in shaping political understanding. While this does not imply that the study of 'major' thinkers and 'classic' texts is worthless, it does emphasise that any interpretation of such thinkers and texts must take account of context, and recognise that, to some extent, all interpretations are entangled with our own values and understanding. The second development is that political theory has become increasingly diffuse and diverse. This has occurred both through the fragmentation of *liberalism and growing debate within a broad liberal tradition, but also through the emergence of new alternatives to liberal theory to add to its established Marxist and conservative rivals, the most obvious examples being feminism, *communitarianism and *ecologism. Finally, modern political theory has lost the bold self-confidence of earlier periods, in that it has effectively abandoned the 'traditional' search for universal values acceptable to everyone. This has occurred through a growing appreciation of the role of *community and local identity in shaping values, brought about, in part, by the impact of *postmodernism.

POSITIVISM

Positivism is the doctrine that the social sciences, and, for that matter, all forms of philosophical enquiry, should strictly adhere to the methods of the natural sciences. The term was introduced by Claud-Henri Saint-Simon (1760–1825) and popularised by his follower, Auguste Comte (1789–1857). Positivism thus assumes that science holds a monopoly of knowledge. In the form of logical positivism, which was advanced in the 1920s and 1930s by a group of philosophers collectively known as the Vienna Circle, it rejected all propositions that are not empirically verifiable as simply meaningless.

Significance

Positivism did much in the twentieth century to weaken the status of *political philosophy and to underpin the emergence of *political science. Normative concepts and theories were discarded as nonsense, on the grounds that they were 'metaphysical' and did not deal with that which is externally measurable. Not only did this undermine the credentials of the philosophical approach to political analysis but it also encouraged philosophers to lose interest in moral and political issues. On the other hand, one of the chief legacies of positivism was the emergence of *behaviouralism and the attempt to develop a value-free science of *politics. However, the influence of positivism upon philosophy and political analysis declined significantly in the second half of the twentieth century. This occurred partly because positivism was associated with a simplistic faith in science's capacity to uncover truth that has come to be regarded as naœve, and partly because, in rejecting altogether the beliefs, attitudes and values of political actors, it drew politics towards dull and exclusively empirical analysis.

POSTMODERNISM

Postmodernism is a controversial and confusing term that was first used to describe experimental movements in Western architecture and cultural development in general. Postmodern thought originated principally in continental Europe, especially France, and constitutes a challenge to the type of academic *political theory that has come to be the norm in the Anglo-American world. Its basis lies in a perceived social shift – from modernity to postmodernity – and a related cultural and intellectual shift – from modernism to postmodernism. Modern societies are seen to have been structured by industrialisation and class solidarity, social identity being largely determined by one's position within the productive system. Postmodern societies, on the other hand, are increasingly fragmented and pluralistic 'information societies' in which individuals are transformed from producers to consumers, and *individualism replaces class, religious and ethnic loyalties. Postmodernity is thus linked to postindustrialism, the development of a society no longer dependent upon manufacturing industry, but more reliant upon knowledge and communication.

The central theme of postmodernism is that there is no such thing as certainty: the idea of absolute and universal truth must be discarded as an arrogant pretence. Although by its nature postmodernism does not constitute a unified body of thought, its critical attitude to truth-claims stems from the general assumption that all knowledge is partial and local, a view it shares with certain forms of *communitarianism. Poststructuralism, a term sometimes used interchangeably with postmodernism, emphasises that all ideas and concepts are expressed in language which itself is enmeshed in complex relations of *power.

Significance

Since the 1970s postmodern and poststructural political theories have become increasingly fashionable. In particular they have attacked all forms of political analysis that stem from modernism. Modernism, the cultural form of modernity, is seen to stem largely from Enlightenment ideas and theories, and has been expressed politically in ideological traditions that offer rival conceptions of the good life, notably *liberalism and *Marxism. The chief flaw of modernist thought, from the most postmodern perspective, is that it is characterised by foundationalism, the belief that it is possible to establish objective truths and universal values, usually associated with a strong faith in progress. Jean-François Lyotard (1984) expressed the postmodern stance most succinctly in defining it as 'an incredulity towards metanarratives'. By this he meant scepticism about all creeds and ideologies that are based upon universal theories of history which view society as a coherent totality.

Postmodernism has been criticised from two angles. In the first place it has been accused of relativism, in that it holds that different modes of knowing are equally valid and thus rejects the idea that even science is able reliably to distinguish between truth and falsehood. Secondly it has been charged with *conservatism, on the grounds that a non-foundationalist political stance offers no perspective from which the existing order may be criticised and no basis for the construction of an alternative social order. Nevertheless, the attraction of postmodern theory is its remorseless questioning of apparent solid realities and accepted beliefs. Its general emphasis upon *discourse, debate and *democracy reflects the fact that to reject hierarchies of ideas is also to reject any political or social hierarchies.

RATIONAL CHOICE

Rational choice is a broad theoretical approach to the study of politics whose principal subdivisions include public choice theory, social choice theory and game theory. Sometimes called formal political theory, it draws heavily upon the example of economic theory in building up models based upon procedural rules, usually about the rationally self-interested behaviour of individuals. Rational choice theorists use a method that dates back to Thomas Hobbes (1588–1679) and is employed in *utilitarianism, in assuming that political actors consistently choose the most efficient means to achieve their various ends. In the form of *public choice* theory it is concerned with the provision of so-called public goods, goods that are delivered by government rather than the market, because, as with clean air, their benefit cannot be withheld from individuals who choose not to contribute to their provision. In the form of *social choice* theory it examines the relationship between individuals' preferences and social choices such as voting. In the form of *game theory* it has developed more from the field of mathematics than from the assumptions of neo-classical economics, and entails the use of first principles to analyse puzzles about individual behaviour. The best-known example of game theory is the 'prisoner's dilemma', which demonstrates that rationally self-interested behaviour can be generally less beneficial than cooperation.

Significance

Rational choice theory emerged as a tool of political analysis in the 1950s and gained greater prominence from the 1970s onwards. Most firmly established in the USA, and associated in particular with the so-called Virginia School, it has been used to provide insights into the actions of voters, lobbyists, bureaucrats and politicians. It has had its broadest impact upon political analysis in the form of what is called institutional public choice theory. Supporters of rational choice theory argue that it has introduced greater rigour into the discussion of political phenomena, by allowing political analysts to develop explanatory models in the manner of economic theory. The rational choice approach to political analysis, however, has by no means been universally accepted.

It has been criticised for overestimating human rationality, in that it ignores the fact that people seldom possess clear sets of preferred goals and rarely make decisions in the light of full and accurate knowledge. Furthermore, in proceeding from an abstract model of the individual, rational choice theory pays insufficient attention to social and historical factors, failing to recognise, amongst other things, that human self-interestedness may be socially conditioned, and not innate. Finally, rational choice theory is sometimes seen to have a conservative value bias, stemming from its initial assumptions about human behaviour, and reflected in its use by theorists such as Buchanan and Tulloch (1962) to defend the free market and support a minimal state.

RATIONALISM

Rationalism is the belief that the world has a rational structure, and that this can be disclosed through the exercise of human reason and critical enquiry. As a philosophical theory, rationalism is the belief that knowledge flows from reason rather than experience, and thus it contrasts with *empiricism. As a general principle, however, rationalism places a heavy emphasis on the capacity of human beings to understand and explain their world, and to find solutions to problems. While rationalism does not dictate the ends of human conduct, it certainly dictates how these ends should be pursued. It is associated with an emphasis upon principle and reason-governed behaviour, as opposed to a reliance upon custom or tradition, or non-rational drives and impulses.

Significance

Rationalism was one of the core features of the Enlightenment, the intellectual movement that reached its height in the eighteenth century and challenged traditional beliefs in religion, politics and learning generally in the name of reason. Enlightenment rationalism provided the basis for both *liberalism and *socialism and established the intellectual framework within which conventional political and social analysis developed. Rationalist approaches to understanding have a number of characteristics. First, they tend to place a heavy emphasis upon progress and reform. Reason not only enables people to understand and explain their world, but it also helps them re-shape the world for the better. Rationalism thus promises to emancipate humankind from the grip of the past and the weight of custom and *tradition. Each generation is able to advance beyond the last as the stock of human knowledge and

understanding progressively increases. Second, rationalism is associated with the attempt to uncover values and structures that are
universally applicable to humankind. Reason, in this sense, constitutes a higher reference point for human conduct than do the inherited values and norms of a particular society. Third, rationalism
highlights the importance of debate and discussion over the use of
force or aggression, and implies a broad faith in *democracy. If
people are reason-guided creatures they have both the ability to
settle disputes through debate and negotiation, and a capacity to
identify and express their own best interests.

However, rationalistic approaches to political understanding
have never been universally accepted. A form of anti-rationalism
took root in the late nineteenth century as thinkers started to reflect
upon the limits of human reason and draw attention to other, perhaps more powerful, drives and impulses. For instance, Friedrich
Nietzsche (1844–1900) proposed that human beings are motivated
by deep-seated emotions, their 'will' rather than the rational mind,
and in particular by what he called the 'will to power'. In their most
extreme form, associated with *fascism, such ideas were manifest in
a reverence for strength and military power and the rejection of
intellectual enquiry as cold, dry and lifeless. In the form of traditional *conservatism, they gave rise to the much more modest
belief that tradition and history are surer guides for human conduct
than reason and principle, because the world is simply too complicated for people fully to grasp. Faith in rationalism also particularly
waned in the final decades of the twentieth century. This occurred,
amongst other things, through a growing acceptance that particular individuals, groups and societies possess their own intrinsic
values and that these are not susceptible to rational ordering,
and through a recognition that rationalism is linked to Western
values and that the Enlightenment project of which it is a part is
merely a form of cultural imperialism. Such reservations about
rationalism have been expressed by both communitarian and postmodern theorists.

REALISM

Realism, sometimes called 'political realism', is a perspective on
international politics that is grounded in an emphasis upon power
politics and the pursuit of national interests. As such it represents

the major alternative to *idealism. The central assumption of realism is that the *state is the principal actor on the international or world stage and, being sovereign, is able to act as an autonomous entity. Moreover, the rise of *nationalism and the emergence of modern *nation-states has transformed the state into a cohesive political community, within which other loyalties and ties are subordinate to those of the *nation. The realist tradition therefore portrays international politics as a 'state of nature', an essentially anarchic system in which each state is forced to help itself and give priority to its own national interests, defined, most basically, as state survival and territorial defence. Realists, as a result, stress the role of *power in international affairs, and tend to understand power largely in terms of military capacity or force.

By no means, however, does international anarchy mean relentless conflict and unending war. Instead, realists insist that the pattern of conflict and cooperation within the state system largely conforms to the requirements of a balance of power. In pursuit of national security, states may enter into alliances which, if balanced against one another, may ensure prolonged periods of peace. Similarly, realists have always acknowledged that the international order is not a classic state of nature because power, wealth and resources are not equally distributed amongst states. The resulting hierarchy of states imposes a measure of order on the international system, reflecting the control that great powers exercise over subordinate ones through trading blocks, 'spheres of influence', and outright colonialism. *Neo-realism*, sometimes called 'new' or structural realism, has modified classical realism in that it tends to explain events in terms of the structure of the international system rather than the goals and make-up of individual states.

Significance

Realism became the dominant perspective on international politics during the twentieth century, receiving its impetus from the First World War and Second World War. These not only undermined the idealist belief in *internationalism and natural harmony, but also provided abundant evidence of the naked pursuit of state aggrandisement, especially in the case of Nazi expansionism. During the Cold War period, realist theories portrayed global politics in terms of a bipolar world order based upon rivalry between the

US and Soviet power blocs. Realists were nevertheless prepared to argue that bipolarity helped to maintain peace as escalating military spending led to an effective system of nuclear deterrents, especially once the condition of mutually assured destruction (MAD) was recognised in the 1960s. A stable hierarchy based upon accepted rules and recognised processes thus kept anarchy at bay, and encouraged realists to adopt the modified idea of what Hedley Bull (1977) termed an 'anarchical society'.

Realism and neo-realism have attracted fierce criticism, however. The central objection is that, in divorcing politics from morality, the realist perspective legitimises military escalation and the hegemonic ambitions of great powers. This view suggests that power politics has not so much maintained peace as kept the world on the verge of nuclear catastrophe. A second critique of realism is advanced by feminist theorists, who contend that power-seeking behaviour and an obsession with national security and military might reflect the worldwide dominance of male politicians whose priorities are essentially aggressive and competitive. The central empirical weakness of realist theories is that, in focusing attention upon the state as the dominant international actor, they have ignored pluralistic tendencies that have reshaped the face of international politics in the late twentieth century. Classical realism has thus largely given away to neo-realism.

SYSTEMS THEORY

Systems theory sets out to explain the entire political process, as well as the function of major political actors, through the application of systems analysis. A 'system' is an organised or complex whole, a set of interrelated and interdependent parts that form a collective entity. To analyse *politics from this perspective is to construct the model of a political system. A political system consists of linkages between what are viewed as 'inputs' and 'outputs' (see Figure 4.1). Inputs into the political system consist of demands and supports from the general public. Demands can range from pressure for higher living standards, improved employment prospects, and more generous welfare payments to greater protection for minority and individual rights. Supports, on the other hand, are ways in which the public contributes to the political system by paying taxes, offering compliance and being willing to participate in

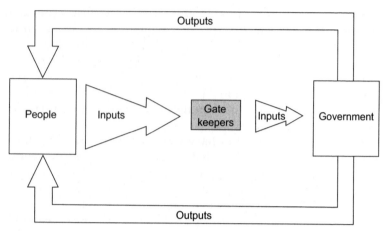

Figure 4.1   The political system

public life. Outputs consist of the decisions and actions of *govern-ment, including the making of *policy, the passing of *laws, the imposition of taxes, and the allocation of public funds. These out-puts generate 'feedback', which in turn shapes further demands and supports. The key insight offered by the systems model is that the political system tends towards long-term equilibrium or politi-cal stability, as its survival depends upon outputs being brought into line with inputs.

Significance

Systems analysis was first employed in political science in the 1950s, the pioneering work having been done by David Easton ([1953] 1981). Linked to *behaviouralism, the systems approach was part of the attempt to introduce more scientific rigour into the study of politics, in this case through the application of models of ecological systems from biology. Systems theory has provided a rich source of insights into, for instance, the role of 'gatekeepers' such as *political parties and *pressure groups, which regulate the flow of inputs into the political system, and into the general policy process and the nature of its outputs. Its strengths include the breadth of its scope, which extends well beyond state institutions and even the class system to include all politically significant actors, and its tendency to foster holistic thinking. However, the systems model is at best a device for drawing out understanding; it does not in itself constitute reliable knowledge. For example, institutions such as parties and pressure groups are more interesting and complex than their designation as 'gatekeepers' suggests; for instance, they play an important role in managing public perceptions and thus help to shape the nature of public demands. Moreover, the systems model is more effective in explaining how and why political systems respond to popular pressures than in explaining why they employ repression and coercion, as, to some degree, all do. Finally, the systems model is implicitly conservative, in that it highlights the responsiveness and inherent stability of *liberal democracy, thereby, arguably, concealing its structural weaknesses and inherent contradictions.

UTILITARIANISM

Utilitarianism is a moral philosophy that suggests that the 'rightness' of an action, policy or institution can be established by its tendency to promote happiness. This is based upon the assumption that individuals are motivated by self-interest and that these interests can be defined as the desire for pleasure, or happiness, and the wish to avoid pain or unhappiness. Individuals thus calculate the quantities of pleasure and pain each possible action would generate and choose whichever course promises the greatest pleasure over pain. Utilitarian thinkers believe that it is possible to quantify pleasure and pain in terms of 'utility', taking account of their intensity, duration and so forth. Human beings are therefore utility maximisers, who seek the greatest possible pleasure and the least possible pain. The principle of utility can be applied to society at large using Jeremy Bentham's (1748–1832) classic formula: 'the greatest happiness for the greatest number'.

Utilitarianism, however, has developed into a cluster of theories. Classical utilitarianism is *act-utilitarianism*, in that it judges an act to be right if its consequences produce at least as much pleasure-over-pain as those of any alternative act. *Rule-utilitarianism*, rather, judges an act to be right if it conforms to a rule which, if generally followed, would produce good consequences. What is called *utilitarian generalisation* assesses an act's rightfulness not in terms of its own consequences, but on the basis of its consequences if the act were to be generally performed. *Motive-utilitarianism* places emphasis upon

the intentions of the actor rather than upon the consequences of
each action.

Significance

Utilitarian theory emerged in the late eighteenth century as a supposedly scientific alternative to natural rights theories. In the UK,
during the nineteenth century, utilitarianism provided the basis
for a wide range of social, political and legal reforms, advanced by
the so-called philosophic radicals. Utilitarianism provided one of
the major foundations for classical *liberalism and remains perhaps
the most important branch of moral philosophy, certainly in terms
of its impact upon political issues.

The attraction of utilitarianism is its capacity to establish supposedly objective grounds upon which moral judgements can be made.
Rather than imposing values on society, it allows each individual to
make his or her own moral judgements as each alone is able to define
what is pleasurable and what is painful. Utilitarian theory thus
upholds diversity and *freedom, and demands that we respect
others as pleasure-seeking creatures. Its drawbacks are philosophical and moral. Philosophically, utilitarianism is based upon a highly
individualistic view of *human nature that is both asocial and ahistorical. It is by no means certain, for instance, that consistently self-
interested behaviour is a universal feature of human society.
Morally, utilitarianism may be nothing more than crass hedonism,
a view expressed by J. S. Mill (1806–73) in his declaration that he
would rather be 'Socrates dissatisfied than a fool satisfied' (although
Mill himself subscribed to a modified form of utilitarianism). Utilitarianism has also been criticised for endorsing acts that are widely
considered wrong, such as the violation of basic *human rights, if
they serve to maximise the general utility of society.

UTOPIANISM

A utopia (from the Greek utopia, meaning 'no place', or the Greek
eutopia, meaning 'good place') is literally an ideal or perfect society.
The term was coined by Thomas More (1478–1535), and was first
used in his Utopia ([1516] 1965). Utopianism is a style of social theorising that develops a critique of the existing order by constructing a

model of an ideal or perfect alternative. As such it usually exhibits
three features. First, it embodies a radical and comprehensive rejection of the status quo; present social and political arrangements are
deemed to be fundamentally defective and in need of root-and-
branch change. Second, utopian thought highlights the potential
for human self-development, based either upon highly optimistic
assumptions about *human nature or optimistic assumptions about
the capacity of economic, social and political institutions to amelio-
rate baser human drives and instincts. Third, utopianism usually
transcends the 'public/private' divide in that it suggests the possibility of complete or near-complete personal fulfilment. For an alternative society to be ideal, it must offer the prospect of emancipation
in the personal realm as well as in the political or public realm.

However, utopianism is not a *political philosophy or an *ideology. Substantive utopias differ from one another, and utopian thinkers have not advanced a common conception of the good life.
Nevertheless, most utopias are characterised by the abolition of
want, the absence of conflict and the avoidance of violence and
oppression. *Socialism in general, and *anarchism and *Marxism
in particular, have a marked disposition towards utopianism,
reflecting their belief in the human potential for sociable, cooperative and gregarious behaviour. Socialist utopias, as a result, are
strongly egalitarian and typically characterised by collective property ownership and a reduction in, or eradication of, political
*authority. *Feminism and *ecologism have also spawned utopian
theories. *Liberalism's capacity to generate utopian thought is
restricted by its stress upon human self-interestedness and competition; however, an extreme belief in free-market *capitalism can be
viewed as a form of market utopianism. Other utopias have been
based upon faith in the benign influence of government and political
authority. More's society, for example, was hierarchical, authoritarian and patriarchal, albeit within a context of economic equality.

Significance

The utopian approach to political understanding was most popular
in the nineteenth century, generally stimulated by the immense political and social upheavals generated by industrialisation. During
the twentieth century, however, utopianism became distinctly un-
fashionable. Criticisms of utopian thought fall into two categories.

The first (in line with the pejorative, everyday use of the term 'uto-pian') suggests that utopianism is deluded or fanciful thinking, a belief in an unrealistic and unachievable goal. Karl Marx (1818–83), for instance, denounced 'utopian socialism' on the grounds that it advances a moral vision that is in no way grounded in histor-ical and social realities. By contrast, 'scientific socialism' sought to explain how and why a socialist society would come into being (Marxism's utopian character is nevertheless evident in the nature of its ultimate goal: the construction of a classless, communist society). The second category of criticisms holds that utopianism is implicitly totalitarian, in that it promotes a single set of indisputa-ble values and so is intolerant of free debate and diversity.

However, a revival of utopianism has occurred since the 1960s associated with the rise of *New Left and the writings of thinkers such as Herbert Marcuse (1898–1979), Ernst Bloch (1885–1977) and Paul Goodman (1911–72). The strength of utopianism is that it enables *political theory to think beyond the present and to chal-lenge the 'boundaries of the possible'. The establishment of 'con-crete' utopias is a way of uncovering the potential for growth and development within existing circumstances. Without a vision of what could be, political theory may simply be overwhelmed by what is, and thereby lose its critical edge.

FURTHER READING

Barry, B. and Hardin, R. (eds), *Rational Man and Irrational Society?* (Beverly Hills, CA: Sage, 1982).

Burchill, S. and Linklater, A., *Theories of International Relations* (London: Macmillan, 1996).

Chalmers, A. F., *What Is This Thing Called Science?* (Milton Keynes: Open University Press, 1986).

Cohen, G. A., *Karl Marx's Theory of History: A Defence* (Oxford: Clarendon Press, 1978).

Dallmayr, F. and McCarthy, T. (eds), *Understanding and Social Inquiry* (Notre Dame, IN: University of Notre Dame Press, 1997).

Dunleavy, P., *Democracy, Bureaucracy and Public Choice: Economic Explana-tions in Political Science* (Hemel Hempstead: Harvester Wheatsheaf, 1991).

Easton, D., *The Political System* (Chicago, IL: Chicago University Press, 1981).

Finifter, A. (ed.), *Political Science: The State of the Discipline* (Washington, DC: American Political Science Association, 1993).

Goodin, R., *Utilitarianism as a Public Philosophy* (Cambridge: Cambridge University Press, 1995).

Harvey, D., *The Condition of Post Modernity* (London: Basil Blackwell, 1989).

Held, D. (ed.), *Political Theory Today* (Oxford: Polity Press, 1991).

Held, D., *Political Theory and the Modern State* (Oxford: Polity Press, 1990).

Heywood, A., *Political Theory: An Introduction* (London: Macmillan, 1999).

Hutcheon, L., *The Politics of Post Modernism* (New York: Routledge, 1989).

Johnson, N., *The Limits of Political Science* (Oxford: Clarendon Press, 1989).

Kegley, C. (ed.), *Controversies in International Relations Theory: Realism and the Neoliberal Challenge* (New York: St Martin's Press, 1995).

Kuhn, T., *The Structure of Scientific Revolutions* (Chicago, IL: Chicago University Press, 1962).

Kumar, K., *Utopianism* (Milton Keynes: Open University Press, 1991).

Kymlika, W., *Contemporary Political Philosophy: An Introduction* (Oxford and New York: Oxford University Press, 1990).

Marsh, D. and Stoker, G. (eds), *Theory and Methods in Political Science* (London: Macmillan, 1995).

Merleau-Ponty, M., *Adventures of the Dialectic* (London: Heinemann, 1993).

Ollman, B., *Dialectical Investigations* (London: Routledge, 1993).

Vincent, A., *Political Theory: Tradition and Diversity* (Cambridge: Cambridge University Press, 1997).

Weaver, R. K. and Rockman, B. A. (eds), *Do Institutions Matter?* (Washington, DC: Brookings Institution, 1993).

Part five

Values

This section examines concepts that are normative principles or political ideals; in many cases, these are the building-blocks of ideological traditions.

VALUES

ACCOUNTABILITY

Accountability means answerability; it implies a duty to explain one's conduct and be open to criticism by another. Accountability requires that the duties, powers and functions of government bodies are defined in such a way that the performance of subordinate ones can be monitored and evaluated by 'higher' bodies. In this sense accountability can operate only in a context of *constitutionalism; being accountable does not mean being subject to arbitrary *authority or capricious punishment. However, accountability may also amount to a weak form of *responsibility, since it establishes a duty to answer and explain one's conduct, but not necessarily to bear guilt and accept punishment.

Significance

Accountability is an important feature of limited *government, effective policy-making and *democracy. It limits government *power by establishing mechanisms of political control through which one institution oversees the working and performance of another. It can promote the quality of public *policy by ensuring that policy proposals are carefully scrutinised and political performance is rigorously monitored. When this is achieved through regular and competitive elections, it amounts to a system of public control, public accountability being the practical face of democratic rule. However, accountability is effective only under certain circumstances. These include that the mechanisms for monitoring performance are rigorous; that 'higher' institutions or bodies have sufficient access to information to make critical and informed judgements; and that appropriate sanctions can be applied in the event of blunders or under-performance. The main drawback of accountability is that it may constrain independent judgement and action. For instance, the accountability of civil servants to ministers can lead to politicisation and allow bureaucratic power to be harnessed to the needs of the government of the day.

AUTONOMY

Autonomy literally means self-rule or self-government. *States, institutions or groups can be said to be autonomous if they enjoy a substantial degree of independence, although autonomy in this connection is sometimes taken to imply a high measure of self-government, rather than sovereign independence. Applied to the individual, autonomy is closely linked with *freedom. However, since it suggests not merely being 'left alone' but being rationally self-willed, autonomy is best classified as a form of positive freedom. By responding to inner or 'genuine' drives, the autonomous individual is seen to achieve authenticity and personal fulfilment.

Significance

In international politics, autonomy is widely used as an index of *sovereignty, autonomous states being independent and self-governing. However, it is now widely accepted that very few, if any, states are autonomous in this sense, and pluralist theorists in particular now use autonomy in a relative, not absolute, sense. As a constitutional principle, referring to institutions or levels of government, autonomy is closely linked to *decentralisation. Autonomy in this context is justified through an essentially liberal belief in fragmenting *power, although the checks and balances thus established imply interdependence as well as independence. The term is also used in the analysis of the state, the autonomy of the state implying that the state articulates its own interests and is not merely an instrument or agent through which powerful groups in society at large act. Liberals have traditionally defended this image of state autonomy against the Marxist theory of the class state, even though modern Marxists are prepared to accept the 'relative autonomy' of the state. Finally, the ideal of personal autonomy can be seen as the underlying value of libertarian and anarchist thought, self-governing individuals needing little or no guidance in the form of political *authority. Autonomy in this sense is often linked with *democracy, but may nevertheless also limit the jurisdiction of democracy, as it emphasises individuality rather than collective or majority rule.

CITIZENSHIP

Citizenship is a relationship between the individual and *state, in which the two are bound together by reciprocal *rights and duties. Citizens differ from subjects and aliens in that they are full members of their political community, or state, by virtue of the possession of basic rights. Citizenship is viewed differently depending upon whether it is shaped by *individualism or *communitarianism. The former, linked to *liberalism, advances the principle of a 'citizenship of rights', and places particular stress upon private entitlement and the status of the individual as an autonomous actor. There are socialist and conservative versions of communitarianism, but each advances the principle of a 'citizenship of duty', highlighting the importance of civic *responsibility. Such theories tend to portray the state as a moral agency, and to underline the need for *community and the role of social existence.

Significance

The idea that citizenship is the proper end of government can be traced back to the political thought of Ancient Greece, and to the belief that an interest in public affairs is a basic feature of individual existence. Recurrent interest in citizenship therefore reflects an enduring concern for, and commitment to, the 'public' face of human life. Controversies about citizenship centre upon the rights it implies and its value as a political principle. The political *right tends to endorse a narrow view of citizenship that stresses only civil and political rights, the rights that are exercised within *civil society and rights of participation. The political *left, by contrast, tends to endorse 'social citizenship', the idea that citizens are entitled to a social minimum, expressed in terms of social and welfare rights. Opponents of the very idea of citizenship include libertarians who reject the notion that individuals have a broader social identity and responsibilities. Marxists may also criticise citizenship on the grounds that it masks the reality of unequal class power, while feminists may do so because it takes no account of patriarchal oppression. Nevertheless, the rise of communitarianism and the emergence of 'new' *social democracy has led to a revival of interest in citizenship, as an attempt to re-establish a 'rights and responsibilities' agenda and to counterbalance the market individualism of the *New Right. This is usually associated with the idea of 'active citizenship', a notion that places particular emphasis upon the social duties and moral responsibilities of citizens.

CIVIL LIBERTY

Civil liberty is a 'private' sphere of existence that belongs to the citizen, not the *state. Civil liberty therefore encompasses a range of 'negative' *rights, usually rooted in the doctrine of *human rights, which demand non-interference on the part of *government. The classic civil liberties are usually thought to include the right to freedom of speech, freedom of the press, freedom of religion and conscience, freedom of movement, and freedom of association. Civil liberties are often confused with civil rights. The former are freedoms *from* government, while the latter are generally 'positive' rights, in the sense that they are rights of participation and access to *power. Civil rights campaigns thus typically call for a widening of voting and political rights and for an end to discrimination, rather than for a broadening of civil liberty.

Significance

The maintenance of key civil liberties is generally seen as vital to the functioning of liberal-democratic societies, since they provide the individual with protection against arbitrary government. In many cases the principle of civil liberty is given constitutional expression through documents such as a *bill of rights, and it is widely seen as a basic justification for judicial independence and a strict separation between *law and *politics. The clarity with which civil liberties are defined, and the effectiveness with which they are upheld, are therefore the crucial index of individual *freedom from the liberal perspective. Reservations about civil liberty have nevertheless been expressed by both conservatives and socialists. Conservatives have argued that the strengthening of civil liberties tends to weaken government and, in particular, hamper the maintenance of domestic order. Socialists, on the other hand, have warned that the doctrine of civil liberty, especially when applied to property rights, can serve as a defence of social inequality and class oppression.

COLLECTIVISM

Collectivism is, broadly, the belief that collective human endeavour is of greater practical and moral value than individual self-striving. It reflects the idea that *human nature has a social core, and implies that social groups, whether *social classes, *nations, *races or whatever, are meaningful political entities. However, the term is used with little consistency. Michael Bakunin (1814–76) used collectivism to refer to self-governing associations of free individuals, describing his form of *anarchism as collectivist anarchism. More commonly, collectivism is treated as the opposite of *individualism, on the grounds that it implies that collective interests should prevail over individual ones. Collectivism in this sense is often linked to the *state, as the mechanism through which collective interests are upheld against the individual interests of *civil society. This suggests, in stark contrast to Bakunin's use of the term, that the growth of state responsibilities marks the advance of collectivism. It also explains why collectivism is often confused with *collectivisation, the extension of state control over the economy (although collectivisation may be seen as a means of advancing collectivist goals).

Significance

Collectivism has been one of the key components of socialist ideology. The socialist case for collectivism is both moral and economic. Morally, collective endeavour in the form of cooperation fosters social solidarity and a *responsibility for fellow human beings, based upon our common humanity. Economically, collectivism enables the collective energies of society to be harnessed in a rational and efficient fashion, by contrast with self-striving which results in wasteful competition. This emphasis upon collectivism is evident in a traditional socialist belief in *equality, *welfare and common ownership. Marxism, indeed, subscribes to a form of methodological collectivism, in that it treats social classes rather than individuals as the principal agents of historical change. However, collectivism is by no means exclusively linked to *socialism, and forms of collectivism can be identified in, for instance, *nationalism, *racialism and *feminism. Two basic objections are usually made to collectivism, both rooted in the ideas of liberal individualism. The first is that collectivism stifles individuality and diversity by insisting upon a common social identity and shared human interests. The second is that collectivism is necessarily, and not accidentally, linked to statism and the erosion of *freedom, as there is no effective means to advance collective interests except through political *authority.

COMMUNITY

A community, in everyday language, is a collection of people in a given location; that is, a village, town, city or even country. As a political or social principle, however, the term community suggests a social group that possesses a strong collective identity based upon the bonds of comradeship, loyalty and duty. Ferdinand Tönnies (1855-1936) distinguished between *Gemeinschaft*, or 'community', typically found in traditional societies and characterised by natural affection and mutual respect, and *Gesellschaft*, or 'association', that is, the looser, artificial and contractual relationships typically found in urban and industrialised societies. Emile Durkheim (1858–1917) emphasised the degree to which community is based upon the maintenance of social and moral codes. If these are weakened, this induces 'anomie', feelings of isolation, loneliness and meaninglessness, which Durkheim associated with the incidence of suicide.

Significance

An emphasis upon community has been a recurrent theme in political thought and can be traced back to Aristotle's (384–322 BCE) assertion that human beings are essentially 'political animals', although the idea of community has often remained vague and ill-defined. Socialists and traditional conservatives have placed particular emphasis upon community. For socialists it implies cooperation and social responsibility and, in its most radical form, it has led to a preference for small, self-managing communities, or communes. For conservatives it is linked to the need to give individuals a secure social identity and sense of rootedness. In the late twentieth century the cause of community was advanced explicitly through the rise of *communitarianism, which set out to redress the 'atomism' which had resulted from the spread of liberal and individualist values.

Critics of the principle of community point out that it is either politically dangerous or intellectually bogus. The danger of community is that it can lead to individual rights and liberties being violated in the name of the collective body. This was most graphically demonstrated through *Nazism's emphasis upon the *Völksgemeinschaft*, or 'national community', which aimed to dissolve individuality, and indeed personal experience, within the social whole. The intellectual limitations of community derive from its tendency to imply the existence of collective identities and social bonds which in fact do not exist. Liberals may therefore point out that there is no such thing as community, but only a collection of individuals. Terms such as 'gay community' and 'black community' have come in for particular criticism in this respect.

CONSENT

To consent means to agree or grant permission. As a political principle, consent is normally linked to *authority, as a means through which people agree to be governed and thus to be bound by political *obligation. In practical terms consent is often associated with *elections. However, voters are generally thought to have consented to be governed not specifically through voting for the winning party or candidate, but through having participated in the electoral mechanism and thereby having accepted it as a legitimate means for selecting leaders or establishing a *government.

Significance

Consent is an important principle of *liberalism. In the liberal view, authority and social relationships should always be based upon consent, representing the voluntary actions of free individuals. This ensures that authority arises 'from below', and is always grounded in *legitimacy. The classic expression of this doctrine is that government must be based upon the 'consent of the governed'. Consent therefore disposes liberals to favour *representation and *democracy. However, they also believe that social bodies and associations should be based upon consent, in that they are formed through contractual agreements willingly entered into by individuals intent on pursuing their own self-interest. In this light, political and other obligations are morally binding because our voluntary agreement implies a promise to uphold them. Objections to the principle of consent stem from the grounds upon which it can be demonstrated and the extent to which individuals can be regarded as free and self-willed actors. Is it, for instance, reasonable to suggest that the act of voting amounts to the granting of consent on the part of the governed? Are those who vote obliged to respect their government and the *laws it makes? Moreover, the idea of consent ignores the capacity of *ideology and government propaganda to shape what people think, and thereby to influence their seemingly voluntary behaviour.

CONSTITUTIONALISM

Constitutionalism, in a narrow sense, is the practice of limited *government brought about through the existence of a *constitution. Constitutionalism in this sense can be said to exist whenever government institutions and political processes are effectively constrained by constitutional rules. More broadly, constitutionalism refers to a set of political values and aspirations that reflect the desire to protect *freedom through the establishment of internal and external checks upon government *power. Constitutionalism is typically expressed in support for constitutional provisions that establish this goal, notably a codified constitution, a *bill of rights, the *separation of powers, *bicameralism and *federalism or *decentralisation.

Significance

Constitutionalism is one of the basic political values of *liberalism and one of the key components of *liberal democracy. Its importance rests upon the underlying fear that government is always liable to become a tyranny against the individual, because power is corrupting in itself. Constitutionalism is thus a vital guarantee of liberty. The forms it takes may nevertheless vary considerably. Liberal constitutionalism is usually associated with a written or codified constitution, a system of checks and balances amongst government institutions and formal, and usually entrenched, guarantees for *civil liberty. Nevertheless, the UK system of government has sometimes been regarded as constitutional even though it has traditionally lacked each of these three features. Critics of constitutionalism have pointed out that it gives attention only to the formal and usually legal organisation of government. For instance, constitutions and institutional fragmentation may be less important in maintaining individual liberty than party competition and *democracy. Constitutionalism has also been criticised by socialists as a means of constraining government power and thus of preventing meaningful reform of the capitalist system.

DEMOCRACY

Democracy literally means rule by the *demos* or people (although the Greeks originally used *demos* to mean 'the poor' or 'the many'). However, the simple notion of 'rule by the people' is vague and has been subject to a bewildering variety of interpretations (indeed, democracy may equally be treated as a 'contested' value or be taken to stand for a variety of systems). Perhaps a more helpful starting point is Abraham Lincoln's Gettysburg Address (1864), which extolled the virtues of what he called 'government of the people, by the people and for the people'. This highlights the importance of three core features of democracy. First, the stress upon 'the people' implies political *equality, an equal distribution of political *power and influence. Second, *government 'by' the people emphasises the importance of popular participation. Third, government 'for' the people highlights the fact that democracy suggests rule in the public interest.

However, there are a number of models of democracy. The most important distinction is between direct democracy and representative democracy. *Direct democracy* (a term that overlaps with classical democracy, radical democracy and participatory democracy) is based upon the direct, unmediated and continuous participation of citizens in the tasks of government. Direct democracy thus obliterates the distinction between government and governed, and between the *state and *civil society; it is a system of popular self-government. It was achieved in ancient Athens through a form of government by mass meeting (Athenian democracy), and its most common modern manifestation is in the use of *referendums. *Representative democracy* (whose most common form is *liberal democracy) is a limited and indirect form of democracy. It is limited in that popular participation in government is infrequent and brief, being restricted to the act of voting every few years. It is indirect in that the public do not exercise power themselves; they merely select those who will rule on their behalf. This form of rule is democratic only insofar as *representation establishes a reliable and effective link between the government and the governed. This is sometimes expressed in the notion of an electoral *mandate.

Significance

The mass conversion of politicians and political thinkers to the cause of democracy was one of the most dramatic and significant events in political history. Well into the nineteenth century the term continued to have pejorative implications, suggesting a system of 'mob rule'. Now, however, we are all democrats. Liberals, conservatives, socialists, communists, anarchists and even fascists are eager to proclaim the virtues of democracy and to demonstrate their democratic credentials. Indeed, 'end of history' theorists interpreted the collapse of *communism in the late twentieth century to imply the worldwide, and final, triumph of liberal democracy. Democratic processes and practices have displaced *authoritarianism basically because political stability in complex and highly differentiated modern societies can be maintained only through a diffusion of *power, a tendency that is strengthened by the development of a better educated and informed and more politically sophisticated citizenry. Overwhelmingly, where democracy has triumphed it has done so in its more practicable, representative form; however, developments in information technology have increasingly made direct democracy more viable, particularly in small communities.

Most of the debates about democracy stem from rivalries between different theories or models of democracy and concern how, and to what extent, democratic practices should be applied. The most common of these deal with the adequacy of representative democracy and, in particular, the link between *elections and democracy, and whether or not democratic principles should be narrowly confined to political matters or extended more widely to cover, say, the family, the workplace and the distribution of economic power. Nevertheless, key debates about the virtues and vices of democracy remain relevant.

Amongst the advantages that have been claimed for democracy are the following:

- it protects the individual from government, and so defends *freedom, by ensuring that power is constrained and subject to popular *consent;
- it promotes education and personal development by allowing citizens, through political participation, to gain insight into how their society operates;
- it strengthens *community and social solidarity by giving all people a stake in society by virtue of having a voice in its decision-making processes;
- it widens social and personal well-being by ensuring that government policies reflect the interests of citizens at large;
- it guarantees political stability by bringing the 'outputs' of government into line with popular 'inputs', so generating equilibrium.

Amongst the criticisms that have been made of democracy are the following:

- as wisdom and knowledge are unequally distributed in society, democracy leads to rule by the ignorant and poorly informed masses;
- it amounts to a 'tyranny of the 51 per cent' because it means that individual liberty and minority rights can be crushed by the majority, in the name of the people;
- it results in excessive government and state control because it articulates the interests of the collective body rather than those of the individual;
- it may result in *dictatorship and repression because it allows demagogues to come to power by appealing to the basest instincts of the masses

EQUALITY

Equality is the principle of uniform apportionment; it does not imply identity or sameness. Equality, however, is meaningless unless we can answer the question: equal in what? The term equality has very different implications, depending upon what is being apportioned. *Foundational equality* is the idea that human beings are 'born equal' in the sense that their lives are of equal moral value. *Formal equality* refers to the formal status of individuals in society in terms of their *rights and entitlements; its clearest expression is in the form of legal equality ('equality before the law') and political equality (universal suffrage and one person one vote, one vote one value). *Equality of opportunity* means that everyone has the same starting-point, or equal life chances. This distinguishes between inequalities that result from unequal social treatment (which are non-legitimate) and ones that result from an unequal distribution of merit, talent and the willingness to work (which are legitimate). *Equality of outcome* refers to an equal distribution of rewards; it is usually reflected in social equality, an equal distribution of income, wealth and other social goods. These different views of equality are sometimes mutually incompatible. For instance, equality of opportunity may justify unequal social outcomes on the grounds of *meritocracy and the need for incentives.

Significance

The idea of equality is perhaps the defining feature of modern political thought. Whereas classical and medieval thinkers took it for granted that hierarchy is natural or inevitable, few modern ones have not been willing to support equality in one of its various forms. In a sense we are all egalitarians now. The modern battle about equality is therefore fought not between those who support the principle and those who reject it, but between different views about where and how equality should be applied. Although foundational equality as a philosophical principle, and formal equality as a legal and political principle, are widely accepted, at least in liberal-democratic societies, deep controversy continues to surround the idea of equality of outcome or rewards. Indeed, many treat the *left/right political spectrum as a reflection of differing attitudes towards social equality, left-wingers broadly supporting it, while right-wingers question or oppose it.

Amongst the arguments in favour of social or material equality are the following:

- it strengthens social cohesion and *community by creating a common identity and shared interests;
- it promotes *justice in that the most obvious forms of social inequality are the result of unequal treatment by society rather than unequal natural endowment;
- it enlarges *freedom in the sense that it safeguards people from poverty and satisfies basic needs, enabling them to achieve fulfilment;
- it is the only meaningful form of equality in that all other equalities rest upon it: genuine legal and political equality require that people have access to equal social resources.

Amongst the arguments against social equality are the following:

- it is unjust because it treats unequals equally and therefore fails to reward people in line with their talents and capacities;
- it results in economic stagnation in that it removes incentives and caps aspirations, amounting to a process of 'levelling down';
- it can be achieved only through state intervention and a system of 'social engineering', meaning that it always infringes upon individual liberty;
- it results in drab uniformity; diversity is vanquished and with it the vigour and vitality of society.

FREEDOM

Freedom or liberty (the two terms are best used interchangeably) is, in its broadest sense, the ability to think or act as one wishes. An important distinction is nevertheless made between negative freedom and positive freedom (Berlin, 1958). *Negative freedom* means non-interference: the absence of external constraints upon the individual. The individual is thus 'at liberty' to act as he or she wishes. The clearest manifestations of negative freedom are in the form of freedom of choice, *civil liberty and privacy. *Positive freedom* is linked to the achievement of some identifiable goal or benefit, usually personal development or self-realisation, although Berlin defined it as self-mastery and linked it to *democracy. For Berlin the negative/positive distinction was reflected in the difference between being free *from* something and being free *to* do something. However, the 'freedom from' and 'freedom to' distinction is misleading, because every example of freedom can be described in both ways. For instance, being free from ignorance means being free to gain an education. G. C. MacCallum (1991) proposed a single, value-free concept of freedom in the form: 'X is free from Y to do or be Z'. This suggests that the apparently deep question 'are we free?' is meaningless, and should be replaced by a more complete and specific statement about what we are free from, and what we are free to do.

Significance

Freedom is often considered the supreme political value in Western liberal societies. Its virtue is that, attached to the idea that human beings are rationally self-willed creatures, it promises the satisfaction of human interests or the realisation of human potential. In short, freedom is the basis for happiness and well-being. However, despite its popularity, different political thinkers and traditions draw quite different conclusions from their belief in freedom. For classical liberals and supporters of the *New Right, who view freedom in strictly negative terms, it implies rolling back the *state and minimising the realm of political *authority. Indeed, for anarchists, who alone regard freedom as an absolute value, it is irreconcilable with any form of political authority. On the other hand, modern liberals and socialists have tended to subscribe to a positive view of freedom that justifies widening the responsibilities of the state, particularly in relation to *welfare and economic management. The state is regarded as the enemy of freedom when it is viewed as an external constraint upon the individual, but as a guarantee of freedom when it lays down the conditions for personal development and self-realisation. Conservatives, for their part, have traditionally endorsed a weak view of freedom as the willing recognition of duties and responsibilities. This position is taken to its extreme by fascists, who portrayed 'true' freedom as unquestioning obedience to the leader and the absorption of the individual into the national *community.

Nevertheless, with the exception of *anarchism, freedom is not regarded as an unqualified blessing. This is reflected in the widely accepted distinction between liberty and licence, the former referring to morally acceptable forms of freedom, the latter to the abuse of freedom or excessive freedom. As R. H. Tawney (1880–1962) put it, 'The freedom of the pike is death to the minnows.' Above all, freedom must be balanced against *order, and the nature of this balance has been one of the central themes in *political theory. Those who believe that this balance should favour freedom, such as liberals and socialists, generally regard human beings as rational and enlightened creatures, capable of making wise decisions in their own interests. Those, in contrast, who emphasise order over freedom, such as traditional conservatives, usually regard human beings as weak, limited or even corrupt creatures, who need authority to be exercised over them.

In addition to philosophical debates about freedom, political thinkers have sometimes discussed its psychological impact. In sharp contrast to the optimistic expectations of liberal thinkers such as J. S. Mill (1806–73) that freedom will result in human flourishing, writers such as Erich Fromm (1984) have drawn attention to the 'fear of freedom'. This is the idea that freedom entails psychological burdens in terms of choice and uncertainty, which at times of political instability and economic crisis may incline people to flee from freedom and seek security in submission to an all-powerful leader or totalitarian state. This has been used as an explanation of the rise of *fascism and of *religious fundamentalism.

HUMAN RIGHTS

Human rights are *rights to which people are entitled by virtue of being human; they are a modern and secular version of 'natural' rights, which were believed to be God-given. Human rights are therefore universal, fundamental and absolute. They are universal in the sense that they belong to all humans everywhere, regardless of nationality, ethnic or racial origin, social background and so on. They are fundamental in that they are inalienable: human rights can be denied or violated but a human being's entitlement to them cannot be removed. They are absolute in that, as the basic grounds for living a genuinely human life, they cannot be qualified (although some argue that all rights are relative as they conflict with one another, rights being a 'zero-sum' game). Human rights can be distinguished from civil rights, on the grounds that the former are moral principles that claim universal jurisdiction, while the latter depend upon the freedoms and status accorded citizens in particular societies. However, the notions of civil rights and *civil liberties often rest upon an underlying belief in human rights, and are viewed as moral principles given legal expression in the form of *citizenship.

Significance

Human rights have come to be accorded in certain parts of the world a near-religious significance. Supporters of human rights argue that they constitute the basic grounds for *freedom, *equality and *justice, and embody the idea that all human lives are worthy of respect. In that sense human rights can be said to give political expression to moral values found in all the world's major religions and which transcend conventional ideological divisions. As such they have been accepted as one of the cornerstones of international *law, sometimes being viewed as superior to state *sovereignty and thereby being used to justify humanitarian and even military intervention (as in cases such as Iraq and Serbia in the 1990s). The most authoritative definition of human rights is found in the United Nations Declaration of Human Rights (1948), although other documents, such as the European Convention on Human Rights and Fundamental Freedoms (1953), have also been influential.

However, the doctrine of human rights has also attracted criticism. A variety of philosophical difficulties have been raised. These include the arguments that human rights are merely moral assertions and lack any empirical justification; that it is difficult to view them as absolute because rights, such as the right to life and the right to self-defence, are often balanced against one another; and that it is not always clear when a person should be regarded as 'human' and therefore entitled to human rights (which is particularly controversial in relation to abortion). Political objections come from conservatives and communitarians, who point out that it is nonsense to suggest that individuals have rights that are separate from the traditions, cultures and societies to which they belong. Marxists, for their part, have traditionally argued that natural or human rights protect private *property by giving all people the right to utilise their unequal social resources. Finally, it is often claimed that human rights are intrinsically linked to the ideas and assumptions of political *liberalism. In this case to portray them as universally applicable is to indulge in a form of ideological imperialism, suggesting that Western liberal values are superior to all others.

INDIVIDUALISM

Individualism is a belief in the primacy, or supreme importance, of the individual over any social group or collective body. It is usually viewed as the opposite of *collectivism. Individualism, however, may be either a descriptive or a normative concept. As a descriptive concept, in the form of *methodological individualism*, it suggests that the individual is central to any political theory or social explanation – all statements about society should be made in terms of the individuals who compose it. As Margaret Thatcher put it, 'there is no such thing as society, only individuals and their families'. As a normative concept, in the form of *ethical individualism*, it implies that society should be constructed so as to benefit the individual, giving priority to the individual's *rights, needs or interests.

What ethical individualism means in practice, nevertheless, depends upon one's view of the individual or theory of *human nature. In its most familiar form, *egoistical individualism* (also called 'market', 'possessive' or 'atomistic' individualism), it stresses human self-interestedness and self-reliance. The individual is the exclusive possessor of his or her own talents, owing nothing to society and being owed nothing in return (this form of individualism overlaps most clearly with methodological individualism). On the other hand, what can be called *developmental individualism* emphasises personal growth and human flourishing, and is expressed in the idea of individuality. As this form of individualism allows for social *responsibility and even altruism, it blurs the distinction between individualism and collectivism.

Significance

The doctrine of individualism emerged in the seventeenth and eighteenth centuries as a result of the development of market or capitalist societies, in which individuals were expected to make a wider range of economic and social choices and to take personal

responsibility for their own lives. It constitutes the basic principle of
*liberalism and, as such, has come to be one of the major compo-
nents of Western political culture. Methodological individualism
has a long and impressive history, having been employed by social
contract theorists such as Thomas Hobbes (1588–1679) and John
Locke (1632–1704), by utilitarians such as Jeremy Bentham
(1748–1832), by economic theorists from Adam Smith (1723–90)
onwards, and by modern *rational choice theorists. Its attraction
as a mode of analysis is that it enables theories to be constructed on
the basis of seemingly empirical, and even scientific, observations
about human behaviour. In short: understand the individual and
social and political institutions and mechanisms become explicable.
However, the drawback of any form of methodological individualism is that it is both asocial and ahistorical. By building political
theories upon the basis of a pre-established model of human
nature, individualists ignore the fact that human behaviour varies
from society to society, and from one historical period to the next.
If experience and the social environment shape human nature, the
individual should be seen as the product of society, not the other
way round.

As an ethical or political principle, however, individualism has
usually had strongly anti-statist implications. For classical liberals,
the *New Right and individualist anarchists, the central thrust of
individualism is to expand the realm of *civil society and the 'private' sphere at the expense of political *authority. Individualism
thus implies negative *freedom, the expansion of individual choice
and responsibilities. However, this egoistical individualism has
been rejected by socialists, traditional conservatives and modern
communitarians. In the view of socialists individualism promotes
greed and competition, weakening the bonds of *community; in
the view of conservatives it produces insecurity and rootlessness
and undermines traditional values; and in the view of communitarians it robs society of its capacity to establish moral order and
encourage collective endeavour.

JUSTICE

Justice is the idea of a morally justifiable distribution of rewards or
punishments. Justice, in short, is about giving each person what he
or she is 'due', often seen as his or her 'just desserts'. In this sense

justice can be applied to the distribution of any 'goods' in society: *freedom, *rights, *power, wealth, leisure and so on. However, as the grounds for just distribution may vary enormously, justice can perhaps be seen as the archetypal 'essentially contested' concept. A distinction can nevertheless be made between procedural and substantive notions of justice. *Procedural justice*, or 'formal' justice, refers to the manner in which outcomes are arrived at, and thus to the rules that govern human conduct and interaction. For instance, any outcome of a sporting competition is considered just so long as it results from the application of fair rules independently adjudicated – in short, there should be a 'level playing field'. *Substantive justice*, or 'concrete' justice, on the other hand, is concerned with the substance of the outcomes themselves; that is, with the nature of the end-point. This can be seen in the idea that the punishment should 'fit' the crime; in other words, that penalties should be appropriate and justifiable in themselves.

The two most common applications of the concept of justice are legal justice and social justice. *Legal justice* refers to the apportionment of punishments and rewards as a result of wrongdoing and, in particular, law-breaking. The judicial system is sometimes therefore described as the administration of justice. However, *law should not be equated with justice: laws may be just or unjust, as may be the court system through which they are administered. *Social justice* refers to a morally justifiable distribution of material or social rewards, notably wealth, income and social status. Many take social justice to imply *equality, even viewing it as a specifically socialist principle. However, concepts of social justice may be inegalitarian as well as egalitarian, and even when socialists use the term it tends to imply a weak form of equality: a narrowing of material inequalities, often justified in terms of equality of opportunity.

Significance

Justice has been portrayed as the master concept of political thought. Since the time of Plato (427–347 BCE) and Aristotle (384–22 BCE), political thinkers have seen the 'good' society as a 'just' society. Much of *political theory therefore consists of a debate about 'who should get what?'. In relation to legal justice this issue has largely been resolved through the development of widely accepted procedural rules about, for example, access to legal advice and representation, judicial neutrality, rules of evidence and the use of juries, although there may be important substantive differences between the laws which operate in liberal-democratic societies and, say, *Sharia* law found in Islamic states.

However, controversies over social justice have been deep and recurrent. Some, including supporters of the *New Right, dismiss the very idea of social justice on the grounds that it is inappropriate to apply moral principles such as justice to the distribution of wealth and income, because these are strictly economic matters and can be judged only by criteria such as efficiency and growth. From this perspective, to portray the poor as 'victims' of injustice is simply absurd. Socialists and modern liberals, in contrast, have been attracted to the idea of social justice precisely because they are unwilling to divorce economics from ethics, and because they are unwilling to leave issues related to wealth and poverty to the vagaries of the *market. Sympathy for social justice therefore usually goes hand-in-hand with support for government intervention in economic and social life. However, there are quite different liberal and socialist models of social justice. The liberal model is rooted in *individualism and is based upon a commitment to *meritocracy, while the socialist model is rooted in *collectivism and exhibits greater support for social equality and *community.

LEADERSHIP

Leadership can be understood as a pattern of behaviour, as a personal quality and as a political value. As a pattern of behaviour, leadership is the influence exerted by an individual or group over a larger body to organise or direct its efforts towards the achievement of desired goals. As a personal attribute, leadership refers to the character traits which enable the leader to exert influence over others. Leadership in this sense is effectively equated with charisma, charm or personal power. As a political value, leadership refers to guidance and inspiration, the capacity to mobilise others through moral authority or ideological insight.

Significance

In some respects the subject of political leadership appears to be outdated. The division of society into leaders and followers is rooted in a pre-democratic culture of deference and respect in which leaders 'knew best' and the public needed to be led, mobilised or guided. Democratic pressures may not have removed the need for leaders, but they have certainly placed powerful constraints upon leadership, notably by making leaders publicly accountable and establishing institutional mechanisms through which they can be removed. In other respects, however, the politics of leadership has become increasingly significant. For instance, to some extent *democracy itself has enhanced the importance of personality by forcing political leaders, in effect, to 'project themselves' in the hope of gaining electoral support. This tendency has undoubtedly been strengthened by modern means of mass communication (especially television) which tend to emphasise personality rather than policies, and provide leaders with powerful weapons with which to manipulate their public images. Furthermore, as society becomes more complex and fragmented, people may increasingly look to the personal vision of an individual leader to give coherence and meaning to the world in which they live.

The question of political leadership is nevertheless surrounded by deep ideological controversy. Its principal supporters have been on the political *right, influenced by a general belief in natural inequality and a broadly pessimistic view of the masses. In its extreme form this was reflected in the fascist 'leader principle', which holds that there is a single, supreme leader who alone is capable of leading the masses to their destiny, a theory derived from Friedrich Nietzsche's (1844–1900) notion of the *Übermensch* ('superman').

Amongst the supposed virtues of leadership are the following:

- it mobilises and inspires people who would otherwise be inert and directionless;
- it promotes unity and encourages members of a group to pull in the same direction;
- it strengthens organisations by establishing a hierarchy of responsibilities and roles.

Liberals and socialists, on the other hand, have usually warned that leaders should not be trusted, and treated leadership as a basic threat to *equality and *justice. Nevertheless, this has not prevented socialist regimes from employing leadership systems, and, in the case of Lenin's (1870–1924) theory of the vanguard party, they have sometimes stressed the need for political leadership.

The alleged dangers of leadership include the following:

- it concentrates *power, and can thus lead to corruption and tyranny, hence the democratic demand that leadership should be checked by *accountability;
- it engenders subservience and deference, thereby discouraging people from taking responsibility for their own lives;
- it narrows debate and argument, because of its emphasis upon ideas flowing down from the top, rather than up from the bottom.

MERITOCRACY

Meritocracy literally means rules by the able or talented, merit being talent plus hard work. The term, however, is most commonly used as a principle of social *justice, implying that social position and material rewards should reflect the distribution of ability and effort in society at large. Different implications can nevertheless be drawn from meritocracy, depending on whether emphasis is placed upon talent or hard work. Meritocratic systems that focus primarily upon talent are designed to encourage people, and particularly the talented, to realise their natural ability to its fullest potential. Ones that primarily emphasise hard work only regard effort as morally laudable, on the grounds that to reward talent is to create a 'natural lottery' (Rawls, 1971). Meritocracy differs from hierarchy, in that it allows for social mobility and a flexible pattern of inequalities, as opposed to fixed and structural gradations in social position and wealth.

Significance

Meritocracy is a key liberal social principle and can be seen as one of the basic values of liberal *capitalism. Its defenders argue that it has both economic and moral virtues, including the following:

- it guarantees incentives by encouraging people to realise their talents and by rewarding hard work;
- it ensures that society is guided by wise and talented people who are better able to judge the interests of others;
- it is just in that distribution according to merit gives each person what he or she is 'due' and respects the principle of equality of opportunity.

However, the principle of meritocracy is by no means universally accepted. Its principal critics have been socialists but traditional conservatives have also objected to it. Amongst their criticisms are the following:

- it threatens *community and social cohesion by encouraging competition and self-striving; R. H. Tawney (1880–1962) called it a 'tadpole philosophy';
- it is unjust because it implies that inequalities reflect unequal personal endowment when, in reality, they usually reflect unequal social treatment;
- it is contradictory because, on the one hand, it justifies social inequality, and on the other it can be achieved only through the redistribution of wealth to create a 'level playing field'.

NEUTRALITY

Neutrality is the absence of any form of partisanship or commitment; it consists of a refusal to 'take sides'. In international relations, neutrality is a legal condition through which a *state declares non-involvement in a conflict or war, and indicates its intention to refrain from supporting or aiding either side. As a principle of individual conduct, applied to the likes of judges, civil servants, the military and other public officials, it implies, strictly speaking, the absence of political sympathies and ideological leanings. Neutral actors are thus political eunuchs. In practice the less exacting requirement of impartiality is usually applied. This allows that political sympathies may be held as long as these do not intrude into a person's professional or public responsibilities.

Significance

The principle of neutrality is crucial to the theory and practice of liberal-democratic *government. At its core is a belief in state neutrality, the idea that the *state harbours no economic, social or other biases and therefore treats all individuals and groups alike. This is reflected in the constitutional principle of neutrality as it applies to state bodies and officials, notably the *judiciary, the civil service, the police and the military. Neutrality thus guarantees that the state is kept separate from the government, in the sense that public officials are not contaminated by the political and ideological enthusiasms of professional politicians. From this perspective, political neutrality has two key benefits. It ensures fairness in the sense that all people are treated equally regardless of social background, race, religion, gender and so on, and it fosters objectivity in allowing decisions to be made on the basis of reason and evidence, rather than irrational prejudice. However, neutrality has been criticised on three grounds. First, Marxists, feminists and others have portrayed it as a façade designed to mask the degree to which the state, often via the structure and composition of state institutions, articulates the interests of powerful or propertied groups in society. Second, some dismiss neutrality as simply a myth, arguing that no one is capable of suppressing values and beliefs that are formed through one's social background and group membership. Third, neutrality may be considered undesirable by those who believe that it engenders indifference or allows public officials to resist the will of democratically elected governments.

OBLIGATION

An obligation is a requirement or duty to act in a particular way. Legal obligations are nevertheless different from moral obligations. *Legal obligations*, such as the requirement to pay taxes and observe other *laws, are enforceable through the courts and backed up by a system of penalties. 'Being obliged' to do something implies an element of coercion; legal obligations may thus be upheld on grounds of simple prudence: whether laws are right or wrong they are obeyed out of a fear of punishment. *Moral obligations*, on the other hand, are fulfilled not because it is sensible to do so, but because such conduct is thought to be rightful or morally correct. 'Having an obligation' to do something suggests only a moral duty. To give a promise, for example, is to be under a moral obligation to carry it out, regardless of the consequences which breaking the promise will entail. The most important form of moral obligation is 'political obligation', the duty of the citizen to acknowledge the *authority of the *state and obey its laws. Obligation can therefore be thought of as one of the key components of *citizenship, the *rights and obligations of the citizen being reverse sides of the same coin.

Significance

The issue of political obligation has been one of the central themes in *political theory. This is because the question of obligations addresses the moral basis of political rule. The classic explanation of political obligation is found in the idea of a 'social contract', an agreement made amongst citizens, or between citizens and the state, through which they accept the authority of the state in return for benefits which only a sovereign power can provide. For Plato (427–347 BCE), the obligation to obey the state is based upon an implicit promise made by the simple fact that citizens choose to remain within its borders; for Hobbes (1588–1679) and Locke (1632–1704), it was based upon the state's ability to deliver *order and stability; and for Rousseau (1712–78), it followed from the state's capacity to articulate the 'general will' or collective good. However, conservatives and communitarians have gone further and suggested that obligation is not merely contractual but is an intrinsic feature of any stable society. From this perspective, obligation is a form of natural duty, reflecting the fact that our values and identities are largely derived from the societies in which we live. The only theorists who reject the very idea of political obligation are philosophical anarchists, who insist upon absolute respect for personal *autonomy.

PROPERTY

Property, in everyday usage, refers to inanimate objects or 'things'. However, property is better thought of as a social institution, defined by custom, convention and, in most cases, by *law. As a political principle, property draws attention to a relationship of ownership that exists between the object in question and the person or group to whom it belongs. In that sense there is a clear distinction between property and simply making use of an object as a possession. For example, to pick up a pebble from the beach, to borrow a pen, or to drive someone else's car, does not establish ownership. Property is thus an established and enforceable claim to an object or possession; it is a *right not a 'thing'. The ownership of property is therefore reflected in the existence of rights and powers over an object, and also the acceptance of duties and liabilities in relation to it.

However, property can be conceived of as private, common or state property. *Private property* is the right of an individual or institution to exclude others from the use or benefit of something. The right to 'exclude' does not necessarily deny access, however. Someone else can use 'my' car – but only with my permission. *Common property* is based upon a shared right of access to property amongst members of a collective body, none of whom can exercise a 'right to exclude', except in relation to non-members. *State property* is private property that belongs to the *state. Ordinary citizens, for instance, have no more right of access to state property such as police cars than they do to any other private vehicle. However, the notions of state property and common property are often confused. Terms such as 'public ownership' or 'social ownership' appear to refer to property owned collectively by all citizens, but in practice usually describe property that is owned and controlled by the state. 'Nationalisation' similarly implies ownership by the *nation, but it invariably operates through a system of state control.

Significance

The question of property has been one of the deepest and most divisive issues in political and ideological debate. Indeed, ideological divisions have traditionally boiled down to where one stands on property, both left-wing and right-wing political creeds practising different forms of the politics of ownership. The clash between *capitalism and *socialism has thus been portrayed as a choice between two rival economic philosophies, the former based upon private property and the latter upon common ownership.

Liberals and conservatives have generally been strong supporters of private property; amongst their arguments are the following:

- property is a right based upon 'self-ownership' – because each person has exclusive rights over his or her self, it follows that such people have an exclusive right to the product of their labour; inanimate objects have been 'mixed' with human labour to create property rights (Locke);
- it is an incentive to labour and thus serves as a guarantee of economic prosperity and efficiency;
- it enlarges individual *freedom in the sense that it promotes independence and self-reliance – people can 'stand on their own two feet';

- it promotes important social values, because property owners have a 'stake' in society and are more likely to maintain *order, be law-abiding and respect the property of others
- it is a means of self-realisation, an exteriorisation of one's personal identity – people 'see' themselves in what they own, their cars, houses, books and so on.

Socialists and communists, on the other hand, have advanced the following arguments in favour of common property:

- it reflects the fact that labour is generally a social and collective activity depending upon cooperation rather than independent effort – what is produced in common should be owned in common';
- it strengthens *community and social cohesion by ensuring that all members of society have a shared interest and a collective identity;
- it guarantees *equality by preventing some from accumulating wealth while others are denied it;
- it allows people to escape from greed and materialism by defining happiness not in terms of the acquisition but on the basis of personal self-development.

Nevertheless, there are clear indications that the politics of ownership has declined in significance. Although its cause was revived in the 1980s by the *New Right's enthusiasm for privatisation, the collapse of *communism in the revolutions of 1989–91 and the de-radicalisation of socialism have resulted in a widespread acceptance of at least the economic virtues of private property and therefore of the disadvantages of both common and state property.

REPRESENTATION

To represent means, in everyday language, to 'portray' or 'make present', as when a picture is said to represent a scene or a person. As a political principle, representation is a relationship through which an individual or group stands for, or acts on behalf of, a larger body of people. Representation differs from *democracy in that, while the former acknowledges a distinction between *government and the governed, the latter, at least in its classical sense, aspires to abolish this distinction and establish popular self-government. Representative democracy may nevertheless constitute a limited and indirect form of democratic rule, provided that representation links government and the governed in such a way that the people's views are effectively articulated or their interests secured.

However, there is no single, agreed theory of representation. The term may have one of four sets of implications. First, a representative may be a trustee, a person who is vested with formal responsibility for another's property or affairs. This was classically expressed by Edmund Burke (1729–97), who argued that representatives serve their constituents by thinking for themselves and using their own, mature judgement. Second, a representative may be a delegate, a person who is chosen to act for another on the basis of clear guidance or instructions. Delegation implies acting as a conduit conveying the views of others, without expressing one's own views or opinions; examples include sales representatives and ambassadors. Third, a representative may be a person who carries out a *mandate, in the sense that such people are obliged to carry out the promises upon which they fought an *election. This theory implies that *political parties rather than individual politicians are the principal agents of representation. Fourth, a representative may typify or resemble the group he or she claims to represent, usually coming from the group itself. This notion is embodied in the idea of a 'representative cross-section', and implies that a representative government or *parliament would constitute a microcosm of the larger society, containing members drawn from all groups and sections in society, and in numbers that are proportional to the size of the groups in society at large.

Significance

Representation is widely viewed as the only practicable form of democracy in modern circumstances. Interest in it developed alongside the wider use of popular election as the principal means of political recruitment, although pre-democratic forms of representation supposedly operated through, for example, the obligation of monarchs to consult major landed, clerical and other interests. The general benefits of representation are that it provides the people with a mechanism through which they can replace unpopular politicians or unsuccessful governments, while relieving ordinary citizens of the everyday burdens of decision-making, thus making possible a division of labour in *politics.

Representation therefore allows governments to be placed in the hands of those with better education, expert knowledge and greater experience.

Nevertheless, there are very different views about what representation does, or should, imply in practice. Burke's model of trusteeship, for instance, views representation as a moral duty that can be invested in an educated and social elite. Its virtue is that it does not bind representatives to the ill-considered and ignorant views of their constituents, but its disadvantage is that it may allow representatives to advance their own interests or defend the general interests of the social elite. Representation as delegations emerged specifically to counter such tendencies by realising the ideal of popular *sovereignty; however, it appears to rob governments and parliaments of their vital deliberative function as forums of debate and discussion. The doctrine of the mandate has the advantage that it helps to imbue elections with meaning by authorising governments only to carry out policies that have been properly endorsed, but it is questionable whether voters are influenced by issues or policies, and, as with delegation, it allows governments little freedom of debate or manoeuvre. The resemblance model supposedly ensures that representatives can fully identify with the group they represent because they have a common background and shared experiences, but the idea that only a woman can represent women, or only a black person can represent other black people, is perhaps unnecessarily narrow as well as simplistic. Others, however, question the very idea of representation. This is done most commonly by those who argue that representation is simply a substitute for democracy, in that the former always has elitist implications because government is carried out by a small group of professional politicians and the people are kept at arm's length from political *power.

RESPONSIBILITY

Responsibility can be understood in three contrasting ways. First, it means to have control or *authority, in the sense of being responsible *for* something or someone. Personal responsibility thus implies being responsible for oneself and one's own economic and social circumstances, while social responsibility implies being responsible for others. Second, responsibility means *accountability or answerability, in the sense of being responsible *to* someone. This suggests the existence of a higher authority to which an individual or body is subject, and by which it can be controlled. Government is responsible in this sense if its actions are open to scrutiny and criticism by a *parliament or assembly that has the ability to remove it from *power. This also has an important moral dimension: it implies that the government is willing to accept blame and bear an appropriate penalty. Third, responsibility means to act in a sensible, reasonable or morally correct fashion, often in the face of pressure to behave otherwise. A government may thus claim to be responsible when it resists electoral pressures and risks unpopularity by pursuing policies designed to meet long-term public interests.

Significance

Responsibility, as it applies to individuals, has different implications depending upon what citizens are deemed to be responsible for, and to whom. However, the idea of responsible government has clearer applications, linked to the wider use of electoral and democratic procedures. Responsible government, in the sense of accountable government, is usually associated with two important benefits. The first is that it facilitates *representation by binding government to the electorate viewed as a higher authority. Responsible government thus means that the government is responsible to, and removable by, the public, presumably through the mechanism of competitive elections. The second advantage is that it exposes government to scrutiny and oversight, checking the exercise of government power and exposing *policy to analysis and debate. This is a function that is usually vested in the parliament; it is carried out through procedures for debate and questioning and, in a more specific manner, by the use of *committees.

In the UK system, responsible government has been elaborated into the conventions of collective and individual ministerial responsibility. Collective responsibility obliges all ministers to 'sing the same song', on the grounds that they are collectively responsible to and removable by Parliament. Individual responsibility holds that ministers are personally responsible to Parliament for departmental blunders or policy failures. Nevertheless, the adequacy of responsible government has been widely doubted. This occurs when doctrines of responsibility lose their political edge and become mere constitutional principles. For instance, UK governments have little fear of collective responsibility so long as they have majority control of the House of Commons; and individual responsibility no longer, at least in its traditional form, results in ministerial resignations. Responsibility in the sense of governments acting in a morally correct fashion has always been deeply controversial. Its danger is that, by contrast with the idea of accountability, it divorces government from the people by suggesting that only the former has the ability to judge the best interests of the latter. Doubtless, all governments would view themselves as responsible in this sense, supported by the knowledge that no other body could challenge this designation.

RIGHTS

A right is an entitlement to act or be treated in a particular way (although in its original meaning it stood for a power or privilege, as in the rights of the nobility or divine right). Rights, however, can be either legal or moral in character. *Legal rights* are laid down in *law or in a system of formal rules and so are enforceable. *Moral rights*, in contrast, exist only as moral claims or philosophical assertions. *Human rights, and their predecessors, natural rights, are essentially moral rights, despite the fact that they have increasingly been translated into international law and sometimes domestic law. A further distinction can be made between negative rights and positive rights. *Negative rights* are rights that mark out a realm of unconstrained action, and thus impose restrictions upon the behaviour of others, particularly the *government. Traditional *civil liberties, such as freedom of speech and freedom of movement, are therefore negative rights; our exercise of them requires that government and fellow citizens leave us alone. *Positive rights* are rights that impose demands upon others, and particularly government, in terms of the provision of resources or supports, and thus extend their responsibilities. Social or welfare rights, such as the right to education or the right to benefits, are positive rights. Our exercise of them requires that the government provides services and guarantees social supports.

Significance

The doctrine of rights emerged in the seventeenth and eighteenth centuries through the idea of natural or God-given rights, particularly as used by social contract theorists. Rights thus developed as, and, in an important sense, remain, an expression of liberal *individualism. However, the language of rights has come to be adopted by almost all political traditions and thinkers, meaning that political debate is littered with assertions of rights – the right to education, the right to free speech, the right to abortion, the rights of animals and so on. This reflects the fact that rights are the most convenient means of translating political commitments into principled claims. The most significant divisions over rights therefore focus not upon whether or not they exist, but upon which rights should be given priority and with what implications. Negative rights, for instance, have traditionally been supported by liberals, who see them as a means of defending the individual from arbitrary government, but have been attacked by socialists on the grounds that they may merely uphold private *property and thus class inequality. Positive rights, on the other hand, are favoured by socialists who wish to defend welfare provision and economic intervention, but are condemned by some liberals and supporters of the *New Right because they breed dependency and weaken self-reliance.

Moreover, whereas liberals treat rights as strictly individual entitlements, others have developed the idea of group rights, as in the case of socialist support for trade union rights and the nationalist emphasis upon the rights of national self-determination. The idea of minority rights, in reference to the rights of groups such as women (a minority, of course, only in terms of elite representation), gays, the disabled, children and ethnic minorities, has provoked particular debate. In many cases these are rights of *equality; demands, in other words, for equal treatment on behalf of people who suffer from some form of discrimination or social disadvantage. In other cases minority rights articulate demands that arise from the special needs of particular groups, examples including contraception and abortion rights for women, and mobility rights for people who use wheelchairs. Further controversy has arisen as a result of attempts by ecologists to apply rights to non-humans, most obviously in the form of animal rights, but also more generally in the idea of the rights of the planet.

Nevertheless, some thinkers object to the very idea of rights. Marxists have traditionally portrayed rights as an example of bourgeois *ideology, in that they establish a bogus *equality that disguises the workings of the capitalist class system; utilitarians

reject rights as nonsense, on the grounds that they constitute untest-
able philosophical assertions; and conservatives and some communitarians have warned that a 'culture of rights' breeds egoism and
weakens social norms, an obsession with individual rights being a
threat to the idea of what is morally right.

TOLERATION

Toleration means forbearance, a willingness to accept views or
actions with which one disagrees or of which one disapproves. Toleration should therefore be distinguished from both permissiveness
and indifference. Permissiveness is a social attitude that allows
people to act as they wish or as they choose; it reflects either moral
indifference (the belief that the actions in question cannot be judged
in moral terms) or moral relativism (the belief that moral judgements can be made only from the perspective of the individuals
concerned). Toleration, on the other hand, is based upon two separate moral judgements. The first is disapproval of a form of behaviour or set of beliefs; the second is a deliberate refusal to impose
one's own views on others. Toleration, thus, does not simply mean
'putting up with' what cannot be changed – for example, a bat-
tered wife who stays with her abusive husband out of fear can
hardly be said to 'tolerate' his behaviour. Moreover, toleration
does not imply non-interference. Although toleration does not
allow for interference with, or constraint upon, others, it allows
influence to be exerted through moral example and rational persuasion. A distinction is sometimes made between 'negative' toleration,
a passive acceptance of diversity or willingness to 'live and let live',
and 'positive' toleration, a celebration of diversity and *pluralism
viewed as enriching for all.

Significance

Toleration is a core principle of *liberalism and one of the central
values of *liberal democracy. Liberals have usually viewed toleration as a guarantee of individual *freedom and a means of social
enrichment. John Locke (1632–1704) defended toleration, particularly religious toleration, on the grounds that the *state has no right
to meddle in 'the care of men's souls'. However, his central argument

was based upon a belief in human rationality. 'Truth' will only emerge out of free competition amongst ideas and beliefs and therefore must be left to 'shift for herself'. John Stuart Mill (1806–73) treated toleration as one of the faces of individual liberty, suggesting that it represents the goal of personal *autonomy, and that, in promoting debate and argument, it stimulates the intellectual development and moral health of society at large. Such views are consistent with support for pluralism in its moral, cultural and political forms.

Nevertheless, even liberals recognise the limits of toleration, particularly in the need to protect toleration from the intolerant. This may, for instance, provide a justification for banning anti-democratic and anti-constitutional *political parties, on the grounds that, if they came to power, they would establish dictatorial rule and abolish toleration. Other concerns about toleration include that it places a heavy, perhaps over-heavy, faith upon *rationalism and the ability of people to resist 'bad' ideas; that it may allow groups with offensive views, such as racists and fascists, to operate legally and gain respectability; and that it weakens society in the sense that it makes it impossible to develop shared values and a common culture.

TRADITION

Tradition refers to ideas, practices or institutions that have endured through time and have therefore been inherited from an earlier period. However, it is difficult to determine precisely how long something has to survive before it can be regarded as a tradition. Tradition is usually thought to denote continuity between generations; traditions are things that have been transmitted from one generation to the next. However, the line between the traditional and the merely fashionable is often indistinct. Tradition should nevertheless be distinguished from both progress and reaction. Whereas progress implies a movement forward, building upon the past, and reaction suggests 'turning the clock back', reclaiming the past, tradition stands for continuity or conservation: the absence of change.

Significance

Tradition is one of the key principles, some would say the defining principle, of *conservatism. The original conservative justification for tradition rested upon the idea of natural *order and the belief that tradition reflected God-given institutions and practices has now effectively been abandoned except by religious fundamentalists. The remaining conservative case for tradition is twofold. First, tradition reflects the accumulated wisdom of the past, institutions and practices that have been 'tested by time' and should be preserved for the benefit of the living and for generations to come. This is embodied in Edmund Burke's (1729–97) assertion that society is a partnership between 'those who are living, those who are dead and those who are to be born'. Second, tradition engenders a sense of belonging and identity in the individual that is rooted in history, and also fosters social cohesion by establishing in society a moral and cultural bedrock. Tradition thus gives people, individually and collectively, a sense of who they are.

However, developments in modern society have generally eroded respect for tradition, lingering forms of traditionalism, such as the neo-conservative defence of traditional values, often being seen as part of the difficult adjustment to a post-traditional society. The most important of these developments has been the accelerating pace of change in technologically advanced societies, and the spread of *rationalism, suggesting that reason and critical understanding are a better test of 'value' than mere survival. The two most common criticisms of tradition are that it amounts to the 'despotism of custom' (J. S. Mill), in that it enslaves the present generation to the past and denies the possibility of progress, and that tradition serves the interests not of the many but of the few, elite groups which dominated past societies.

WELFARE

Welfare, in its simplest form, means happiness, prosperity or well-being in general; it implies not merely physical survival but some measure of health and contentment as well. As a political principle, however, welfare stands for a particular means through which social well-being is maintained: collectively provided welfare, delivered by *government, through what is termed a welfare state. The term 'welfare state' is used either to refer to a *state that assumes broad responsibilities for the social well-being of its citizens, or, more narrowly, to the health, education, housing and social security systems through which these responsibilities are carried out.

Welfare states nevertheless come in many different shapes or forms. Esping-Andersen (1990) distinguished between three types of welfare state: liberal or 'limited' welfare states (as in the USA and Australia) aim to provide little more than a 'safety net' for those in need; conservative or 'corporate' welfare states (as in Germany) provide a comprehensive range of services that depend heavily upon the 'paying-in' principle and link benefits closely to jobs; and social democratic or 'Beveridge' welfare states (as traditionally existed in Sweden and the UK, modelled on the 1942 Beveridge Report) incorporate a system of universal benefits and are based upon national insurance and full employment.

Significance

Interest in welfare emerged during the nineteenth century as industrialisation created a spectre of urban poverty and social division that, in different ways, disturbed conservative, liberal and socialist politicians. Early support for social reform and welfare reflected elite fears about the danger of social *revolution and the desire to promote national efficiency in both economic and military terms, as well as the more radical wish to abolish poverty and counter the injustices of the capitalist system. This, in turn, gave rise to quite different forms of welfare support in different states. Although a welfare *consensus developed in the early post-1945 period as paternalistic conservatives, modern liberals and social democrats unified in support for at least the principle of welfare, the 1980s and 1990s witnessed a general retreat from welfare, even among socialists, brought about in part by the pressures of economic *globalisation. Nevertheless, welfare remains one of the central faultlines in ideological debate, dividing pro-welfarist social democrats and modern liberals from anti-welfarist libertarians and supporters of the *New Right.

Amongst the arguments in favour of welfare are the following:

- it promotes social cohesion and national unity, in that it gives all citizens a 'stake' in society and guarantees at least basic social support;
- it enlarges *freedom in the sense that it safeguards people from poverty and provides conditions in which they can develop and realise their potential;

- it ensures prosperity by countering the effects of social deprivation and helping those who cannot help themselves;
- it serves as a redistributive mechanism that promotes greater *equality and strengthens a sense of social responsibility.

Arguments against welfare include the following:

- it creates a culture of dependency and so restricts freedom in the sense of individual responsibility and self-reliance;
- it amounts to legalised theft, and so is unjust, in that it transfers resources from the prosperous to the lazy without their consent;
- it is economically damaging because welfare spending pushes up taxes and fuels inflation;
- it is inefficient because it is provided through monopolistic public bureaucracies that are not geared to the profit motive.

FURTHER READING

Arblaster, A., *Democracy* (Milton Keynes: Open University Press, 1994).
Barbalet, J. M., *Citizenship* (Milton Keynes: Open University Press, 1988).
Barker, J., *Arguing for Equality* (London and New York: Verso, 1987).
Barry, N., *Welfare* (Milton Keynes: Open University Press, 1990).
Bellamy, R. (ed.), *Theories and Concepts of Politics* (Manchester: Manchester University Press, 1993).
Birch, A. H., *Representation* (London: Macmillan, 1972).
Freeden, M., *Rights* (Minneapolis, MN: University of Minnesota Press, 1991).
Goodin, R. E. and Pettit, P., *A Companion to Contemporary Political Philosophy* (Oxford: Blackwell, 1995).
Gray, T., *Freedom* (London: Macmillan, 1990).
Held, D. (ed.), *Political Theory Today* (Cambridge: Polity Press, 1991).
Heywood, A., *Political Theory: An Introduction* (London: Macmillan, 1999).
Horton, J., *Political Obligation* (London: Macmillan, 1992).
Kingdom, J., *No Such Thing as Society? Individualism and Community* (Buckingham: Open University Press, 1992).
Mendus, S., *Toleration and the Limits of Liberalism* (London: Macmillan, 1989).
O'Neill, J. (ed.), *Modes of Individualism and Collectivism* (London: Gregg Revivals, 1993).
Rawls, J., *A Theory of Justice* (London: Oxford University Press, 1971).
Ryan, A., *Property* (Milton Keynes: Open University Press, 1987).

Part six

SYSTEMS

This section examines concepts that refer to the organisation of political power, or the wider institutional arrangements of government.

SYSTEMS

ABSOLUTISM

Absolutism is the theory or practice of absolute government. *Government is 'absolute' in the sense that it possesses unfettered *power: government cannot be constrained by a body external to itself. The most prominent manifestation of absolute government is the absolute *monarchy. However, there is no necessary connection between monarchy and absolute government. Although unfettered power can be placed in the hands of the monarch, it can also be vested in a collective body such as the supreme legislature. Absolutism nevertheless differs from modern versions of *dictatorship, notably *totalitarianism. Whereas absolutist regimes aspire to a monopoly of political power, usually achieved by excluding the masses from *politics, totalitarianism involves the establishment of 'total power' through the politicisation of every aspect of social and personal existence. Absolutism thus differs significantly from, for instance, *fascism.

Significance

Absolutism was the dominant political form in Europe in the seventeenth and eighteenth centuries. It was usually linked to the claim that *sovereignty, representing unchallengeable and indivisible legal *authority, resided in the monarchy. Absolutist rule was justified by both rationalist and theological theories. Rationalist theories of absolutism, such as those of Jean Bodin (1530–96) and Thomas Hobbes (1588–1679), advanced the belief that only absolute government can guarantee *order and social stability. Divided sovereignty or challengeable power is therefore a recipe for chaos and disorder. Theological theories of absolutism were based upon the doctrine of divine right, according to which the absolute control

a monarch exercises over his or her subjects derives from, and is analogous to, the power of God over his creation.

However, absolutist theories are now widely regarded as politically redundant and ideologically objectionable. They are politically redundant because the advance of *constitutionalism and
*representation has fragmented power and resulted in a strength-
ening of checks and balances, and because where dictatorship has
survived it has assumed a quite different political character. It is
ideologically objectionable because absolutism serves as a cloak for
tyranny and arbitrary government, and is, by definition, irreconcilable with ideas such as individual *rights and democratic
accountability. Nevertheless, a form of constitutional absolutism
can be seen to survive in political systems based upon respect for
the principle of parliamentary sovereignty.

AUTHORITARIANISM

Authoritarianism is a belief in, or the practice of, government 'from
above', in which political rule is imposed upon society regardless
of its *consent. Authoritarianism thus differs from *authority.
The latter rests upon *legitimacy, and in that sense arises 'from
below'. Authoritarianism is a very broad classification of government. It can be associated with monarchical *absolutism, traditional *dictatorships and most forms of military rule; and left-wing
and right-wing versions of authoritarianism can be identified, associated, respectively, with *communism and *capitalism. However,
authoritarianism is usually distinguished from *totalitarianism, on
the grounds that it is primarily concerned with the repression of
opposition and political liberty, rather than with the more radical
goal of obliterating the distinction between the *state and *civil
society. Authoritarian regimes may therefore tolerate a significant
range of economic, religious and other freedoms.

Significance

Authoritarianism was the dominant political form in pre-
constitutional and pre-democratic societies, usually taking the form
of monarchical rule and aristocratic privilege. Theories of authoritarianism can be traced back to thinkers such as Joseph de Maistre

(1753–1821), who argued that the belief in the principle of authority, as opposed to individual *freedom, is the only reliable means of securing *order. In modern politics, however, authoritarianism is usually viewed as a regime type that differs from both *democracy and totalitarianism. The value of the term is nevertheless limited by the fact that, although authoritarian regimes rely upon command and obedience, they exhibit a wide range of political and ideological features. For example, so-called 'old' authoritarian regimes, such as Franco's Spain, were often conservative in that they set out to protect traditional elites and de-politicise the masses, while 'new' authoritarian regimes, commonly found in the developing world, aim to bring about economic mobilisation and, to some extent, rely upon political agitation. Indeed, such regimes may develop authoritarian-populist features which resemble Bonapartism (after Louis Napoleon's regime in France, 1848–70), a style of government that fused personal leadership with conservative *nationalism, or Peronism (after Juan Peron's regime in Argentina, 1946–55), a dictatorship that based its support upon the impoverished masses and the promise of economic and social progress.

However, the stark authoritarian/democratic distinction is often misleading because authoritarian traits can be identified in democratic regimes. Examples of this include the McCarthyite 'witch hunts' of the 1950s in the USA and Thatcherism in the UK, whose combination of neo-liberal economics and neo-conservative social policies has been interpreted as a form of 'authoritarian populism' (Hall and Jacques, 1983). Finally, authoritarianism has also been viewed as a psychological or sociological phenomenon linked to either a disposition to obey orders unthinkingly or a rigid insistence upon obedience from subordinates. The classic contribution to this approach to authoritarianism was the idea of the 'authoritarian personality', developed by Adorno et al. (1950), which explains unquestioning obedience and rigidity of character in terms of an 'extreme intolerance to ambiguity'; in other words, it is a response to deep insecurities precipitated by uncertainty and choice.

CAPITALISM

Capitalism is an economic system as well as a form of property ownership. Its central features include the following. First, it is based upon generalised commodity production, a 'commodity' being a good or service produced for exchange – it has market value rather than use value. Second, productive wealth in a capitalist economy is predominantly held in private hands. Third, economic life is organised according to impersonal market forces, in particular the forces of demand (what consumers are willing and able to consume) and supply (what producers are willing and able to produce). Fourth, in a capitalist economy material self-interest and profit maximisation provide the main motivation for enterprise and hard work.

However, there is no such thing as a 'pure' capitalist system, that is, one not contaminated by socialist and other impurities, such as public ownership, economic management, or collective practices. Moreover, all economic systems are shaped by the historical, cultural and ideological context in which they operate. At least three types of capitalist system can therefore be identified in the modern world. *Enterprise capitalism*, or free-market capitalism (found in the USA and, since the 1980s, the UK) is characterised by faith in the untrammelled workings of market competition, minimal public ownership, safety-net welfare provision and weak trade unions. *Social capitalism*, or Rhine–Alpine capitalism (found throughout continental Europe and especially in Germany) is characterised by the idea of a social market; that is, it attempts to balance the disciplines of market competition against the need for social cohesion and solidarity guaranteed by economic and social intervention. *Collective capitalism*, or 'tiger' capitalism (found in East Asia generally, and increasingly in China) is characterised by what had been called 'relational markets', close connections between industry and finance, and between producers and government, and by an emphasis upon collaborative effort sometimes dubbed 'peoplism'.

Significance

Capitalist economic forms first emerged in seventeenth-century and eighteenth-century Europe, developing from within predominantly feudal societies. Capitalist practices initially took root in the form of commercial agriculture that was orientated towards the *market, and increasingly relied upon waged labour instead of bonded serfs. Developed or industrial capitalism started to emerge from the mid-nineteenth century onwards, first in the UK but soon in the USA and across Europe, with the advent of machine-based factory production and the gradual shift of populations from the land to the expanding towns and cities. Having defied socialist predictions about its inevitable demise, and withstood the twentieth-century ideological battle against *communism, capitalism has, since the Eastern European Revolutions of 1989–91, emerged as a global system without serious rivals. The dual secrets of its success have been its flexibility, which has enabled it to absorb non-capitalist 'impurities' and adapt to a variety of cultures, and its seemingly relentless capacity to generate technological development, which has enabled it to deliver widespread, if uneven, prosperity.

Few issues have polarised political debate so effectively as capitalism; indeed, the *left/right ideological divide is commonly interpreted as a battle between anti-capitalist and pro-capitalist positions. Three broad stances have been adopted in relation to capitalism. The first, taken up by fundamentalist socialists, rejects capitalism out of hand on the grounds that it amounts to a system of mass exploitation. Karl Marx (1818–83) was undoubtedly the foremost exponent of this view, arguing that capitalism, like all other class societies, is doomed because it is based upon a fundamental contradiction between oppressors (the bourgeoisie) and the oppressed (the proletariat). The second stance, adopted in different ways by parliamentary socialists, modern liberals and paternalist conservatives, can be summed up in the assertion that capitalism is a good servant but a bad master. This view accepts that capitalism is the most reliable, perhaps only reliable, mechanism for generating wealth, but emphasises that unregulated capitalism is chronically unstable and prone to high unemployment and wide material inequalities. Associated with the ideas of J. M. Keynes (1883–1946), this perspective suggests that the issue is not so much capitalism but how and to what extent the capitalist system should be reformed or 'humanised'. The third stance, adopted by classical liberals, the *New Right and, in its most extreme form, by anarcho-capitalists, is that capitalism is a self-regulating mechanism and should therefore be encumbered as little as possible by external controls, an idea summed up in the principle of *laissez-faire*, literally meaning 'leave to do'. The earliest and most influential exponent of this view was Adam Smith (1723–90), who argued that the market is regulated by 'an invisible hand' and so tends towards long-run equilibrium.

COLLECTIVISATION

Collectivisation is a system in which *property is owned and controlled by a collective body, usually through the mechanism of the *state. Collectivisation is therefore a comprehensive form of nationalisation, in that it brings the entirety of economic life, and not merely selected industries, under state control. Collectivised economies are organised on the basis of planning rather than the *market, and therefore seek to allocate resources on a rational basis in accordance with clearly defined goals.

Significance

The best examples of collectivisation were found in orthodox communist states, such as the USSR, which operated a system of central planning. Collectivisation was introduced in the USSR under Stalin through a series of Five Year Plans, the first of which was announced in 1928. All Soviet enterprises – factories, farms, shops and so on – were set planning targets, ultimately by Gosplan (the State Planning Committee), and these were administered by a collection of powerful economic ministries. The attraction of collectivisation was that it promised to achieve an important range of socialist goals, notably to gear the economy to the wider needs of society, as opposed to private profit, and to ensure that material inequalities were abolished or substantially reduced. However, collectivisation effectively collapsed with the Eastern European Revolutions of 1989–91 and, where communism survived, as in China and Cuba, it did so in part by abandoning collectivisation. The major criticisms of collectivisation are that it is inherently inefficient because it is not orientated around profit and allows little scope for material incentives, and that it is implicitly totalitarian because state control of the economy is a fundamental threat to *civil society, the absence of economic freedom imposing an inevitable threat to political freedom.

CONSOCIATIONALISM

Consociationalism is a form of *government that contrasts with the majoritarianism of Westminster-style systems and is particularly suited to the needs of divided or plural societies. Lijphart (1977) identified two major features of what he called 'consociational democracy'. The first is executive power-sharing, usually through a grand coalition that represents all significant segments of society, although in *presidential systems this may be accomplished through the distribution of other high offices. The second is that the various segments of society enjoy a large measure of autonomy, guaranteed, for instance, by territorial divisions such as *federalism or *devolution. Two more minor features may also be present. These are, first, representative mechanisms that ensure proportionality and guarantee that minorities have a political voice, and second, a minority veto to prevent the vital interests of small sections of society being violated by the will of the majority.

Significance

Consociationalism has been widely practised, particularly in continental Europe since 1945. Examples include Austria in the 1945–66 period, Belgium since 1918, Netherlands and Luxembourg in the 1917–67 period, and, in certain respects, modern-day Israel and Canada. The conditions that particularly favour consociationalism are the existence of a relatively small number (ideally between three and five) of roughly equal-sized and geographically concentrated segments; a disposition to seek national *consensus based upon overarching loyalties; the absence of major socio-economic inequalities; and a relatively small total population.

The strength of consociationalism is that it offers an institutional solution to the problems of divided societies that is both stable and democratic. This it achieves by balancing compromise against *autonomy: matters of common or national concern are decided jointly by representatives of all key segments, whilst allowing the segments the greatest possible independence in relation to other concerns. Two main criticisms have been advanced of consociationalism. First, the combination of conditions that favour it is so complex that it is appropriate only to very particular societies, and for limited periods of time. In other words, it may not be a solution that is suitable for all divided societies. Second, consociationalism has been criticised as being inherently unstable, its emphasis upon power-sharing and the protection of minority interests having the potential to create an arena for struggle amongst rival segments rather than the basis for compromise.

CORPORATISM

Corporatism, in its broader sense, is a means of incorporating organised interests into the processes of *government. The core bases of
corporatism are therefore a recognition of the political significance
of functional or socio-economic divisions in society, and the notion
that these divisions can be reconciled through institutions that aim
to map out a higher national interest. However, there are two faces
of corporatism: authoritarian corporatism and liberal corporatism. *Authoritarian corporatism* (sometimes termed state corporatism)
is an *ideology or economic form closely associated with Italian
*fascism. It set out to establish what Mussolini called a 'corporate
state', which claimed to embody the organic unity of Italian society
but, in practice, operated through the political intimidation of
industry and the destruction of independent trade unions. *Liberal
corporatism* (sometimes termed 'societal' corporatism or neo-corpor-
atism) refers to the tendency found in mature *liberal democracies
for organised interests to be granted privileged and institutionalised
access to policy formulation. The mechanisms through which this
form of group politics is achieved vary considerably, as does the
degree of integration between groups and government. In contrast
to its authoritarian variant, liberal corporatism is often viewed as a
'bottom-up' form of corporatism that strengthens groups in relation
to government, not the other way round.

Significance

The idea of corporatism originated in Mussolini's Italy and was
associated with a fascist version of Catholic social theory. This
emphasised the importance of groups rather than individuals and
stressed the need for social balance or harmony. In practice, however, fascist corporatism amounted to little more than a means
through which the Mussolini state could exercise control over the
Italian economy. Attempts to export this authoritarian model of
corporatism to Salazar's Portugal or to post-1964 Brazil, Mexico
and Peru proved to be similarly short-lived and unsuccessful, at
least in terms of promoting economic growth.

Liberal corporatism, on the other hand, proved to be politically much more significant, especially in the early post-1945

period. Some commentators regard corporatism as a state-specific phenomenon, shaped by particular historical and political circumstances. They thus associated it with countries such as Austria, Sweden and the Netherlands and, to some extent, Germany and Japan in which the government has customarily practised a form of economic management. Others, however, view corporatism as a general phenomenon that stems from tendencies implicit in economic and social development, and therefore believe that it is manifest, in some form or other, in all advanced industrial societies. From this perspective, corporatist tendencies may merely reflect the symbiotic relationship that exists between groups and government. Groups seek 'insider' status because it gives them access to policy formulation, which enables them better to defend the interests of their members. Government, for its part, needs groups both as a source of knowledge and information and because the compliance of major economic interests is essential if *policy is to be workable. Supporters of corporatism have thus argued that a close relationship between groups and government facilitates both social stability and economic development.

However, the general drift towards corporatism in advanced capitalist states has been reversed since the 1970s, with corporatist ideas and structures being subject to growing criticism. Concerns about corporatism have been many and various. It has been criticised for narrowing the basis of representation by leading to a form of tripartitism that binds together government, business and the unions but leaves consumer and promotional groups out in the cold and restricts institutionalised access to so-called 'peak' associations. A second problem is that the distinction between liberal and authoritarian corporatism may be more apparent than real, in that the price that group leaders pay for privileged access to government is a willingness to deliver the compliance of their members. Thirdly, corporatism may weaken the formal processes of representation by allowing decisions to be made outside the reach of democratic control and through a process of bargaining that is in no way subject to political scrutiny. Finally, New Right theorists argue that corporatism is responsible for the problem of government 'overload', in which government is effectively 'captured' by consulted groups and is unable to resist their demands. Corporatism thus fuels interventionism, which, in turn, stifles competition and the natural vigour of the *market.

DICTATORSHIP

A dictatorship is, strictly, a form of rule in which absolute *power is vested in a single individual; in this sense dictatorship is synonymous with autocracy. Originally, the term was associated with the unrestricted emergency powers granted to a supreme magistrate in the early Roman Republic, which created a form of constitutional dictatorship. In the modern usage of the term, however, dictators are seen as being above the *law and acting beyond constitutional constraints. More generally, dictatorship is characterised by the arbitrary and unchecked exercise of power, as in the ideas of the 'dictatorship of the proletariat', 'military dictatorship' and 'personal dictatorship'. A distinction is sometimes drawn between traditional dictatorships and totalitarian dictatorships. *Traditional dictatorships* aim to monopolise government power and conform to the principles of *authoritarianism. *Totalitarian dictatorships* seek 'total power' and extend political control to all aspects of social and personal existence.

Significance

Dictators have been found throughout political history. Classic examples include Sula, Julius Caesar and Augustus Caesar in Rome, Cromwell after the dissolution of Parliament in 1653, Napoleon Bonaparte, Napoleon III and Bismarck in the nineteenth century, and in the twentieth century Hitler, Stalin and Saddam Hussein. Although all dictators depend upon fear and operate through the control of coercive power, the modern phenomenon of dictatorship is often linked to charismatic leadership and the idea that the leader in some way embodies the destiny or 'general will' of the people. Totalitarian dictatorships may thus masquerade as 'perfect democracies' and enjoy a significant measure of popular support based, crucially, upon strict control of the means of mass communication. However, the personal aspect of dictatorship should not be over-emphasised, as most modern dictatorships are usually military dictatorships or operate through a monopolistic party. In these cases unrestrained power is vested in the armed forces or the party–state apparatus (or a combination of the two), with leadership sometimes being shared amongst a group of people, the classic example of which is the military junta. There is evidence, nevertheless, that dictatorship as the principal alternative to *democracy is of declining significance. Its impact upon the twentieth century was linked to the, now largely spent, ideological forces of *fascism and *communism, meaning that dictatorship is now mainly a developing-world phenomenon. The glaring moral defect of dictatorship is its link to repression and tyranny; its major structural defect is its inability to generate or deal with the pressures generated by social and economic development.

ELITISM

The term elite originally meant, and can still mean, the highest, the best or the excellent. Used in a neutral or empirical sense, however, it refers to a minority in whose hands *power, wealth or privilege is concentrated, justifiably or otherwise. Elitism is a belief in, or practice of, rule by an elite or minority. At least three forms of elitism can exist. *Normative elitism* is a political theory that suggests that elite rule is desirable, usually on the grounds that power should be vested in the hands of a wise or enlightened minority (in this sense, elitism could be regarded as a value or even an ideology). This implies that *democracy is undesirable, and is, for example, evident in Plato's (427–347 BCE) belief in rule by a class of benign philosopher-kings. *Classical elitism* claimed to be empirical (although normative beliefs often intruded), and saw elite rule as being inevitable, an unchangeable fact of social existence. This implies that egalitarian ideas such as democracy and *socialism are impossible. The chief exponents of this view were Vilfredo Pareto (1848–1923), Gaetano Mosca (1857–1941) and Robert Michels (1876–1936). *Modern elitism* has also developed an empirical analysis, but it is more critical and discriminating about the causes of elite rule, usually linking these to particular economic and political structures rather than the inevitable structure of society. Modern elitists, such as C. Wright Mills (1916–62) have often been concerned to highlight elite rule in the hope of both explaining and challenging it. What is called variously 'pluralist', 'competitive' or 'democratic' elitism is a development within modern elitism that acknowledges that modern elites are typically fractured or divided rather than unified and coherent, and that rivalry amongst elites can, to some extent, ensure that non-elite groups are given a political voice.

Significance

Normative elitism has largely been abandoned given the advance of democratic values and practices, although representative democracy can be seen to embody residual elitist assumptions, in that it ensures that government decisions are made by educated and well-informed professional politicians rather than by the public directly. Classical elitism has had a considerable impact upon social and *political theory, being used, amongst other things, to reject the Marxist idea of a classless, communist society. Mosca argued that the resources or attributes that are necessary for rule are always unequally distributed, and that a cohesive minority will always be able to manipulate and control the masses, even in a parliamentary democracy. Pareto linked elite rule to two psychological types: 'foxes', who rule by cunning and manipulation, and 'lions', who dominate through coercion and violence. Michels developed what he termed the 'iron law of oligarchy', the idea that in all organisations power is concentrated in the hands of a small group of leaders. However, such arguments have been criticised for generalising on the basis of assumptions about *human nature or organisation, and because they are difficult to reconcile with modern democratic practices.

Modern elitism nevertheless offers an important critique of both *pluralism and democracy. The democratic elitism of Joseph Schumpeter (1883–1950) offered a 'realistic' model of democracy, which emphasises that although elections can decide which elite rules, they cannot change the fact that power is always exercised by an elite. This gave rise to the 'economic theory of democracy', which applies *rational choice theories to *politics by treating electoral competition as a political market. The 'power elite' model advanced by theorists such as Mills (1956) departed from Marxism insofar as it rejected the idea of an economically defined 'ruling class', but nevertheless drew attention to the disproportionate influence of the military–industrial complex. Attempts to provide empirical support for elite theory have been provided by a variety of community power studies. However, although it is still influential in the USA in particular, the elitist position has its drawbacks. These include that it is less theoretically sophisticated than, say, *Marxism or pluralism, and that empirical evidence to sustain elitist conclusions, especially about the distribution of power at national level, is as yet unconvincing.

LIBERAL DEMOCRACY

Liberal democracy is a form of democratic rule that balances the principle of limited *government against the ideal of popular *consent. Its 'liberal' features are reflected in a network of internal and external checks upon government that are designed to guarantee liberty and afford citizens protection against the *state. Its 'democratic' character is based upon a system of regular and competitive elections, conducted on the basis of universal suffrage and political *equality. Although it may be used to describe a political principle, the term liberal democracy more commonly describes a particular type of regime.

The core features of a liberal-democratic regime are the following:

- constitutional government based upon formal, usually legal, rules;
- guaranteed civil liberties and individual *rights;
- institutional fragmentation and a system of checks and balances;
- regular *elections respecting the principles of universal suffrage and 'one person, one vote';
- political *pluralism in the form of electoral choice and party competition;
- a healthy *civil society in which organised groups and interests enjoy independence from government;
- a capitalist or private enterprise economy organised along *market lines.

Significance

Liberal democracy is the dominant political force found in the developed world, and increasingly in the developing world. Indeed, the collapse of *communism and the advance of 'democratisation' (usually understood to imply liberal-democratic reforms, that is, electoral democracy and economic liberalisation) in Asia, Latin America and Africa, especially during the 1980s, led 'end of history' theorists such as Francis Fukuyama (1989) to proclaim the worldwide triumph of Western liberal democracy. In Fukuyama's view, liberal democracy is 'the final form of human government'. The remarkable success of liberal democracy stems from two chief factors. First, liberal democratic systems are highly responsive, in that they establish a number of channels of communication between government and the governed. Second, because liberal democracy invariably goes hand-in-hand with *capitalism, it is associated with widespread consumer prosperity. Liberal-democratic theorists point out that it is the only political system that is capable of delivering both political *freedom and economic opportunity, and that liberal-democratic processes are sufficiently responsive and robust to articulate the concerns of all significant sections of society. Amongst the strongest advocates of liberal democracy have been pluralist theorists, who praise its capacity to ensure a wide distribution of political power amongst competing groups.

Nevertheless, liberal democracy does not command universal approval or respect. Its principal critics have been elitists, Marxists, radical democrats and feminists. Elitists have drawn attention to the capacity of electoral democracy to replace one elite with another, but not challenge the fact of elite rule. From this perspective, the principle of political *equality and the process of electoral competition upon which liberal democracy is founded are nothing more than a sham. The traditional Marxist critique of liberal democracy has focused upon the inherent contradiction between democracy and capitalism. The egalitarianism of political democracy merely masks a reality of unequal class power; the dominant economic class 'rules' democratic governments through its control of wealth and other resources. Radical democrats object to the limited and non-participatory character of liberal democracy, pointing out that the act of voting every few years is a poor manifestation of popular rule and no means of securing genuine *accountability. Feminists, for their part, have drawn attention to the patriarchal character of liberal-democratic systems that apply democracy only to traditionally male realms such as government and the *state, whilst ignoring the structures of male power that traditionally operate through the family and domestic life.

MILITARISM

The term militarism can be used in two ways. First, it refers to the achievement of ends by the use of military force. Any attempt to solve problems by military means can be described as militarism in this sense. Second, and more commonly, militarism is a cultural and ideological phenomenon in which military priorities, ideals and values come to pervade the larger society. This typically includes the glorification of the armed forces, a heightened sense of national *patriotism, the recognition of war as a legitimate instrument of *policy, and an atavistic belief in heroism and self-sacrifice. In some cases, but not all, militarism is characterised by the abuse by the military of its legitimate functions, and its usurpation of responsibilities normally ascribed to civilian politicians.

Significance

Militarism, in it cultural or ideological sense, is a common feature of military regimes and totalitarian *dictatorships. The defining feature of military rule is that members of the armed forces displace civilian politicians, meaning that the leading posts of government are filled on the basis of the person's position within the military chain of command. However, military rule may take a variety of forms, including collective military government, classically in the form of a military junta (from the Spanish *junta*, meaning 'council' or 'board'), a military dictatorship dominated by a single individual (for example, Colonel Papadopoulis in Greece, 1974–80, General Pinochet in Chile, 1973–90, and General Abacha in Nigeria, 1993–98), and situations in which the armed forces 'pull the strings' behind the scenes whilst allowing civilian political leaders to retain formal positions of power.

In such circumstances militarism is a direct means of legitimising the military's control of political life. In the case of totalitarian dictatorships, charismatic leaders such as Mussolini, Hitler and Saddam Hussein have used militarism in more subtle ways to consolidate power. By wearing military uniforms, associating themselves with the armed forces and using martial and militaristic rhetoric, they have attempted to imbue their regimes and societies with military values such as discipline, obedience and a heightened sense of collective purpose, usually linked to chauvinist *nationalism. However, militarism as a mechanism of regime consolidation is likely to be effective only in a context of war or intensifying international conflict, as is demonstrated by the fact that militarism is invariably accompanied by terroristic policing and widespread repression. Marxists have sometimes highlighted a link between militarism, in the limited sense of a disposition towards war and the use of military means, and *capitalism, on the grounds that only high levels of defence spending, justified by the regular use of the military, ensure that domestic demand is buoyant and that profit levels remain high.

PARLIAMENTARY GOVERNMENT

A parliamentary system of government is one in which the *government governs in and through the *parliament or assembly, thereby 'fusing' the legislative and executive branches. Although they are formally distinct, the parliament and the *executive (usually seen as the government) are bound together in a way that violates the doctrine of the *separation of powers, setting parliamentary systems of government clearly apart from *presidential government.

The chief features of a parliamentary system are as follows:

- governments are formed as a result of parliamentary elections, based upon the strength of party representation – there is no separately elected executive;
- the personnel of government are drawn from the parliament, usually from the leaders of the party or parties that have majority control;
- the government is responsible to the parliament, in the sense that it rests upon the parliament's confidence and can be removed (generally by the lower chamber) if it loses that confidence;

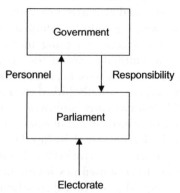

Figure 6.1   Parliamentary government

- the government can, in most cases, 'dissolve' the parliament by calling a general election, meaning that electoral terms are usually flexible within a maximum limit;
- parliamentary executives are generally collective in that they accept at least the formal principle of cabinet government;
- the posts of head of government (usually a prime minister) and head of state are separate, the latter being either a constitutional monarch or a non-executive president.

Significance

Most *liberal democracies have adopted some form of parliamentary government. These are often seen as 'Westminster model' systems of government, in that they are based upon the example of the UK Parliament, sometimes portrayed as the 'mother of parliaments'. However, the full 'Westminster model' also relies upon features such as a two-party system, parliamentary *sovereignty and collective *responsibility that may be absent in other parliamentary systems, such as those in Germany, Sweden, India, Japan, New Zealand and Australia. The chief strength of parliamentary government is that it supposedly delivers strong but responsible government. Government is strong in that it rests upon the confidence of the parliament and so can, in most cases, ensure that its legislative programme is passed. In short, governments can get things done. However, responsible government is maintained because the government can govern only as long as it retains the confidence of the parliament. In theory the parliament has the upper hand because it has a power it does not possess in a presidential system: the ability to remove the government or executive. Moreover, parliamentary government is often seen to promote *democracy, parliamentary democracy being a form of responsible and representative government in which the parliament plays a vital deliberative role as a forum for national debate, constituting a popular check upon government.

However, the workings of parliamentary government depend upon a number of other factors, notably the nature of the party system and the *political culture. Parliamentary government can, for instance, become a form of party government. This occurs when the government is formed from a single, ideologically and organisationally cohesive party, which operates on the basis of a direct *mandate from the electorate, rather than on the basis of parliamentary *authority. Parliamentary government is also often associated with the problem of executive domination, what Lord Hailsham (1976), in the case of the UK system, referred to as 'elective dictatorship'. If governments have majority control and can maintain party discipline (easier in the case of single-party government) the parliament can be reduced to little more than a 'talking shop' and its members may become mere 'lobby fodder'. Finally, parliamentary systems have also been linked with weak government and political instability. This usually occurs when the party system is fractured, and is often associated with highly proportional electoral systems. In the French Fourth Republic (1945–58), for instance, 25 governments came and went in little over 12 years, and Italy had no fewer than 52 governments between 1945 and 1996. Parliamentary government can thus, ironically, result in either excessive executive power or excessive legislative power.

PATRIARCHY

Patriarchy literally means rule by the *pater* (Latin) or father, and refers to the domination of the husband–father within the family, and the subordination of his wife and his children. However, the term is usually used in the more general sense of 'rule by men', drawing attention to the totality of oppression and exploitation to which women are subject. The use of the patriarchy thus implies that the system of male power in society at large both reflects and stems from the domination of the father in the family. This is reflected in the radical feminist slogan: 'the personal is the political'. Kate Millett (1970) argued that patriarchy contains two principles: 'male shall dominate female, elder male shall dominate younger male', suggesting that a patriarchal society is characterised by interlocking systems of sexual and generational oppression.

Significance

The concept of patriarchy was introduced into wider political discourse through the emergence of so-called second-wave *feminism in the 1960s. Its value is that it draws attention to the political significance of *gender and to the political relationship between women and men. Whereas conventional *political theory treats gender relations as natural, feminist theorists, through the notion of patriarchy, view them as part of the political institution of male power. However, patriarchy is interpreted differently by different schools of feminism. For radical feminists patriarchy is a key concept, in that it emphasises that gender inequality is systematic, institutionalised and pervasive; many radical feminists argue that patriarchy is evident in all social institutions and in every society, both contemporary and historical. Patriarchy thus expresses the belief that gender divisions are deeper and more politically significant than divisions based, say, upon nationality, *social class, *race or *ethnicity. Socialist feminists, in contrast, highlight links between gender inequality and social inequality, seeing patriarchy and *capitalism as interdependent systems of domination. Liberal feminists, on the other hand, are sometimes reluctant to use the term patriarchy, on the grounds that they are less likely to prioritise gender divisions over other forms of inequality, and because they understand it in terms of the unequal distribution of *rights and entitlements, rather than systematic and institutionalised oppression. Post-feminist theorists have also argued that the advances that women have made, in developed societies at least, mean that patriarchy is no longer a useful or appropriate term, patriarchal institutions and practices having been substantially reformed.

PLURALISM

Pluralism can broadly be defined as a belief in, or commitment to, diversity or multiplicity – the existence of many things. The term, however, is complex, because it can be used in both a normative and descriptive sense (and sometimes combines descriptive observations with normative endorsements), and because it has a variety of applications. As a normative term it implies that diversity is healthy and desirable in itself, usually because it safeguards individual *freedom and promotes debate, argument and understanding. As a descriptive term it can assume a variety of forms. *Political pluralism* denotes the existence of electoral choice and a competitive party system. *Moral pluralism* refers to a multiplicity of ethical values. *Cultural pluralism* suggests a diversity of lifestyles and cultural norms.

Pluralism, however, is used more narrowly as a theory of the distribution of political *power. *Classical pluralism* holds that power is widely and evenly dispersed in society, rather than concentrated in the hands of an elite or a ruling class. In this form pluralism is usually seen as a theory of group politics, in which individuals are largely represented through their membership of organised groups, and all such groups have access to the policy process.

The main assumptions of the pluralist perspective are as follows:

- all citizens belong to groups and many will have multiple group membership;
- there is rough equality amongst groups, in that each group has access to *government and no group enjoys a dominant position;
- there is a high level of internal responsiveness within groups, leaders being accountable to members;
- the *state is neutral amongst groups and the governmental machine is sufficiently fragmented to offer groups a number of access points;
- although groups have competing interests, there is a wider *consensus amongst groups on the nature of the political system and the values of openness and competition.

Reformed pluralism, or neo-pluralism, has revised classical pluralism in that it acknowledges that the distribution of power in modern societies is imperfect, elite and privileged interests persisting within a broader context of group competition. Western democracies are thus viewed as 'deformed polyarchies' in which major corporations in particular exert disproportionate influence.

Significance

Pluralist ideas can be traced back to early liberal *political philosophy, and notably to the ideas of John Locke (1632–1704) and C.-L. Montesquieu (1689–1775). Their first systematic development, however, was in the contributions of James Madison (1751–1836) to *The Federalist Papers* (1787–89), in which he advocated a system of divided government based upon the *separation of powers, *bicameralism and *federalism in order to resist majoritarianism and to provide minority interests with a guaranteed political voice. The link between pluralism and *democracy has been emphasised by modern pluralist theorists such as Robert Dahl (1956). Political pluralism is widely regarded as the key feature of *liberal democracy, in that it both allows electors to express independent views and gives them a mechanism through which they can remove unpopular governments. Nevertheless, pluralist thinkers generally emphasise that democracy in modern societies operates less through formal or electoral machinery and more through a constant interplay between government and organised groups or interests. In this sense pluralist democracy can be seen as an alternative to parliamentary democracy and to any form of majoritarianism. Pluralist ideas and values have in many ways been revived by the emergence of *postmodernism, which rejects all monolithic theories of society and extols the virtues of debate and *discourse.

Pluralism has also been subject to a variety of criticisms, however. As a theory of the distribution of power, pluralism has been attacked by elitists, Marxists and the *New Right. Elitists point out that many interests in society, such as the unemployed, the homeless or consumers, have no meaningful political voice because they are either unorganised or poorly organised, and that business groups which control employment and investment decisions in society are invariably dominant. Marxists, for their part, highlight the structural inequalities that flow from the system of ownership within *capitalism, and argue that the state is invariably biased in favour of business interests. The New Right's critique of pluralism draws attention to the problem of 'pluralistic stagnation', the growth of rival group pressures upon government resulting in 'overload', and a spiralling increase in public spending and state intervention. In many ways neo-pluralism has emerged as a response to such criticisms.

Although the spread of liberal-democratic values means that political pluralism attracts near-universal approval, the same cannot be said of moral and cultural pluralism. While liberals believe that diversity in moral and cultural life is an essential expression of *toleration, traditional conservatives have argued that it may weaken the foundations of society which relies for its stability upon shared values and a common culture. Religious fundamentalists have developed a similar attack upon Western pluralism, believing that it fosters moral relativism and is unable to provide individuals with ethical guidance.

POPULISM

Populism (from the Latin *populus*, meaning 'the people') has been used to describe both a particular tradition of political thought and distinctive political movements and forms of rule. As a political tradition, populism reflects the belief that the instincts and wishes of the people provide the principal legitimate guide to political action. Movements or parties described as populist have therefore been characterised by their claim to support the common people in the face of 'corrupt' economic or political elites. Populist politicians thus make a direct appeal to the people and claim to give expression to their deepest hopes and fears, all intermediary institutions being distrusted.

Significance

The populist political tradition can be traced back to Rousseau's (1712–78) notion of a 'general will' as the indivisible collective interest of society. Populism thus aims to establish an unmediated link between a leader and his or her people, through which the leader gives expression to the innermost hopes and dreams of the people. Populist *leadership can be seen in its most developed form in totalitarian *dictatorships that operate through the appeal of charismatic leaders, but it can also be found in democratic systems in which leaders cultivate a personal image and ideological vision separate from and 'above' parties, *parliaments and other government institutions. Indeed, the wider use of focus groups and the increasing sophistication of political presentation and communication, particularly linked to the activities of so-called 'spin doctors', have provided greater impetus for populism in modern politics generally.

If populism is defended, it is on the basis that it constitutes a genuine form of *democracy, intermediate institutions tending to pervert or misrepresent the people's will. More commonly, however, populism is subject to criticism. Two main criticisms are made of it. First, populism is seen as implicitly authoritarian, on the grounds that it provides little basis for challenging the leader's claim to articulate the genuine interests of the people. Second, it debases *politics both by giving expression to the crudest hopes and fears of the masses and by leaving no scope for deliberation and rational analysis. 'Populist democracy' is thus the enemy of both pluralist democracy and parliamentary democracy.

PRESIDENTIAL GOVERNMENT

A presidential system of government is characterised by a constitutional and political *separation of powers between the legislative and executive branches of government. Executive *power is thus vested in an independently elected *president who is not directly accountable to, or removable by, the assembly or *parliament.

The principal features of presidential government are the following:

- the executive and the legislature are separately elected, and each is invested with a range of independent constitutional powers;
- there is a formal separation of personnel between the legislative and executive branches;
- the executive is not constitutionally responsible to the legislature and cannot be removed by it (except through the exceptional process of impeachment);
- the president or executive cannot 'dissolve' the legislature, meaning that the electoral terms of both branches are fixed;
- executive authority is concentrated in the hands of the president – the *cabinet and ministers merely being advisors responsible to the president;
- the roles of head of state and head of government are combined in the office of the presidency – the president wears 'two hats'.

Presidential government can clearly be distinguished from *parliamentary government. However, there are a number of hybrid systems that combine elements of the two, notably semi-presidential systems. *Semi-presidential government* operates on the basis of a 'dual

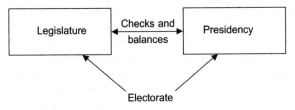

Figure 6.2   Presidential government

executive', in which a separately elected president works in conjunction with a *prime minister and cabinet drawn from and accountable to the parliament. In some cases policy-making responsibilities are divided between the president and the cabinet, ensuring that the former is largely concerned with foreign affairs whilst the latter deals primarily with domestic issues.

Significance

Presidential government is the principal alternative to parliamentary government in the liberal-democratic world. However, presidentialism is rarer than parliamentarianism. The USA is the classic example of a presidential system, and it is a model that has been adopted in many parts of Latin America. Semi-presidential systems can be found in *states such as France and Finland. The principal strength of presidential government is that, by separating legislative power from executive power, it creates internal tensions that help to protect individual *rights and liberties. This, indeed, was the intention of the so-called 'founding fathers' of the US Constitution, who wished to prevent the presidency assuming the mantle of the British *monarchy. In the USA the danger of executive domination is protected against by the range of powers that are vested in the Congress. For instance, Congress has the right to declare war and raise taxes, the Senate may ratify treaties and confirm presidential appointments, and the two houses can combine to charge and impeach the president. Further advantages are that the president, as both head of state and head of government and as the single politician who is nationally elected, serves as a strong focus for patriotic loyalty and national unity. The dispersal of power between the executive and the legislature also allows government to be more democratic in the sense that it is responsive to competing minorities.

However, presidential systems may also be ineffective and cumbersome, because they offer an 'invitation to struggle' to the executive and legislative branches. Critics of the US system, for example, argue that, since 'the president proposes and Congress disposes', it is nothing more than a recipe for institutional deadlock, or 'government gridlock'. This may be more likely when the White House (the presidency) and Capitol Hill (Congress) are controlled by rival parties, but it can also occur, as the Carter administration (1977–81) demonstrated, when both branches are controlled by

the same party. To some extent semi-presidential systems were constructed to overcome this problem. However, similar institutional
tensions have been generated in France when presidents have been
forced to work with prime ministers and cabinets drawn from a rival
party or parties, giving rise to the phenomenon of 'cohabitation'.

REPUBLICANISM

Republicanism refers, most simply, to a preference for a republic
over a *monarchy. However, the term republic suggests not merely
the absence of a monarch but, in the light of its Latin root, *res publica*
(meaning common or collective affairs), it implies a distinctively
public arena and popular rule. Republicanism has thus developed
into a broader school of *political theory that advocates certain
moral precepts and institutional structures. The moral concern of
republicanism is expressed in a belief in civic virtue, understood to
include public spiritedness, honour and *patriotism. Above all, it is
linked to a stress upon public activity over private activity. The institutional focus of republicanism has, however, shifted its emphasis
over time. Whereas classical republicanism was usually associated
with mixed government that combined monarchical, aristocratic
and democratic elements, the American and French revolutions
reshaped republicanism by applying it to whole nations rather than
small communities, and by endorsing the implications of modern
democratic government. In its US version this means an acceptance
of divided government achieved through *federalism and the
*separation of powers; in its French version it is more closely asso-
ciated with radical democracy and the idea of the 'general will'.

Significance

Republican political ideas can be traced back to the ancient Roman
Republic, its earliest version being Cicero's (106–43) defence of
mixed government developed in *The Republic*. It was revived in
Renaissance Italy as a model for the organisation of Italian city-
states that supposedly balanced civic *freedom against political
stability. Further forms of republicanism were born out of the
English, American and French revolutions. The major defence of
republican forms of government, particularly in their anti-monarch-
ical form, is their emphasis upon civic freedom. Republican freedom

combines liberty in the sense of protection against arbitrary and tyrannical government with the full and active participation of citizens in public and political life. In the form of 'civic republicanism',
advocated since the 1960s particularly by communitarian thinkers,
it amounts to the attempt to re-establish the public domain as the
principal source of personal fulfilment, and thus rejects the tendency towards privatisation and the 'rolling back' of the political
sphere, as advocated by the *New Right. Republicanism is therefore associated with the notion of active *citizenship. The main
criticisms of republicanism are that it is politically incoherent, in
that it has been associated with such a wide variety of political
forms, and that it is illiberal in that it rejects the idea of freedom as
privacy and non-interference, and has been used to justify the
expansion of government responsibilities.

REVOLUTION

The term revolution, in its earliest usage, meant cyclical change
(from the verb 'to revolve'), as in the restoration of 'proper' political
order in the so-called Glorious Revolution of 1688 in England. The
French Revolution (1789), however, established the modern concept of revolution as a process of dramatic and far-reaching
change, involving the destruction and replacement of old order.
Revolutions, nevertheless, may have a political, social or cultural
character. *Political revolutions* are popular uprisings involving extra-
legal mass actions; they are often, although not necessarily, violent
in character. This distinguishes a revolution from a coup d'état, a
seizure of *power by a small band. Revolutions differ from rebel-
lions and revolts in that they bring about fundamental change, a
change in the political system itself, as opposed to merely the displa-
cement of a governing elite or a change of policy.

Social revolutions are changes in the system of ownership or the
economic system; in Marxist theory they are changes in the 'mode
of production', as when *capitalism replaced feudalism and when
*communism replaces capitalism. For Marxists, social revolutions
are more fundamental than political ones, the latter being the political manifestation of a deeper and more long-term transformation
of the class system. *Cultural revolutions* involve the rooting out of
values, doctrines and beliefs that supported the old order, and the
establishment in their place of a set of new ones. All revolutions

have a crucial cultural dimension, reflecting the fact that any stable system of rule must, to some extent, be culturally and ideologically embedded. Many political revolutions are consolidated through a conscious process of re-education to establish a new set of system-sustaining values and aspirations.

Significance

The modern world has been formed through a series of crucial revolutions. These commenced with the English Revolution of the 1640s and 1650s, which overthrew monarchical *absolutism and established early principles of *constitutionalism and *parliamentary government. The American Revolution (1776) led to the creation of a constitutional republic independent from Britain, and gave practical expression to the principle of representation. The French Revolution set out to destroy the old order under the banner of 'liberty, equality and fraternity', advanced democratic ideals and sparked an 'age of revolution' in early nineteenth-century Europe. The Russian Revolution (1917), the first 'communist' revolution, provided a model for many of the subsequent twentieth-century revolutions, including the Chinese Revolution (1949), the Cuban Revolution (1959), the Vietnamese Revolution (1972) and the Nicaraguan Revolution (1979).

Debate about revolutions centres upon their causes and their consequences. Amongst the general theories of revolutions are the following. The Marxist theory of revolution holds that they are essentially social phenomena that arise out of contradictions which exist in all class societies. Systems theorists argue that revolution results from 'disequilibrium' in the political system, brought about by economic, social, cultural or international changes to which the system itself is incapable of responding – the 'outputs' of government become structurally out of line with the 'inputs'. The idea of a 'revolution of rising expectations' suggests that revolutions occur when a period of economic and social development is abruptly reversed, creating a widening gap between popular expectations and the capabilities of government. The social-structural explanation implies that regimes usually succumb to revolution when, through international weakness and/or domestic ineffectiveness, they lose the ability, or the political will, to maintain control through the exercise of coercive power.

The consequences of revolution also cause deep disagreement. Revolutionaries themselves argue that revolution is by its nature a popular phenomenon, the unleashing of naked democratic pressure. They also tend to portray revolution as a purifying and ennobling struggle, a rooting-out of corruption, injustice and oppression; for this reason revolutionary movements usually subscribed to some form of *utopianism. Critics of revolution, however, point out that revolutions in practice invariably fail to live up to the high ideals of their perpetrators. This occurs for a variety of reasons. These include that, despite the image of popular revolt, revolutions are invariably brought about by small cliques which are typically unwilling to relinquish their newly won power; that any regime that is established through the use of force and violence is compelled to continue using them and is thus forced down the road of *authoritarianism; and that revolutions dismantle or crucially weaken institutions and governmental structures, leaving revolutionary leaders with potentially unchecked power.

TOTALITARIANISM

Totalitarianism is an all-encompassing system of political rule that is typically established by pervasive ideological manipulation and open terror and brutality. Totalitarianism differs from both autocracy and *authoritarianism, in that it seeks 'total power' through the politicisation of every aspect of social and personal existence. Totalitarianism thus implies the outright abolition of *civil society: the abolition of 'the private'. Friedrich and Brzezinski (1966) defined totalitarianism in terms of a six-point 'syndrome of inter-related traits and characteristics':

- the existence of an 'official' *ideology;
- a one-party state, usually led by an all-powerful leader;
- a system of terroristic policing;
- a monopoly of the means of mass communication;
- a monopoly of the means of armed combat;
- state control of all aspects of economic life.

Significance

The phenomenon of totalitarianism is usually believed to have arisen in the twentieth century, pervasive ideological manipulation and

systematic terror requiring the resources of a modern industrialised *state. The idea of totalitarianism originated in fascist Italy as
a belief in the state as an all-consuming 'ethical community' that
reflects the altruism and mutual sympathy of its members. This
was developed into the doctrine: 'everything for the state, nothing
outside the state, nothing against the state'. The term was subsequently adopted to describe the perhaps uniquely oppressive character of twentieth-century *dictatorships, in particular Hitler's
Germany and Stalin's USSR. Totalitarian analysis achieved greatest prominence in the 1950s and 1960s, when it was widely used
to highlight totalitarian parallels between *fascism and *communism, and to divide the world into rival democratic (liberal
democratic) and totalitarian states.

However, the totalitarian classification has a number of drawbacks. First, it became part of Cold War ideology and was used as
a sometimes crude form of anti-communist propaganda. Second, it
tended to obscure important differences between fascism and communism, particularly in relation to their ideological orientation and
the degree to which they tolerated *capitalism. Third, the idea of
'total' state power is misleading because some form of resistance or
*opposition always persists, even in the most technologically
advanced and brutal of states. Nevertheless, even though the apparent precision of the six-point syndrome is misleading, the concept of
totalitarianism is useful in highlighting distinctions between
modern and traditional dictatorships and in drawing attention to
the importance of charismatic leadership. The latter consideration
has given rise to the idea of 'totalitarian democracy', the phenomenon whereby a leader justifies his unchecked power through a
claim to possess a monopoly of ideological wisdom and to articulate
the 'true' interests of his people. A very different theory of totalitarianism was advanced by Herbert Marcuse (1964), who identified
totalitarian tendencies in advanced industrial societies, viewing
them as 'one-dimensional societies' in which rising affluence helps
to subdue argument and debate and absorb all forms of opposition.

FURTHER READING

Beetham, D. (ed.), *Defining and Measuring Democracy* (London: Sage, 1994).
Birch, A. H., *Representative and Responsible Government: An Essay on the British Constitution* (London: Allen and Unwin, 1964).

Bottomore, T., *Elites and Society* (London: Routledge, 1993).
Bottomore, T., *Theories of Modern Capitalism* (London: Allen & Unwin, 1985).
Calvert, P., *Revolution and Counter-Revolution* (Buckingham: Open University Press, 1990).
Friedrich, C. J. and Brzezinski, Z. (eds), *Totalitarian Dictatorship and Autocracy* (Cambridge, MA: Harvard University Press, 1966).
Holden, B., *Understanding Liberal Democracy* (Hemel Hempstead: Harvester Wheatsheaf, 1993).
Lijphart, A., *Democracy in Plural Societies: A Comparative Exploration* (New Haven, CT: Yale University Press, 1977).
McLennan, G., *Pluralism* (Buckingham: Open University Press, 1995).
Millett, K., *Sexual Politics* (London: Virago, 1970).
Pettit, P., *Republicanism: A Theory of Freedom and Government* (Oxford: Oxford University Press, 1997).
Pinkney, R., *Right-Wing Military Government* (London: Pinter, 1990).
Saunders, P., *Capitalism: A Social Audit* (Buckingham: Open University Press, 1995).
Schmitter, P. C. and Lehmbruch, G. (eds), *Trends Towards Corporatist Intermediation* (London: Sage, 1979).
Tormey, S., *Making Sense of Tyranny: Interpretations of Totalitarianism* (Manchester and New York: Manchester University Press, 1995).
Verney, D. V., *The Analysis of Political Systems* (London: Routledge & Kegan Paul, 1959).

Part seven

STRUCTURES

This section examines concepts that stand for particular institutions or governmental bodies; these are often the component features of systems.

STRUCTURES

BICAMERALISM

Bicameralism is the fragmentation of legislative *power, established through the existence of two chambers or houses in the *parliament. Bicameral systems are usually classified according to the role, powers and composition of the 'second' chamber or 'upper' house. Most second chambers are constitutionally and politically subordinate to the first chamber, which is usually seen as the locus of popular *authority. This is particularly the case in *parliamentary systems in which government is generally responsible to, and drawn, largely or wholly, from the lower house. Second chambers often also exercise limited legislative power, meaning that they function essentially as 'revising' chambers. Not uncommonly, such weaker versions of bicameralism reflect the restrictive representative basis of the upper house, which may be selected through indirect elections, partial elections, appointment or, though rarely, inheritance. A stronger version of bicameralism is found in assemblies with two popularly elected chambers that have broadly equal powers. The US Congress is perhaps the only example of a legislative that has a dominant upper chamber (although all taxation must be introduced in the House of Representatives, the Senate alone exercises ratification and confirmation powers).

Significance

Bicameralism is usually seen as a centrle principle of liberal *constitutionalism. The chief benefits of bicameralism are that second chambers can check the power of first chambers and prevent majoritarian rule; that bicameral assemblies more effectively check the power of the executive; that the existence of two chambers widens the basis of *representation and interest-articulation; that

the legislative burden of the first chamber can be relieved and legislation can be more thoroughly scrutinised; and that the second
chamber can act as a constitutional safeguard, preventing or delay-
ing the passage of controversial legislation. The representative
advantages of bicameralism may be particularly important in systems in which *federalism or *devolution operate, as the second
chamber can help to overcome conflict between the centre and the
periphery by representing provincial or regional interests at
national level.

However, there was a clear trend towards unicameralism in the
post-1945 period (with second chambers being abolished in New
Zealand, Denmark and Sweden). Bicameralism has been criticised
for a number of reasons. Unicameral assemblies may be more efficient, because the existence of a second chamber can make the legislative process unnecessarily complex and difficult. Second chambers
may act as a check on democratic rule, particularly when their members are non-elected or indirectly elected. Bicameral parliaments
may be a recipe for institutional conflict in the parliament, and may
make strong or effective government impossible. The existence of
two, co-equal chambers may narrow access to policy-making by forcing joint committees to make decisions when there is disagreement
between the chambers. Finally, second chambers may introduce a
conservative political bias by upholding existing constitutional
arrangements and, sometimes, the interests of social elites.

BILL OF RIGHTS

A bill of rights is a legal document that specifies the privileges,
*rights and liberties of the individual. As such, it defines the rela-
tionship between the *state and the citizen and establishes the
legal extent of *civil liberty. Bills of rights may either be entrenched
or statutory. An *entrenched bill of rights* has the status of 'higher' or
constitutional law and often comprises part of a written *constitution. The first ten amendments of the US Constitution, which spe-
cify a collection of individual rights and freedoms, thus came to be
known as the Bill of Rights, with the Fourteenth, Fifteenth and
Nineteenth Amendments subsequently being accorded the same
status. Entrenched rights are binding on the legislature, can usually
be introduced, amended or removed only through a complex, constitutional process, and are ultimately upheld by a supreme or

constitutional court. A *statutory bill of rights* has the same legal status as any other legislature-made *law and can therefore be changed through the normal legislative process. Sometimes called a statute of rights, such a bill of rights can operate in the absence of a written constitution and a constitutional court, as in the case of the Human Rights Act (1998) in the UK, which incorporated the European Convention on Human Rights into British law. In other cases *advisory bills of rights* may operate, which oblige *government formally to consider individual rights in the process of policy formulation without being bound to respect them.

Significance

Bills of rights are often considered a valuable, and perhaps essential, means of guaranteeing limited government and of protecting *freedom. Not only does a bill of rights provide the individual with a means of defence against overbearing public *authority, but it also has an educational value in heightening sensitivity towards individual rights within government, amongst the *judiciary and, most importantly, amongst the public at large. Underlying this argument is often a belief in the doctrine of *human rights, the idea that there are certain fundamental, inviolable human rights to which all human beings are entitled, and that these should enjoy the protection of both international and state law. Opponents of this view may either question the validity of the idea of human rights or suggest that rights are adequately protected by common law and, in relation to entrenched bills of rights, by statute law. Other criticisms are that bills of rights compromise the *neutrality of judges and inevitably draw them into political disputes; that rights are better left in the hands of elected politicians rather than non-elected judges; and that bills of rights legally embed ideological biases (for instance, in relation to property rights) that are difficult to remove and may precipitate conflict.

BUREAUCRACY

Bureaucracy (literally 'rule by officials') is, in everyday language, a pejorative term meaning pointless administrative routine, or 'red tape'. In the social sciences the concept of bureaucracy is used in a more specific and neutral sense, but refers to phenomena as different

as rule by non-elected officials, the administrative machinery of
*government, and a rational mode of organisation. Despite dis-
agreement about its location and character, it is generally accepted
that abstract organisation and rule-governed professional administration are features of bureaucracy. There are fewer difficulties with
the use of the term bureaucracy in the field of comparative government. Here, it refers to the administrative machinery of the *state,
bureaucrats being non-elected state officials or civil servants.

Significance

The core function of the bureaucracy is to implement or execute
*law and *policy. The broadening of the responsibilities of govern-
ment has therefore been accompanied by a general increase in the
size of bureaucracies across the globe. However, the political significance of the bureaucracy largely stems from its role as the chief
source of policy information and advice available to governments.
The principal sources of bureaucratic power therefore include the
ability of civil servants to control the flow of information and thus
determine what their political masters know; the logistical advantages that they enjoy as permanent and full-time public officials;
and their status as experts and supposed custodians of the national
interest. The growth in bureaucratic power during the twentieth
century is usually explained in terms of the increased premium put
upon expertise and specialist knowledge by the fact that the task of
policy-making in modern societies has become increasingly complex
and demanding. This has made the control of the bureaucracy an
important issue in all political systems. The principal means through
which this control is exerted include mechanisms of public accountability to ministers, assemblies, the courts or sometimes an ombuds-
man; the politicisation (either formally or informally) of senior
bureaucratic posts; and the construction of counter-bureaucracies
that provide politicians with alternative sources of advice.

The political role and impact of bureaucracy has been the source
of considerable debate. Max Weber's (1864–1920) classic account
of bureaucracy portrayed it as a reliable, efficient and, above all,
rational means of social organisation that is characterised by rule-
governed behaviour, an ordered hierarchy, the use of written documents and a filing system, and an impersonal authority system in
which appointment and advancement are based upon professional

criteria. Socialists and particularly Marxists, on the other hand, have viewed bureaucracy as a power-bloc that can resist political control and reflects broader class interests, through either the social composition of the senior civil service or structural links between government departments and business interests. However, as communist regimes demonstrated, bureaucracy cannot be viewed as a narrowly capitalist phenomenon. Public choice theorists have interpreted bureaucracy in terms of career self-interest on the part of civil servants. In this view the growth of government intervention is essentially a manifestation of bureaucratic power and the extent to which top bureaucrats are able to resist political control.

CABINET

A cabinet is a *committee of senior ministers who represent the various government departments or ministries (it should not to be confused with *cabinet*, as used in France and the EU to denote groups of policy advisers who support individual ministers). In *presidential systems the cabinet usually exists to serve the *president by acting as a policy adviser rather than a policy-maker. Such cabinets function largely as an administrative tool and a 'sounding board', but are constitutionally subordinate to the president who monopolises formal policy-making responsibility. In contrast, the cabinet, in theory at least, is the apex of the *executive in states that respect the principle of cabinet government. 'Cabinet government' is characterised by two features. First, the cabinet constitutes the principal link between the legislative and executive branches of *government; its members are drawn from and accountable to the *parliament, but also serve as the political heads of the various government departments. Second, the cabinet is the senior executive organ and policy-making responsibility is shared within it, the *prime minister being merely 'first' in name only. This system is usually underpinned by collective responsibility – all cabinet ministers (and sometimes non-cabinet ministers) are required to 'sing the same song' and support official government policy.

Significance

The widespread use of cabinets reflects the political and administrative need for collective procedures within the political executive.

In the first place, cabinets enable government to present a collective face to parliaments and the public. Without a cabinet, government could appear to be a personal tool wielded by a single individual. Second, cabinets are an administrative device designed to ensure the effective co-ordination of government *policy. In short, in the absence of a cabinet, government would consist of rival bureau-cratic empires each bent upon self-aggrandisement. The virtues of cabinet government are therefore that it encourages full and frank policy debate within the *democracy of a cabinet meeting, subject-ing proposals to wide and effective scrutiny; and that it guarantees the unity and cohesion of government, since the cabinet makes deci-sions collectively, and collectively stands by them. Cabinet govern-ment has nevertheless been criticised because it acts as a cloak for prime-ministerial power by forcing dissenting ministers to support agreed government policy in public, and because it makes govern-ment policy incoherent and inconsistent, as decisions tend to be based upon compromises between competing ministers and depart-mental interests.

Whether or not cabinets are invested with formal policy-making responsibility, they have struggled to maintain their political role and status. This is largely a consequence of the growing prominence of the chief executive (whether a president or prime minister), result-ing from the media's and particularly television's tendency to focus upon personality and image, and the need for clear policy *leader-ship in an era of complex and widespread government intervention and global interdependence. Cabinets have also been weakened by the increased size and importance of government departments and other agencies, meaning that policy proposals emerge pre-packaged, with meaningful debate and scrutiny having happened elsewhere. However, cabinets continue to fulfil a residual and irre-ducible function as a means of policy co-ordination, and, especially when they contain members with significant party or public sup-port, or when the chief executive's *authority is weak, they may exert decisive policy influence.

COALITION

A coalition is a grouping of rival political actors brought together either through the perception of a common threat, or the recogni-tion that their goals cannot be achieved by working separately.

Electoral coalitions are alliances through which *political parties agree not to compete against one another with a view to maximising their joint *representation. *Legislative coalitions* are agreements between two or more parties to support a particular bill or programme. *Government coalitions* are formal agreements between two or more parties that involve a cross-party distribution of ministerial portfolios. A 'grand coalition' or 'national government' comprises all the major parties, but they are usually formed only at times of national crisis or economic emergency.

Significance

Most debate about the political impact of coalitions centres upon the workings of government coalitions. These are usually formed to ensure majority control of the *parliament, and are therefore usually found in political systems that employ proportional representation, or which have fragmented party systems. Coalitions have been criticised on the grounds that, as they do not command a unified parliamentary majority, they result in weak and ineffective *government; that conflict between coalition partners tends to produce instability; and that they prevent the development of bold, if controversial, policy initiatives. However, coalition governments may have the advantage that they promote compromise and consensus-building across the political spectrum; that they command wide, if diverse, public support; and that they more rigorously and effectively scrutinise policy proposals. Successful coalition governments usually operate in the context of a broad ideological *consensus, in which parties act as 'brokers' for particular interests and are accustomed to compromise and flexibility. Coalition government is often seen to be particularly appropriate to divided societies.

COMMITTEE

A committee is a small work group composed of members drawn from a larger body and charged with specific responsibilities. Whereas ad-hoc committees are set up for a particular purpose, and disbanded when that task is completed, permanent or standing committees have enduring responsibilities and an institutional role. However, the responsibilities entrusted to committees range from formal decision-making (as in the case of some *cabinets), policy analysis and debate, to administrative co-ordination and information exchange. Not uncommonly, committees operate within a larger committee system of specialist committees, co-ordinating committees and sub-committees.

Significance

Committee structures have become increasingly prominent in legislative and executive branches of government, as deliberative and consultative forums and also as decision-making bodies. It is generally accepted that the wider and more formal use of committees has become an administrative necessity given the size and complexity of modern *government. The major advantages of committees include the following. They allow a range of views, opinions and interests to be represented; provide the opportunity for fuller, longer and more detailed debate; encourage decisions to be made more efficiently and speedily; and make possible a division of labour that encourages the accumulation of expertise and specialist knowledge. However, committees have also been criticised. For instance, they can easily be manipulated by those who set up and staff them, and they can encourage centralisation by allowing a chairperson to dominate proceedings behind a mask of consultation. Moreover, they may narrow the range of views and interests that are taken into account in decision-making, particularly as their members may become divorced from the larger body, creating a form of sham *representation.

CONSTITUTION

A constitution is, broadly, a set of rules that seek to establish the duties, powers and functions of the various institutions of *government, regulate the relationships between them, and define the relationship between the *state and the individual. Constitutions thus lay down certain meta-rules for the political system; in effect, these are rules that govern the government. Just as government establishes ordered rule in society at large, a constitution brings stability, predictability and *order to the actions of government. The most common way of classifying constitutions is to distinguish between codified and uncodified, or written and unwritten, constitutions.

Codified constitutions draw together key constitutional provisions within a single, legal document, popularly known as a 'written' constitution or 'the constitution'. These documents are authoritative in the sense that they constitute 'higher' law – indeed, the highest law of the land. This, in turn, entrenches the provisions of the constitution, in that they can only be amended or abolished using a process more complicated than that employed for statute *law. Finally, the logic of the codification dictates that, as the constitution sets out the duties, powers and functions of government institutions in terms of 'higher' law, it must be justiciable, meaning that all political bodies must be subject to the authority of the courts, and in particular a supreme or constitutional court.

Uncodified constitutions are now found in only two *liberal democracies (Israel and the UK) and a handful of non-democratic states. In the absence of a 'written' constitution, uncodified constitutions draw upon a variety of sources (in the UK these include statute law, common law, conventions, works of authority and EU law). Laws of constitutional significance are thus not entrenched: they may be changed through the ordinary legislative process. Most importantly, this means that *sovereignty, or unchangeable legal *authority, is vested in the *parliament. The parliament has the right to make or unmake any law whatsoever, no body, including the courts, having the ability to override or set aside its laws. Alternative ways of classifying constitutions deal with the ease with which the constitution can be changed (whether it is rigid or flexible), the degree to which the constitution is observed in practice (whether it is effective, nominal or a façade constitution), or the basis of its contents (whether it is monarchical or republican, federal or unitary, or parliamentary or presidential).

Significance

Although the evolution of the British constitution is sometimes traced back to the Bill of Rights of 1689, or even the Magna Carta of 1215, it is more helpful to think of constitutions as late eighteenth-century creations. The 'age of constitutions' was initiated by the enactment of the first 'written' constitutions: the US Constitution in 1787 and the French Declaration of the Rights of Man and the Citizen in 1789. Constitutions play a number of vital roles in the workings of modern political systems. The most basic of these is that they mark out the existence of a *state and make claims concerning its sphere of independent authority. Constitutions also establish, implicitly or explicitly, a broader set of political values, ideals and goals (in the case of 'written' constitutions, this is usually accomplished in preambles that serve as statements of national ideals). Moreover, by serving as 'organisational charts' or 'institutional blueprints', constitutions introduce a measure of stability and predictability to the workings of government and enable conflicts to be resolved more speedily and efficiently.

However, constitutions are chiefly valued because they are a means of constraining government and protecting *freedom. By laying down the relationship between the state and the individual, often through a *bill of rights, they mark out their respective spheres of government authority and individual liberty. Nevertheless, the mere existence of the constitution does not guarantee *constitutionalism. Constitutions are only a device of limited government when they fragment government authority and create effective checks and balances throughout the political system, and when, through whatever means, they ensure that *civil liberty is clearly defined and legally upheld.

Other debates about the constitution focus upon the implications of codification. Codified or written constitutions are seen to have the following strengths:

● as major principles and key constitutional provisions are entrenched, they are safeguarded from interference by the government of the day;
● the legislature is denied sovereignty and is thus unable to extend its own power at will;
● non-political judges are able to police the constitution to ensure that its provisions are upheld by other public bodies;
● individual liberty is more securely protected by an entrenched bill of rights;
● the codified document has a wider educational value, in that it highlights the central values and overall goals of the political system.

However, codification may also have drawbacks, the most important of which include the following:

● a codified constitution is rigid, and may therefore be less responsive and adaptable to changing circumstances than an uncodified one;

- constitutional supremacy ultimately resides with non-elected judges rather than democratically accountable politicians;
- as constitutional documents are inevitably biased, they may either promote ideological hegemony or precipitate more conflicts than they resolve;
- establishing a codified constitution requires that all major parties agree about important features of the political system, which may not be the case.

ELECTION

An election is a device for filling an office or post through choices made by a designated body of people, the electorate. Elections may nevertheless be either democratic or non-democratic. Democratic elections are conducted according to the following principles: universal adult suffrage (however 'adult' is defined); one person one vote, one vote one value; the secret ballot; and electoral choice offered by competition between both candidates and *political parties. Non-democratic elections may therefore exhibit any of the following features: the right to vote is restricted on grounds such as property ownership, education, gender or racial origin; a system of plural voting is in operation or constituency sizes vary significantly; voters are subject to pressure or intimidation; or only a single candidate or single party can contest the election.

There are, however, a variety of democratic electoral systems. These differ in a variety of ways. Voters may be asked to choose between candidates or between parties; they may either select a single candidate, or vote preferentially, ranking the candidates they wish to support in order; the electorate may or may not be grouped into electoral units or constituencies; constituencies may return a single member or a number of members; and the level of support needed to elect a candidate may vary from a plurality (the largest single number of votes or a 'relative' majority) to an overall or 'absolute' majority or a quota of some kind. However, the most common way of distinguishing between electoral systems is on the basis of how they convert votes into seats.

Majoritarian systems enable larger parties to win a significantly higher proportion of seats than the proportion of votes they gain in the election. This increases the chances of a single party gaining a parliamentary majority and being able to govern on its own.

Examples of majoritarian systems include the simple plurality system ('first-past-the-post'), the second ballot system and the alternative vote (AV). *Proportional systems* guarantee an equal, or at least more equal, relationship between seats and votes. In a pure system of proportional representation (PR), a party that gains 45 per cent of the votes would win exactly 45 per cent of the seats. Examples of proportional systems include the party list system, single transferable vote (STV) and the additional member system (AMS).

Significance

Elections are often seen as nothing less than *democracy in practice. The conventional view is that elections, when they are fair and competitive, are a mechanism through which politicians can be called to account and forced to introduce policies that somehow reflect public opinion. This emphasises the 'bottom-up' functions of elections. In this view elections are the major source of political recruitment, a means of making *governments and of transferring government *power, a guarantee of *representation, and a major determinant of government *policy. On the other hand, the 'radical' view of elections portrays them as largely a mechanism through which governments and political elites can exercise control over their populations. This view emphasises the 'top-down' functions of elections. These are that they have the capacity to build *legitimacy for the regime, to enable the government to 'educate' the electorate and shape public opinion, and to neutralise political discontent and opposition by channelling them in a constitutional direction. In reality, however, elections have no single character: they are neither simply mechanisms of public *accountability nor a means of ensuring political control. Like all channels of political communication, elections are a 'two-way street' that provide the government and the people, the elite and the mass, with the opportunity to influence one another.

Much of the debate about elections centres upon the merits of different electoral systems, and in particular the choice between majoritarian and proportional systems. Majoritarian systems have the advantage that they allow governments to be formed that have a clear *mandate from the electorate. They also increase the likelihood of strong and effective government, in that a single party usually has majority control of the *parliament, and produce stable government in that single-party governments rarely collapse through internal disunity. In contrast, proportional systems are 'fairer' in that party representation is reliably linked to electoral support, and ensure that governments have broader and usually majority support amongst the electorate. Moreover, by increasing the likelihood of coalition government, they institutionalise checks on *power and encourage policy to be made through a process of bargaining and consensus-building. Nevertheless, there is no such thing as a 'best' electoral system. The electoral systems debate is, at heart, a debate about the desirable nature of government, and about the respective merits of 'representative' government and 'effective' government. Finally, the impact of particular electoral systems will vary from *state to state, and possibly over time, depending upon factors such as the *political culture, the nature of the party system and the economic and social context within which politics is conducted.

EXECUTIVE

The executive, in its broadest sense, is the branch of *government responsible for the implementation of laws and policies made by the *parliament. The executive branch extends from the head of government, or chief executive, to the members of enforcement agencies such as the police and the military, and includes both ministers and civil servants. More commonly, the term is now used in a narrower sense to describe the smaller body of decision-makers who take overall responsibility for the direction and coordination of government policy. This core of senior figures is often called the *political executive* (roughly equivalent to the 'government of the day', or, in presidential systems, 'the administration'), as opposed to the *official executive*, or *bureaucracy. The term 'core executive' is sometimes used to refer to the coordinating and arbitrating mechanisms that lie at the heart of central government and straddle the 'political/ official' divide by including the chief executive, the *cabinet, senior officials in key government departments and the security and intelligence services, and networks of political advisers.

However, the organisation of the political executive differs significantly depending upon whether it operates in a *parliamentary or a *presidential system of government. *Parliamentary executives* have the following features:

- the personnel of the political executive is drawn from the parliament, usually on the basis of their status and position within the leading party or parties;
- the executive is directly accountable to the parliament (or at least its lower chamber), in the sense that it survives in government only as long as it retains the confidence of the parliament;
- the *cabinet is often regarded as the formal apex of the executive, thereby upholding the idea of collective *leadership;
- as the *prime minister is a parliamentary officer, a separate head of state, in the form of a constitutional monarch or non-executive president, is required to fulfil ceremonial duties and carry out state functions.

Presidential executives are characterised by the following features:

- the *president as chief executive is elected separately from the parliament and there is a formal separation of personnel between the legislative and executive branches;
- the executive is invested with a range of independent constitutional powers and is not removable by the parliament;
- executive authority is concentrated in the hands of the president, the cabinet and other ministers being merely advisers responsible to the president;
- the roles of head of state and head of government are combined in the office of the presidency.

Semi-presidential executives are headed by a separately elected president who presides over a government drawn from, and accountable to, the parliament. The balance of *power between the president and the prime minister, in such circumstances, depends upon factors such as the formal powers of the presidency, which may include the ability to dissolve the parliament, and the party composition of both institutions.

Significance

The executive is the irreducible core of government. Political systems can operate without *constitutions, parliaments, *judiciaries and even *political parties, but they cannot survive without an executive branch. This is because the key function of the political executive is to direct and control the policy process, both formulating government *policy and ensuring that it is implemented. In short, the executive is expected to 'govern'. The political executive is looked to, in particular, to develop coherent economic and social programmes that meet the needs of complex and politically sophisticated societies, and to control the *state's various external relationships in an increasingly interdependent world. One important consequence of this has been the growth of the executive's legislative powers, and its encroachment upon the traditional responsibilities of the parliament. Other important functions of the political executive include overseeing the implementation of policy and strategic control of the bureaucratic machinery of government, the provision of leadership in the event of either domestic or international crises, and the carrying out of various ceremonial and diplomatic responsibilities in which heads of state, chief executives and, to a lesser extent, senior ministers 'stand for' the *state. Moreover, the popularity of the political executive, more than any other part of the political system, is crucial to the character and stability of the regime as a whole. The ability of the executive to mobilise support ensures the compliance and cooperation of the general public, and, more importantly, the political executive's popularity is a crucial determinant of the *legitimacy of the broader regime.

Such is the potential power of executives that much of political development has taken the form of attempts to check or constrain them, either by forcing them to operate within a constitutional framework, or by making them accountable to a popularly elected parliament or democratic electorate. Nevertheless, as the source of political leadership, the executive's role has been greatly enhanced by the widening responsibilities of the state in both domestic and international realms, and the media's tendency to portray politics in terms of personalities. This, in turn, has led to contradictory shifts in the location of executive *power. The official executive, as the source of expertise and specialist knowledge, has been strengthened at the expense of the political executive, but, regardless of the parliamentary/presidential distinction, power has also been concentrated in the hands of the chief executive as the popular face of modern politics. However, the hopes and expectations focused upon executives may also prove to be their undoing. In many political systems, leaders are finding it increasingly difficult to 'deliver the goods'. This is linked both to the growing complexity of modern society and to the fact that, through the impact of *globalisation, the capacity of national governments to solve problems has declined.

GENDER

Gender refers to distinctions between males and females in terms of their social role and status. Although the terms gender and sex are often used interchangeably in everyday language, the distinction between them is crucial to social and political analysis. Gender highlights social or cultural differences between women and men, while sex denotes biological, and therefore ineradicable, differences. Gender is thus a social construct and usually operates through stereotypes of 'femininity' and 'masculinity'.

Significance

Gender was largely ignored by political thinkers until the re-emergence of the women's movement and the revival of *feminism in the 1960s. Since then, it has become a central concept in feminist theory and has received wider attention in mainstream political analysis. For most feminists, gender highlights the fact that biological or physical differences between women and men ('sexual' differences) do not imply, or legitimise, their different social roles and positions ('gender' differences). In short, the quest for gender *equality, which is basic to most forms of feminism, reflects the belief that sexual differences have no political or social significance; biology is not destiny. Radical feminists view gender divisions as the deepest and most politically significant of all social cleavages; gender is thus a 'political' category imposed by *patriarchy and reproduced through a process of conditioning that operates mainly through the family. Gender, for radical feminists, plays the same role as *social class does in Marxist analysis, 'sisterhood' being equivalent to 'class consciousness'. Socialist feminists, on the other hand, argue that gender divisions are intrinsically linked to *capitalism, and therefore treat gender and class as interrelated social cleavages. Liberal feminists and mainstream political analysts understand gender divisions less in terms of structural oppression and more in terms of an unequal distribution of *rights and opportunities that prevents the full participation of women in the 'public' realm.

From this perspective, gender politics draws attention to issues such as women's rights and the under-representation of women in *politics and in general professional and managerial positions.

HEGEMONY

Hegemony (from the Greek *hegemonia*, meaning 'leader') is, in its simplest sense, the ascendancy or domination of one element of the system over others. For example, a *state which is predominant within a league, confederation or region can be said to enjoy hegemony. In Marxist theory the term is used in a more technical and specific sense. In the writings of Antonio Gramsci (1891–1937), hegemony refers to the ability of a dominant *social class to exercise *power by winning the consent of those it subjugates, as an alternative to the use of coercion. As a non-coercive form of class rule, hegemony is typically understood as a cultural or ideological process that operates through the dissemination of bourgeois values and beliefs throughout society. However, it also has a political and economic dimension: consent can be manipulated by pay increases or by political or social reform.

Significance

The idea of ideological hegemony is used by Marxist theorists as an alternative to the more conventional notion of *political culture. It is based upon Marx's (1818–83) concept of *ideology, which acknowledges that the ruling class is not only the ruling material force in society, but also its ruling intellectual force. This implies both that ideas, values and beliefs are class-specific, in the sense that they reflect the distinctive social existence of each class, and that the ideas of the ruling class enjoy a decisive advantage over those of other classes, thereby becoming the 'ruling ideas of the age'. Capitalist societies are thus dominated by bourgeois ideology. Gramsci's *Prison Notebooks* ([1929–35] 1971) drew attention to the degree to which the class system is upheld not simply by unequal economic and political power, but also the ruling class's spiritual and cultural supremacy, understood as hegemony. Bourgeois values and beliefs pervade *civil society (the *mass media, churches, youth movements, trade unions and so on), extending beyond formal learning and education and becoming the very common sense of the age. For *socialism to be achieved, a 'battle of ideas' therefore has to be waged through which proletarian principles, values and theories displace, or at least challenge, bourgeois ones. The main criticisms of the idea of hegemony are that it overestimates the role of ideas in *politics, amounting to a form of 'ideologism', and that it underestimates the cultural diversity of capitalist societies that have, over time, become increasingly complex and pluralistic.

JUDICIARY

The judiciary is the branch of *government that is empowered to decide legal disputes. The central function of judges is therefore to adjudicate the meaning of *law, in the sense that they interpret or 'construct' law. Although the role of the judiciary varies from *state to state and from system to system, the judiciary is often accorded unusual respect and is regarded as distinct from other political institutions. This is because of the supposed link between law and *justice, reflected in the capacity of judges to decide disputes in a fair and balanced fashion. Judiciaries and court systems are invariably structured in a hierarchical fashion, reflecting the different types and levels of law, allowing for an appeals process and ensuring consistency of interpretation through the overriding authority of a supreme or high court. Increasingly, however, national judiciaries are subject to the authority of supranational courts, such as the European Court of Justice, the European Court of Human Rights and the World Court.

Significance

The two chief issues concerning the judiciary are whether judges are political and whether they are policy-makers. Certain political systems make no pretence of judicial *neutrality or impartiality. For example, in orthodox communist regimes the principle of 'socialist legality' dictated that judges interpret law in accordance with Marxism–Leninism, subject to the ideological authority of the *state's communist party. Judges thus became mere functionaries who carried out the political and ideological objectives of the regime itself, as was demonstrated by the 'show trials' of the 1930s in the USSR. The German courts during the Nazi period were similarly used as instruments of ideological repression and political persecution.

Liberal-democratic states, however, have emphasised the principles of judicial independence and neutrality. Judicial independence is the principle that there should be a strict separation between the judiciary and other branches of government, and is thus an application of the *separation of powers. Judicial neutrality is the principle that judges should interpret law in a way that is uncontaminated by social, political and other biases. Taken together, these principles are meant to establish a strict separation between law and *politics, and to guarantee that the rule of law is upheld. The devices used to ensure judicial objectivity range from security of tenure and the independence of the legal profession (as in the USA and the UK) to specialised professional training (as widely adopted in continental Europe). However, the image of judicial objectivity is always misleading. The judiciary is best thought of as a political, not merely a legal, institution. The main ways in which political influences intrude into judicial decision-making are through breaches in independence, often linked to the appointment system or the wider use of judges in state roles, and to the threat to neutrality that is posed by the fact that judges everywhere are socially and educationally unrepresentative of the larger society.

The image of judges as simple appliers of law has also always been a myth. Judges cannot apply the so-called 'letter of the law', because no law, legal term or principle has a single, self-evident meaning. In practice, judges impose meaning on law through a process of 'construction' that forces them to choose amongst a number of possible meanings or interpretations. In this sense all law is judge-made law. However, two major factors affect the degree to which judges make *policy. The first is the clarity and detail with which law is specified. Generally, broadly framed laws or constitutional principles allow greater scope for judicial interpretation. The second factor is the existence of a codified or 'written' *constitution. The existence of such a document significantly enhances the status of the judiciary, investing it with the power of judicial review. Judicial review is the ability of the judiciary to consider and possibly invalidate laws, decrees and the actions of other branches of government if they are incompatible with the constitution. In its classical sense this implies that the judiciary is the supreme constitutional arbiter. A more modest form of judicial review, found in uncodified constitutional systems, is restricted to the review of executive actions in the light of ordinary law, using the principle of *ultra vires* (beyond the powers).

MANDATE

A mandate is an instruction or command from a higher body that demands compliance. Policy mandates can be distinguished from governing mandates. A *policy mandate* arises from the claim on behalf of a winning party in an *election that its manifesto promises have been endorsed, giving it authority to translate these into a programme of government. This is sometimes portrayed as a 'popular' mandate or 'democratic' mandate. A *governing mandate* is, in effect, a mandate to govern. It is more flexible in that it attaches to an individual leader (in the case of a 'personal' mandate) or to a *political party or *government, rather than a set of *policies. Whereas policy mandates bind politicians and parties and limit their freedom of manoeuvre, it is difficult to see how governing mandates in any way restrict politicians once they are in power.

Significance

The doctrine of the mandate is an important model of *representation. It holds that politicians serve their constituent not by thinking for themselves or acting as a channel to convey their views, but by remaining loyal to their party and its policies. The strength of the mandate doctrine is that it takes account of the undoubted practical importance of party labels and party policies. Moreover, it provides a means of imposing some kind of meaning upon election results, as well as a way of keeping politicians to their word. The doctrine of the mandate thus guarantees responsible party government, in that the party in power can only act within the mandate it has received from the electorate. Nevertheless, the doctrine has also stimulated fierce criticism. First, it is based upon a highly questionable model of voting behaviour, insofar as it suggests that voters select parties on the grounds of policies and issues, rather than on the basis of 'irrational' factors such as the personality of leaders, the image of parties, habitual allegiances and social conditioning.

Second, the doctrine imposes a straitjacket upon government, in that it leaves no scope for policies to be adjusted in the light of changing circumstances. What guidance do mandates offer in the event of, say, international or economic crises? Third, the doctrine of the mandate can be applied only in the case of majoritarian electoral systems in which a single party wins power, and its use even there may appear absurd if the winning party fails to gain 50 per cent of the vote. Fourth, policy mandates are always in danger of being translated into governing mandates, which are open to clear abuse and have only a tenuous link to representation.

MARKET

A market is a system of commercial exchange which brings buyers wishing to acquire a good or service into contact with sellers offering the same for purchase. In all but the most simple markets, money is used as a convenient means of exchange rather than barter. Markets are impersonal mechanisms in that they are regulated by price fluctuations that reflect the balance of supply and demand, so-called market forces. The terms market economy and *capitalism are often used interchangeably, but market forms may also develop in other social systems (as the idea of market *socialism demonstrates), and capitalist systems themselves subject markets to a greater or lesser degree of regulation.

Significance

The market is the central organising principle within a capitalist economy. It has been applied to the organisation of some socialist societies, as well as to public services such as education and health (using the idea of 'internal markets'). Market forms and market structures have become increasingly prominent in modern society given the failure of alternative planning arrangements, most spectacularly in the collapse of *communism in the revolutions of 1989–91, and also because *globalisation has gone hand-in-hand with marketisation. This has occurred through the market's capacity to regulate highly complex interactions amongst human beings in a way that balances dynamism against equilibrium, a capacity that appears to outstrip that of rational human agents, however well informed and technologically advanced they may be.

Nevertheless, although support, sometimes grudging, for the market now extends to many socialists, the market continues to stimulate deep political and ideological controversy. Supporters of the market argue that its advantages include the following:

- it promotes efficiency through the discipline of the profit motive;
- it encourages innovation in the form of new products and better production processes;
- it allows producers and consumers to pursue their own interests and enjoy freedom of choice;
- it tends towards equilibrium through the coordination of an almost infinite number of individual preferences and decisions.

Critics nevertheless point out that the market has serious disadvantages, including the following:

- it generates insecurity because people's lives are shaped by forces they cannot control and do not understand;
- it widens material inequality and generates poverty;
- it increases the level of greed and selfishness, and ignores the broader needs of society;
- it promotes instability through periodic booms and slumps.

Mass media

The media comprises those societal institutions that are concerned with the production and distribution of all forms of knowledge, information and entertainment. The 'mass' character of mass media is derived from the fact that the media channel communication towards a large and undifferentiated audience using relatively advanced technology. Grammatically and politically, the mass media are plural. The *broadcast media*, including television, radio and, increasingly, electronic forms of communications such as the internet, can be distinguished from the *print media*, which encompass newspapers, magazines and publishing generally. Similarly, different messages may be put out by, for instance, public and private television channels and by tabloid and broadsheet newspapers.

Significance

Interest in the political impact of the mass media burgeoned during the twentieth century, initially through the growth of the popular press, but subsequently because of the growing penetration of television in particular throughout modern society. There can be no doubt that most political information is now disseminated by the mass media. When communication systems are subject to formal political control – as in state socialist, fascist or authoritarian regimes – the media become little more than a propaganda machine. However, there is considerable debate about its impact in liberal-democratic regimes. Some view the media's influence as broadly positive. Pluralist theorists, for instance, tend to argue that, so long as the media are independent from the *state, they serve to promote *democracy and protect *freedom by providing a forum that allows a variety of political views to be debated and discussed. Moreover, as most forms of media are privately owned and so are sensitive to market demand, the media do not impose their own views but merely reflect those of their audience, listeners or readers.

Nevertheless, both left-wing and right-wing critics have complained about media bias, stemming from the fact that all forms of communication involve the selection, prioritisation and interpretation of information. The most common version of this view, advanced especially by Marxists, regards the mass media as perhaps the key means of propagating bourgeois ideas and maintaining capitalist *hegemony. Such ideas generally highlight the political *power that flows from media ownership. An alternative version of the media bias argument holds that the mass media articulate the values of groups that are disproportionally represented amongst its senior professionals, be they left-leaning intellectuals, middle-class conservatives, or men. A more subtle, but nevertheless important form of media influence is summed up in Marshall McLuhan's famous aphorism – 'the medium is the message'. For example, the political impact of television may be less related to its content and more linked to its tendency to privatise leisure time and reduce achievement levels in children, thereby creating a 'post-civic' generation.

MONARCHY

A monarchy is a system of rule dominated by a single individual (it literally means 'rule by one person'). In general usage, however, it is the institution through which the post of head of state is filled through inheritance or dynastic succession. Absolute monarchies nevertheless differ from constitutional monarchies. *Absolute monarchies* are ones in which the monarch claims a monopoly of political *power; the monarch is thus literally a sovereign. The classical basis of monarchical *absolutism is the doctrine of divine right, the belief that the monarch has been chosen by God and so rules with God's *authority on earth. *Constitutional monarchies* are ones in which *sovereignty is vested elsewhere, and the monarch fulfils an essentially ceremonial role largely devoid of direct political significance. In some cases constitutional monarchs may carry out residual political functions, such as selecting the *prime minister, while in other cases they serve as nothing more than formal heads of state.

Significance

Absolute monarchy was the dominant form of government from the sixteenth century to the nineteenth century, but now only exists in a handful of *states, examples including Saudi Arabia, Nepal and Morocco. The dynamics of monarchical absolutism are complex, however. Although the monarch is in theory absolute, in practice power is usually shared between the monarch, economic elites (generally the landed aristocracy), and the established church, the formal source of the monarch's authority. Absolute monarchy was nevertheless unable to withstand the pressures generated by the modernisation process, meaning that when monarchy survived in developed states such as the UK, the Netherlands and Spain, it has done so in a strictly constitutional form. In the UK, although the royal prerogative is now exercised by the prime minister and other ministers accountable to Parliament, the monarch retains potentially significant political influence in her or his ability to choose a prime minister and dissolve Parliament in the event of a 'hung' Parliament (when no party has majority control of the House of Commons).

The advantages associated with the constitutional monarchy include the following:

- it provides a solution to the need for a non-partisan head of state who is 'above' party politics;
- the monarch embodies traditional authority, and so serves as a symbol of patriotic loyalty and national unity;

- the monarch constitutes a repository of experience and wisdom, especially in relation to constitutional matters, available to elected governments.

The disadvantages of a constitutional monarchy include the following:

- it violates democratic principles in that political authority is not based upon popular *consent and is no way publicly accountable;
- the monarch symbolises (and possibly supports) conservative values such as hierarchy, deference and respect for inherited wealth and social position;
- the monarchy binds nations to outmoded ways and symbols of the past, thus impeding modernisation and progress.

OPPOSITION

Opposition, in its everyday sense, means hostility or antagonism. However, in its political sense opposition usually refers to antagonism that has a formal character and operates within a constitutional framework. This is clearest in relation to *parliamentary systems of *government in which the *political parties outside of government are generally viewed as opposition parties, the largest of them sometimes being designated as 'the opposition'. In two-party systems, parliamentary procedures often take account of formal rivalry between the two major parties acting, respectively, as government and opposition, with the opposition sometimes replicating the structure of government by forming a 'shadow' cabinet and operating as a 'government in waiting'.

The notion of opposition is usually less formally developed in multi-party systems and in *presidential systems of government. In multi-party systems the government-versus-opposition dynamic is weakened by the fact that government, being a *coalition, is not a cohesive force but contains internal sources of rivalry, and that there is rarely a single opposition party that has the potential to form a government on its own. In presidential systems the opposition party is technically the party that does not hold the presidency; however, this party may nevertheless be the majority party in the legislature and thereby be able to wield considerable policy-making influence. Opposition may, on the other hand, have an extra-parliamentary and anti-constitutional character. In such cases it refers to political groupings, movements or parties that reject established political procedures and challenge, sometimes through *revolution, the principles upon which the political system is based.

Significance

Opposition is a vital feature of liberal-democratic government. It serves three major functions. First, it helps to ensure limited government and so protect *freedom by serving as a formal check upon the government of the day. Second, it guarantees scrutiny and oversight, improving the quality of public *policy and making government accountable for its blunders. Third, it strengthens democratic *accountability by creating a more informed electorate and offering a choice between meaningful parties of government. In addition, especially in two-party systems, parliamentary opposition ensures a smooth and immediate transfer of power because an alternative government is always available. There are, nevertheless, concerns about the effectiveness and value of constitutional opposition. Some argue that parliamentary opposition is merely tokenistic, in that, behind a façade of debate and antagonism, both government and opposition support the existing constitutional arrangements and, as long as power alternates, both benefit from them. Much opposition is therefore a parliamentary ritual that has little impact upon the content of public policy. An alternative concern is that opposition, particularly in a two-party context, may result in adversary politics, a style of politics that turns political life into an ongoing battle between major parties aimed at winning electoral support. When oppositions oppose for the sake of opposing, political debate is reduced to what has sometimes been called 'ya-boo politics'.

PARLIAMENT

The terms parliament, assembly and legislature are often used interchangeably, but they have, to some extent, different implications. An assembly, in its simplest sense, is a collection or gathering of people, as in, for example, a school assembly. As a political term, assembly has come to be associated with representative and popular *government, an assembly being viewed as a surrogate for the people. For this reason the term is sometimes reserved for the lower, popularly elected chamber in a bicameral system, or for the single chamber in a unicameral system. A legislature is a law-making body; however, even when assemblies are invested with formal and possibly supreme legislative authority, they never monopolise law-making power and rarely in practice control the legislative process. Parliament (from the French *parler*, meaning 'to speak') implies consultation and deliberation, and thus suggests that the primary role of an assembly is to act as a debating chamber in which policies and political issues can be openly discussed and scrutinised. Parliaments are generally categorised according to their capacity to influence *policy. Policy-making parliaments enjoy significant *autonomy and have an active impact upon policy. Policy-influencing parliaments can transform policy but only by reacting to executive initiatives. Executive-dominated parliaments exert marginal influence or merely 'rubber-stamp' executive decisions.

Significance

Parliaments occupy a key position in the machinery of government. Traditionally they have been treated with special respect and status as the public, even democratic, face of government. Parliaments are respected because they are composed of lay politicians who claim to represent the people rather than trained or expert government officials. As such, parliaments provide a link between government and the people; that is, they are a channel of communication that can both support government and uphold the regime, and force government to respond to popular demands. The chief functions of a parliament are to enact legislation, act as a representative body, oversee and scrutinise the *executive, recruit and train politicians, and assist in maintaining the political system's *legitimacy.

However, parliaments are often subordinate bodies in modern political systems. Examples of policy-making assemblies are rare (the US Congress and the Italian Senate are exceptions). Most can be classified as either policy-influencing or executive-dominated parliaments. The amount of *power a parliament has is determined by a variety of state-specific factors. These include the extent of the parliament's constitutional authority, its degree of political independence from the executive (notably whether it operates within a *parliamentary or a *presidential system), the nature of the party system, and the parliament's level of organisational coherence (particularly the strength of its committee system).

Most commentators agree that parliaments generally lost power during the twentieth century. This decline occurred because of the executive's greater capacity to formulate policy and provide *leadership; because of the growth in the role of government and the consequent increase in the size and status of *bureaucracies; because of the emergence of disciplined *political parties; and because of the increased strength of *pressure groups, and the rise of the *mass media as an alternative forum for political debate and discussion. There is, nevertheless, also evidence of a revival in parliamentary power, through, for instance, the strengthening of specialist *committees and a trend towards professionalisation. This reflects the recognition of a link between the legitimacy and stability of a political system and the effectiveness of its parliament.

POLITICAL CULTURE

Culture, in its broadest sense, is the way of life of a people. Sociologists and anthropologists tend to distinguish between 'culture' and 'nature', the former encompassing that which is passed on to one generation to the next by learning, the latter referring to that which is acquired through biological inheritance. Political scientists use the term in a narrower sense to refer to a people's psychological orientation, political culture being the general 'pattern of orientations' to political objects such as parties, *government and the *constitution, expressed in beliefs, symbols and values. Political culture differs from public opinion in that it is fashioned out of long-term values rather than simply people's reactions to specific issues and problems.

Significance

Interest amongst political scientists in the idea of political culture emerged in the 1950s and 1960s as new techniques of behavioural analysis displaced more traditional, institutional approaches to the subject. The classic work in this respect was Almond and Verba's *The Civic Culture* (1963) (subsequently updated as *The Civic Culture Revisited* (1980)), which used opinion surveys to analyse political attitudes in democracy in five countries: the USA, the UK, West

Germany, Italy and Mexico. The civic culture model identified three general types of political culture: participant culture, subject culture and parochial culture. A 'participant' political culture is one in which citizens pay close attention to politics and regard popular participation as both desirable and effective. A 'subject' political culture is characterised by more passivity amongst citizens, and the recognition that they have only a very limited capacity to influence government. A 'parochial' political culture is marked by the absence of a sense of *citizenship, with people identifying with their locality rather than the region, and having neither the desire nor the ability to participate in politics. Almond and Verba argued that the 'civic culture' is a blend of all three in that it reconciles the participation of citizens in the political process with the vital necessity for government to govern. Although interest in political culture faded in the 1970s and 1980s with the declining influence of *behaviouralism, the debate was revitalised in the 1990s. This occurred both as a result of efforts by post-communist states to foster democratic values and expectations, and because of growing anxiety in mature democracies, such as the USA, about the apparent decline of social capital and civic engagement.

However, the civic-culture approach to the study of political attitudes and values has been widely criticised. In the first place Almond and Verba's 'sleeping dogs' theory of democratic culture, which emphasises the importance of passivity and deference, has been rejected by those who argue that political participation is the very stuff of *democracy. Low electoral turn-outs, for example, may reflect widespread alienation and ingrained disadvantage, rather than political contentment. Second, a civic culture may be more a consequence of democracy than its cause. In other words, the assumption that political attitudes and values shape behaviour, and not the other way round, is unproven. Third, this approach tends to treat political culture as homogeneous; that is, as little more than a cipher for national culture or national character. In so doing, it pays little attention to political sub-cultures and tends to disguise fragmentation and social conflict. Finally, the civic-culture model has been condemned as politically conservative. Marxists in particular reject the 'bottom-up' implications of Almond and Verba's work, and adopt instead a dominant-ideology model of political culture, which highlights the role of ideological *hegemony and draws attention to the link between unequal class power and cultural and ideological bias.

POLITICAL PARTY

A political party is a group of people that is organised for the purpose of winning government *power, by electoral or other means.
Parties are often confused with *pressure groups or *social movements. Four characteristics usually distinguish parties from other
groups. First, parties aim to exercise government power by winning
office (although small parties may use *elections more to gain a
platform than to win power). Second, parties are organised bodies
with a formal 'card-carrying' membership. This distinguishes them
from broader and more diffuse social movements. Third, parties
typically adopt a broad issue focus, addressing each of the major
issues of government policy (small parties, however, may have a
single-issue focus, thus resembling pressure groups). Fourth, to
varying degrees, parties are united by shared political preferences
and a general ideological identity.

However, political parties can be classified as mass and cadre
parties, as representative and integrative parties, and as constitutional and revolutionary parties. A *mass party* places a heavy
emphasis upon broadening membership and constructing a wide
electoral base, the earliest examples being European socialist parties which aimed to mobilise working-class support, such as the
UK Labour Party and the German Social Democratic Party
(SPD). Such parties typically place heavier stress upon recruitment
and organisation than on *ideology and political conviction.
Kirchheimer (1966) classified most modern parties as 'catch-all
parties', emphasising that they have dramatically reduced their
ideological baggage in order to appeal to the largest number of
voters. A *cadre party*, on the other hand, is dominated by trained
and professional party members who are expected to exhibit a high
level of political commitment and doctrinal discipline, as in the case
of communist and fascist parties.

Neumann (1956) offered the alternative distinction between
representative parties, which adopt a catch-all strategy and place
pragmatism before principle, and *integrative parties*, which are pro-
active rather than reactive, and attempt to mobilise, educate and
inspire the masses, instead of merely responding to their concerns.
Occasionally, mass parties may exhibit mobilising or integrative
tendencies, as in the case of the UK Conservatives under Margaret
Thatcher in the 1980s. Finally, parties can be classified as *constitutional parties* when they operate within a framework of constraints

imposed by the existence of other parties, the rules of electoral competition and, crucially, a distinction between the party in power (the government of the day) and state institutions (the *bureaucracy, *judiciary, police and so on). *Revolutionary parties*, by contrast, adopt an anti-system or anti-constitutional stance, and when such parties win power they invariably become 'ruling' or regime parties, suppressing rival parties and establishing a permanent relationship with the state machinery.

Significance

The political party is the major organising principle of modern politics. As political machines organised to win (by elections or otherwise), and wield government power, parties are virtually ubiquitous. The only parts of the world in which they do not exist are those where they are suppressed by *dictatorship or military rule. Political parties are a vital link between the *state and *civil society, carrying out major functions such as representation, the formation and recruitment of political elites, the articulation and aggregation of interests and the organisation of government. However, the role and significance of parties varies according to the party system. In one-party systems they effectively substitute themselves for the government, creating a fused party–state apparatus. In two-party systems the larger of the major parties typically wields government power, while the other major party constitutes the opposition and operates as a 'government in waiting'. In a multiparty system the parties tend to act as brokers representing a narrower range of interests, and exert influence through the construction of more or less enduring electoral alliances or formal *coalitions.

Criticisms of political parties have either stemmed from an early liberal fear that parties would promote conflict and destroy the underlying unity of society, and make the politics of individual conscience impossible, or that they are inherently elitist and bureaucratic bodies. The latter view was most famously articulated by Robert Michels ([1911] 1962) in the form of the 'iron law of oligarchy'. Some modern parties, notably Green parties, style themselves as 'anti-party parties', in that they set out to subvert traditional party politics by rejecting parliamentary compromise and emphasising popular mobilisation. Amongst the strongest supporters of the political party has been Lenin ([1902] 1968), who advocated the construction of a tightly knit revolutionary party, organised on the basis of democratic centralism, to serve as the 'vanguard of the working class'. Nevertheless, the late twentieth century provided evidence of a so-called 'crisis of party politics', reflected in a seemingly general decline in party membership and partisanship, and in the contrasting growth of single-issue protest groups and rise of new social movements. This has been explained on the basis that, as bureaucratised political machines, parties are unable to respond to the growing appetite for popular participation and activism; that their image as instruments of government means that they are inevitably associated with power, ambition and corruption; and that, given the growing complexity of modern societies and the decline of class and other traditional social identities, the social forces that once gave rise to parties have now weakened. Such factors are nevertheless more likely to lead to a transformation in the role of political parties and in the style of party politics, than to make them redundant.

PRESIDENT

A president is a formal head of state, a title which is held in other *states by a monarch or emperor. However, constitutional presidents differ from executive presidents. *Constitutional presidents*, or non-executive presidents (found in India, Israel and Germany, for example), are a feature of *parliamentary government and have responsibilities that are largely confined to ceremonial duties. In these circumstances the president is a mere figurehead, and executive power is wielded by a *prime minister and/or a *cabinet. *Executive presidents* wear 'two hats', in that they combine the formal responsibilities of a head of state with the political power of a chief executive. Presidencies of this kind constitute the basis of *presidential government and conform to the principles of the *separation of powers.

Significance

US-style presidential government has spawned imitations throughout the world, mainly in Latin America and, more recently, in post-communist states such as Poland, the Czech Republic and Russia. In investing executive *power in a presidency, the architects of the

US constitution were aware that they were, in effect, creating an 'elective kingship'. The president was invested with an impressive range of powers, including those of head of state, chief executive, commander-in-chief of the armed forces and chief diplomat, and was granted wide-ranging powers of patronage and the right to veto legislation. However, the modern presidency, in the USA and elsewhere, has been shaped by wider political developments as well as by formal constitutional rules. The most important of these developments have been growing government intervention in economic and social life, an increasingly interdependent or globalised international order, and the rise of the *mass media, particularly television, as political institutions. Within the constraints of their political system, presidents have therefore become deliverers of national prosperity, world statesmen and national celebrities. By the 1970s this led to alarm, in the USA in particular, about the emergence of an 'imperial presidency', a presidency capable of emancipating itself from its traditional constitutional constraints. However, subsequent setbacks for presidents such as Nixon and Carter in the USA re-emphasised the enduring truth of Neustadt's (1980) classic formulation of presidential power as the 'power to persuade', that is, the ability to bargain, encourage and even cajole, but not dictate. Although presidents appear to be more powerful than prime ministers, this is often an illusion. Combining state and governmental *leadership in a single office perhaps so raises political expectations that it may make failure inevitable, and it should not disguise the fact that, unlike prime ministers, presidents do not wield direct legislative power.

Presidentialism has a number of clear advantages. Chief amongst these is that it makes personal leadership possible. *Politics becomes more intelligible and engaging precisely because it takes a personal form: the public associates more readily with a person than it does with a political institution, such as a cabinet or *political party. Linked to this is the capacity of a president to become a national figurehead, a symbol of the nation embodying both ceremonial and political *authority. Presidents may thus have particularly pronounced mobilising capacities, especially important in times of economic crisis and war. Finally, concentrating executive power in a single office ensures clarity and coherence, as opposed to the unsatisfactory and perhaps unprincipled compromises that are the stuff of collective cabinet government. On the other hand, presidentialism has its dangers. One of the most obvious of these is that personalising politics risks devaluing it. Elections, for instance, may turn into mere beauty contests and place greater emphasis upon image and personal trivia than upon ideas and policies. The other drawback of presidentialism is that it is based upon a perhaps outdated notion of leadership, in that it implies that complex and pluralistic modern societies can be represented and mobilised through a single individual. If politics is ultimately about conciliation and bargaining, this may be better facilitated through a system of collective leadership rather than personal leadership.

Pressure Group

A pressure group or interest group (the terms are often but not always used interchangeably) is an organised association which aims to influence the policies or actions of *government. Pressure groups differ from *political parties in that they seek to exert influence from outside, rather than to win or exercise government *power. Further, pressure groups typically have a narrow issue focus, in that they are usually concerned with a specific cause or the interests of a particular group, and seldom have the broader programmatic or ideological features that are generally associated with political parties. Pressure groups are distinguished from *social movements both by their greater degree of formal organisation and by their methods of operation. Pressure groups that operate at the international level (particularly in relation to development and environmental issues) have increasingly been accorded formal recognition as non-governmental organisations (NGOs). Nevertheless, not all pressure groups have members in the formal sense; hence the preference of some commentators for the looser term 'organised interests'.

Pressure groups appear in a variety of shapes and sizes. The two most common classifications of pressure groups are between sectional and promotional groups, and between 'insider' and 'outsider' groups. *Sectional groups* (sometimes called protective, functional or interest groups) exist to advance or protect the (usually material) interests of their members. The 'sectional' character of such groups derives from the fact that they represent a section of society: workers, employers, consumers, an ethnic or religious group, and so on. In the USA, sectional groups are often classified as 'private interest groups', to stress that their principal concern is the betterment and well-being of their members, not of society in general. *Promotional groups* (sometimes termed cause or attitude groups) are set up to advance shared values, ideals and principles. In the USA, promotional groups are dubbed 'public interest groups', to emphasise that they promote collective, rather than selective benefits; they aim to help groups other than their own members. Nevertheless, many pressure groups straddle the sectional/promotional divide, in that they both represent their members' interests and are concerned with ideals and broader causes. Trade unions, for instance, often address the issue of social *justice as well as matters such as wages, conditions and job security.

Alternatively, pressure groups can be classified on the basis of their relationship to government. *Insider groups* enjoy privileged and usually institutionalised access to government through routine consultation and representation on government bodies. Such groups either tend to represent key economic interests or to possess specialist knowledge and information necessary to government in the process of *policy formulation. *Outsider groups*, on the other hand, are either not consulted by government or consulted only irregularly, and not usually at a senior level. Lacking formal access to government, these groups are forced to 'go public' in the hope of exercising indirect influence on the policy process via media and public campaigns.

Significance

Pressure groups are found only in liberal-democratic political systems, in which the *rights of political association and freedom of expression are respected. However, the role pressure groups play and the importance they exert varies considerably. Amongst the factors that enhance group influence are a *political culture that recognises them as legitimate actors and encourages membership and participation, a fragmented and decentralised institutional structure that gives groups various points of access to the policy process, a party system that facilitates links between major parties and organised interests, and an interventionist style of public policy that requires that the government consults and cooperates with key interests, often through the emergence of *corporatism.

The most positive perspective on group politics is offered by pluralist theories. These not only see organised groups as the fundamental building blocks of the political process, but also portray them as a vital guarantee of liberty and *democracy. Arguments in favour of pressure groups include the idea that they strengthen *representation by articulating interests and advancing views ignored by political parties; that they promote debate and discussion and thus create a more informed electorate; that they broaden the scope of political participation; that they check government *power and maintain a vigorous and healthy *civil society; and that they promote political stability by providing a channel of communication between government and the people. A more critical view of pressure groups is advanced by corporatist, *New Right and Marxist theorists. Corporatism highlights the privileged position that certain groups enjoy in relation to government and portrays pressure groups as hierarchically ordered and dominated by leaders who are not directly accountable to members. The New Right draws attention to the threat that groups pose in terms of over-government and economic inefficiency. Marxists argue that group politics systematically advantages business and financial interests that control the crucial employment and investment decisions in a capitalist society, and that the *state is biased in favour of such interests through its role in upholding the capitalist system which they dominate.

PRIME MINISTER

A prime minister (sometimes referred to as a chancellor, as in Germany, a minister-president, as in the Netherlands, or called by a local title such as the Irish Taoiseach) is a head of government whose *power derives from his or her *leadership of the majority party, or coalition of parties, in the *parliament or assembly. Prime ministers are formal chief executives or heads of government, but their position differs from that of a *president in a number of respects. First, prime ministers work within *parliamentary systems of government, or semi-presidential ones, and therefore govern in and through the parliament and are not encumbered by a constitutional *separation of powers. Second, prime ministers usually operate within a formal system of cabinet government, meaning that, in theory at least, executive authority is shared collectively within the *cabinet. Third, prime ministers are invested with more modest constitutional powers than presidents, and are therefore typically more reliant upon the exercise of informal powers, especially those linked to their role as party leaders. Fourth, because prime ministers are parliamentary officers they are not heads of state, the latter post generally being held by a non-executive president or a constitutional monarch.

Significance

As the job of prime minister can only have a loose constitutional description, there is some truth in the old adage that the post is what its holder chooses to make of it, or, more accurately, is able to make of it. In practice, prime-ministerial power is based upon the use made of two sets of relationships. The first set are with the cabinet, individual ministers and the government departments; the second with his or her party and, through it, the parliament and the public. The support of the cabinet is particularly crucial to prime ministers who operate within a system of collective cabinet government. In these cases their power is a reflection of the degree to which, by patronage, cabinet management and the control of the machinery of government, they can ensure that ministers serve 'under' them. Nevertheless, there is no doubt that the cornerstone of prime-ministerial power lies in his or her position as party leader. Indeed, the modern premiership is largely a product of the emergence of disciplined political parties. Not only is the post of prime minister allocated on the basis of party leadership, but it also provides its holder with a means of controlling the parliament and a base from which the image of national leader can be constructed. The degree of party unity, the parliamentary strength of the prime minister's party (in particular, whether it rules alone or is a member of a *coalition), and the *authority vested in the parliament or at least its first chamber, are therefore the key determinants of prime-ministerial power.

Most commentators agree that prime ministers have steadily become more significant political actors. This results in part from the tendency of the broadcast media in particular to focus upon personalities, meaning that prime ministers become a kind of 'brand image' of their parties. The growth of international summitry and foreign visits has also provided prime ministers with opportunities to cultivate their statesmanship, and given them scope to portray themselves as national leaders. In some cases this has led to the allegation that prime ministers have effectively emancipated themselves from cabinet constraints and established a form of prime-ministerial government. Prime-ministerial government has two key features. First, by controlling the parliament as well as the bureaucratic machine, the prime minister is the central link between the legislative and executive branches of government. Second, executive power is concentrated in the prime minister's hands through the effective subordination of the cabinet and departmental ministers.

Such developments have led to the phenomenon of 'creeping presidentialism', in that prime ministers, under media and other pressures, have increasingly distanced themselves from their parties, cabinets and governments by cultivating a personal appeal based upon their ability to articulate their own political and ideological vision. Nevertheless, although prime ministers who command cohesive parliamentary majorities and are supported by unified cabinets wield greater power than many a president, their power is always fragile because it can be exercised only in favourable political circumstances. Ultimately, prime ministers are vehicles through which parties win and retain power; prime ministers who fail in these tasks, or become unmindful of the role, rarely survive long.

RACE/ETHNICITY

Race refers to physical or genetic differences amongst humankind that supposedly distinguish one group of people from another on biological grounds such as skin and hair colour, physique and facial features. A race is thus a group of people who share a common ancestry and 'one blood'. The term is, however, controversial both scientifically and politically. Scientific evidence suggests that there is no such thing as 'race' in the sense of a species-type difference between peoples. Politically, racial categorisation is commonly based upon cultural stereotypes, and is simplistic at best and pernicious at worst. The term ethnicity is therefore sometimes preferred.

Ethnicity is the sentiment of loyalty towards a distinctive population, cultural group or territorial area. The term is complex because it has both cultural and racial overtones. The members of ethnic groups are often seen, correctly or incorrectly, to have descended from common ancestors, and the groups are thus thought of as extended kinship groups. More commonly, ethnicity is understood as a form of cultural identity, albeit one that operates at a deep and emotional level. An 'ethnic' culture encompasses values, traditions and practices but, crucially, also gives a people a common identity and sense of distinctiveness, usually by focusing upon their origins and descent.

Significance

The link between race and *politics was first established by the European *racialism of the nineteenth century. This preached doctrines of racial superiority/inferiority and racial segregation, in the twentieth century mixing with *fascism to produce *Nazism, and helping to fuel right-wing nationalist or anti-immigration movements. The central idea behind such movements is that only a racially or ethnically unified society can be cohesive and successful, multiculturalism and multiracialism always being sources of conflict and instability. Very different forms of racial or ethnic politics have developed out of the struggle against *colonialism in particular and as a result of racial discrimination and disadvantage in general. However, the conjunction of racial and social disadvantage has generated various styles of political activism.

These range from civil-rights movements, such as that led in the USA in the 1960s by Martin Luther King, to militant and revolutionary movements, such as the Black Power movement and the Black Moslems (now the Nation of Islam) in the USA, and the struggle of the African National Congress (ANC) against apartheid in South Africa up to 1994. Ethnic politics, however, has become a more generalised phenomenon in the post-1945 period, associated with forms of *nationalism that are based upon ethnic consciousness and regional identity. This has been evident in the strengthening of centrifugal tendencies in *states such as the UK, Belgium and Italy, and has been manifest in the rise of particularist nationalism. In the former USSR, Czechoslovakia and Yugoslavia, it led to state collapse and the creation of a series of new *nation-states. The two main forces fuelling such developments are uneven patterns of social development in so-called 'core' and 'peripheral' parts of the world, and the weakening of forms of 'civic' nationalism resulting from the impact of *globalisation.

REFERENDUM

A referendum is a vote in which the electorate can express a view on a particular issue of public *policy. It differs from an *election in that the latter is essentially a means of filling a public office and does not provide a direct or reliable method of influencing the content of policy. The referendum is therefore a device of direct *democracy. However, it is typically used not to replace representative institutions, but to supplement them. Referendums may either be advisory or binding; they may also raise issues for discussion, or be used to decide or confirm policy questions (propositions or plebiscites). Whereas most referendums are called by the government, initiatives (used especially in Switzerland and California) are placed on the ballot through some form of popular petition.

Significance

The use of the referendum can be traced back to sixteenth-century Switzerland. However, referendums have always had a dual character. On the one hand, they are a form of popular government in that they give expression to 'bottom-up' pressures within the political system. On the other hand, they have been used as 'top-down' instruments of political control. This was clearest in the case of Hitler and other 1930s dictators, who used plebiscites as a means of legitimising *dictatorship, but it has also applied to democratic politicians who wish to neutralise opposition within representative institutions.

The wider use of referendums is supported for a number of reasons, including the following:

- they strengthen democracy by allowing the public to speak for themselves rather than through the inevitably distorted views of their representatives;
- they check the *power of elected governments, keeping them in line with public opinion between elections;
- they promote political participation, thus helping to create a more engaged and better-educated and -informed electorate;
- unlike elections they provide the public with a way of expressing their views about specific issues;
- they provide a means of settling major constitutional questions.

On the other hand, referendums have been associated with the following disadvantages and dangers:

- they place political decisions in the hands of those who have least education and experience, and are most susceptible to media and other influences;

- they provide, at best, only a snapshot of public opinion at one point in time;
- they allow politicians to absolve themselves of *responsibility for making difficult decisions;
- they enable leaders to manipulate the political agenda (especially when governments call referendums and can use public resources and their publicity machine to back their preferred outcome);
- they tend to simplify and distort political issues, reducing them to questions that have a simple yes/no answer.

SEPARATION OF POWERS

The separation of powers is a doctrine that proposes that the three chief functions of *government (legislation, execution and adjudication) should be entrusted to separate branches of government (the legislature, the *executive and the *judiciary, respectively). In its formal sense the separation of powers demands independence, in that there should be no overlap of personnel between the branches. However, it also implies interdependence, in the form of shared powers to ensure that there are checks and balances. The

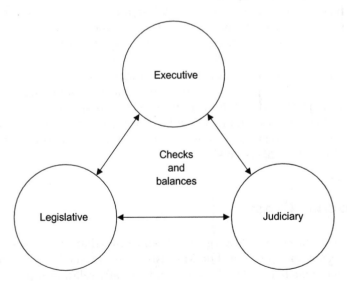

Figure 7.1 Separation of power

separation of powers is applied most strictly in *presidential systems of government, as in the USA, where it is the basis of the *constitution, but the principle is respected in some form in all *liberal democracies, notably in the principle of judicial independence. A full separation of powers requires the existence of a written constitution to define the formal powers and responsibilities of each of the branches of government.

Significance

The principle of the separation of power can be found in the writings of Locke (1632–1704) but was more fully elaborated by Montesquieu (1689–1775). The separation of powers is one of the classic means of fragmenting government *power in order to defend liberty and keep tyranny at bay. An important feature of liberal *constitutionalism, its advantages are that it both cuts the power of any branch of government down to size and establishes a network of internal tensions that ensure that the exercise of power is never unchecked. This is evident in Richard Neustadt's (1980) description of the US system as 'separated institutions sharing powers'. However, few liberal democracies operate on the basis of a strict separation of powers. Its major drawback is that it offers an 'invitation to struggle' to the executive and legislative branches of government. It may therefore be nothing more than a recipe for institutional conflict, or 'government gridlock'. From this point of view it is a device which may suit only large and highly differentiated societies such as the USA, in which political stability requires that competing groups and interests have a wide variety of access points to government. Elsewhere, institutionalised links have been forged between the legislature and executive through *parliamentary systems or hybrid semi-presidential systems.

SOCIAL CLASS

A social class is, broadly, a group of people who share a similar social and economic position. For Marxists, class is linked to economic power, which is defined by the individual's relationship to the means of production. From this perspective, class divisions are divisions between capital and labour, that is, between the owners of productive wealth (the bourgeoisie) and those who live off the sale of their labour power (the proletariat). Non-Marxist definitions of class are usually based upon income and status differences between occupational groups. The most common notion of occupational class distinguishes between 'middle' class, white-collar (or non-manual) workers and 'working' class, blue-collar (or manual) workers. A more sophisticated marketing-based distinction, used, with variations, by sociologists and political scientists, is made between higher professionals (class A), professionals (B), clerical workers (C1), skilled manual workers (C2), semi-skilled and unskilled workers (D), and those who are unemployed, unavailable for work or unable to work (E).

Significance

The leading proponents of the theory of class politics have been Marxists. Marxists regard social class as the most fundamental, and politically the most significant, social division. In Marx's (1818–83) view, classes are the key actors on the political stage, and they have the ability to make history. The proletariat was destined to be the 'grave digger' of *capitalism. It would fulfil this destiny once it had achieved 'class consciousness' and became aware of its genuine class interests, thus recognising the fact of its own exploitation. The proletariat would therefore be transformed from a 'class in-itself' (an economically defined category) to a 'class for-itself' (a revolutionary force). This, Marx believed, would be a consequence of the deepening crisis of capitalism and the declining material conditions, or immiseration, of the working class. The Marxist two-class model has, however, been discredited by the failure of Marx's predictions to materialise, and by declining evidence of class struggle, at least in advanced capitalist societies. Modern Marxists have attempted to refine the crude two-class model, while still emphasising the importance of wealth ownership, accepting, for instance, that an 'intermediate' class of managers and technicians has emerged, and that there are internal divisions within both the bourgeoisie and the proletariat.

The decline in class politics is usually linked to the emergence of a post-industrial society, a society no longer dependent upon manufacturing industry, but more reliant upon knowledge and communication. The solidaristic class culture that was rooted in clear political loyalties and, usually, strong union organisation has thus been displaced by more individualistic and instrumentalist attitudes. For some this is reflected in a transition from a 'Fordist' to a 'post-Fordist' era, from a system of mass production and mass consumption to one characterised by social and political fragmentation. One aspect of this has been the phenomenon of class de-alignment, the weakening of the relationship between social class and party support, evident in the UK, the USA and elsewhere since the 1970s. Another aspect is growing political interest in the so-called 'underclass', those who suffer from multiple deprivation (unemployment or low pay, poor housing, inadequate education and so on) and are socially marginalised – 'the excluded'. However, whereas left-wing commentators define the underclass in terms of structural disadvantage and the changing balance of the global economy, right-wing commentators tend to explain the emergence of the underclass largely in terms of welfare dependency and personal inadequacy.

Social Movement

A social movement is a particular form of collective behaviour in which the motive to act springs largely from the attitudes and aspirations of members, typically acting within a loose organisational framework. Being part of a social movement requires a level of commitment and political activism, rather than formal or card-carrying membership; above all, movements move. A movement is different from spontaneous mass action (such as an uprising or rebellion) in that it implies a measure of intended or planned action in pursuit of a recognised social goal. Not uncommonly, social movements embrace *pressure groups and may even spawn *political parties; trade unions and socialist parties, for instance, can be seen as part of a broader labour movement. So-called *new social movements* – the women's movement, the ecological or green movement, the peace movement, and so on – differ from more traditional social movements in three respects. First, they typically attract support from the young, the better-educated and the relatively affluent, rather than the oppressed or disadvantaged. Second, they usually have a post-material orientation, being more concerned with 'quality of life' issues than with material advancement. Third, while traditional movements had little in common and seldom worked in tandem, new social movements subscribe to a common, if not always clearly defined, set of *New Left values and beliefs.

Significance

Social movements can be traced back to the early nineteenth century. The earliest were the labour movement, which campaigned for improved conditions for the growing working class, various nationalist movements, usually struggling for independence from multinational European empires, and, in central Europe in particular, a Catholic movement that fought for emancipation through the granting of legal and political rights to Catholics. In the twentieth century it was also common for fascist and right-wing authoritarian groups to be seen as movements rather than as conventional political parties. However, the experience of *totalitarianism in the interwar period encouraged mass society theorists such as Erich Fromm (1900–80) and Hannah Arendt (1906–75) to see movements in distinctly negative terms. From the mass society perspective, social movements reflect a 'flight from freedom', an attempt by alienated individuals to achieve security and identity through fanatical commitment to a cause, and obedience to a (usually fascist) leader.

In contrast, new social movements are generally interpreted as rational and instrumental actors, whose use of informal and unconventional means merely reflects the resources available to them. The emergence of new social movements is widely seen as evidence of the fact that *power in postindustrial societies is increasingly dispersed and fragmented. The class politics of old has thus been replaced by a 'new politics', which turns away from 'established' parties, pressure groups and representative processes towards a more innovative and theatrical form of protest politics. Not only do new movements offer new and rival centres of power, but they also diffuse power more effectively by resisting bureaucratisation and developing more spontaneous, effective and decentralised forms of organisation. Nevertheless, although the impact of movements such as the women's movement and the gay and lesbian movement cannot be doubted, it is difficult to assess in practical terms because of the broad nature of their goals and the less tangible character of the cultural strategies they tend to adopt.

FURTHER READING

Baggott, R., *Pressure Groups Today* (Manchester and New York: Manchester University Press, 1995).

Ball, A. and Millward, F., *Pressure Politics in Industrial Societies* (London: Macmillan, 1986).

Blau, P. and Meyer, M. (eds), *Bureaucracy in Modern Society* (New York: Random House, 1987).

Bogdanor, V. (ed.), *Constitutions in Democratic Politics* (Aldershot: Gower, 1988).

Elgie, R., *Political Leadership in Liberal Democracies* (London: Macmillan, 1995).

Gibbins, J. (ed.), *Contemporary Political Culture: Politics in a Post-Modern Age* (London: Sage, 1989).

Graham, B. D., *Representation and Party Politics: A Comparative Perspective* (Oxford: Blackwell, 1993).

Hague, R., Harrop, M. and Breslin, S., *Comparative Government and Politics: An Introduction* (London: Macmillan, 1992).

Hennessy, P., *Cabinet* (Oxford: Blackwell, 1986).

Laclau, E. and Mouffe, C., *Hegemony and Socialist Strategy* (London: Verso, 1985).

LeDuc, L., Niemi, R. and Norris, P. (eds), *Comparing Democracies: Elections and Voting in Global Perspective* (London: Sage, 1996).

Lijphart, A. (ed.), *Parliamentary versus Presidential Government* (Oxford: Oxford University Press, 1992).

McDowell, L. and Pringle, R. (eds), *Defining Women: Social Institutions and Gender Divisions* (Cambridge: Polity Press, 1992).

Nairn, T., *The Enchanted Glass: Britain and its Monarchy* (London: Picador, 1988).

Negrine, R., *The Communication of Politics* (London: Sage, 1996).

Norton, P. (ed.), *Legislatures* (Oxford: Oxford University Press, 1990).

Norton, P. (ed.), *Parliaments in Western Europe* (London: Frank Cass, 1990).

Pakulski, J., *Social Movements: The Politics of Protest* (Melbourne: Longman, 1990).

Rex, J. and Mason, D. (eds), *Theories of Race and Ethnic Relations* (Cambridge: Cambridge University Press, 1992).

Rose, R., *The Postmodern Presidency: The White House Meets the World* (New York: Chartham House, 1991).

Rose, R. and Suleiman, E. N. (eds), *Presidents and Prime Ministers* (Washington, DC: American Enterprise Institute, 1980).

Sartori, G., *Parties and Party Sytems: A Framework for Analysis* (Cambridge: Cambridge University Press, 1976).

Saunders, P., *Social Class Stratification* (London: Routledge, 1990).

Thompson, G., Frances, J., Levacic, R. and Mitchell, J., *Markets, Hierarchies and Networks: The Coordination of Social Life* (London: Sage, 1991).

Waltman, J. and Holland, K. (eds), *The Political Role of Law Courts in Modern Democracies* (New York: St Martin's Press, 1988).

Weller, P., *First Among Equals: Prime Ministers in Westminster Systems* (Sydney: Allen & Unwin, 1985).

Part eight

LEVELS

This section examines concepts that relate to the territorial organisation of political power and the different levels at which government authority is, or should be, exercised.

LEVELS

CENTRALISATION/DECENTRALISATION

Centralisation is the concentration of political *power or govern-ment *authority within central institutions. These institutions are normally considered to be central because they operate at the national level; however, the term centralisation is sometimes used to describe the concentration of power or authority within the national level of government, as, for instance, when *executives dominate legislatures or *parliaments, or when *cabinets are sub-ordinate to chief executives. Decentralisation is usually understood to refer to the expansion of local *autonomy through the transfer of powers and responsibilities away from national bodies. Centralisa-tion and decentralisation thus highlight different territorial divi-sions of power within the *state between central (national) and peripheral (regional, provincial or local) institutions.

Significance

All modern states contain territorial divisions. The nature of these divisions nevertheless varies enormously. The divisions are structured by the constitutional framework within which centre–periphery relationships are conducted; the distribution of functions and responsibilities between the levels of *government; the means by which their personnel are appointed and recruited; the political, economic, administrative and other powers the centre can use to control the periphery; and the independence that peripheral bodies enjoy. What is clear, however, is that neither central nor per-ipheral bodies can be dispensed with altogether. In the absence of central government a state would not be able to function as an actor on the international or world stage.

The case for centralisation is that:

- central government alone articulates the interests of the whole rather than its various parts, that is, the interests of the *nation rather than those of sectional, ethnic or regional groups;
- only central government can establish uniform *laws and public services which help people to move easily from one part of the country to another;
- central government is able to rectify inequalities that arise from the fact that the areas with the greatest social needs are invariably those with the least potential for raising revenue to meet them;
- economic development and centralisation invariably go hand-in-hand; only central government, for instance, can manage a single currency, control tax and spending policies with a view to ensuring sustainable growth, and provide an economic infrastructure.

The case for decentralisation includes the following:

- local or regional government is more effective than central government in providing opportunities for citizens to participate in the political life of their community, thus creating a better-educated and a more informed citizenry
- peripheral institutions are usually 'closer' to the people and are more sensitive to their needs;
- decisions made at a local level are more likely to be seen as intelligible and therefore legitimate, whereas central government may appear to be remote, both geographically and politically;
- decentralisation protects *freedom by dispersing government power and creating a network of checks and balances; peripheral bodies check central government as well as each other.

DEVOLUTION

Devolution is the transfer of power from central government to subordinate regional institutions (to 'devolve' means to pass powers or duties down from a higher authority to a lower one). Devolved bodies thus constitute an intermediate level of *government between central and local government. Devolution differs from *federalism in that, although their territorial jurisdiction may be similar, devolved bodies have no share in *sovereignty; their responsibilities and powers are devolved from, and are conferred by, the centre. In its weakest form, that of *administrative devolution*, devolution implies only that regional institutions implement policies decided elsewhere. In the form of *legislative devolution* (sometimes called 'home rule'), devolution involves the establishment of elected regional assemblies invested with policy-making responsibilities and, usually, a measure of fiscal independence.

Significance

Devolution, at least in its legislative form, establishes the greatest possible measure of *decentralisation within a unitary system of government; that is, one in which sovereign power is vested in a single, national institution. Devolved assemblies have usually been created in response to increasing centrifugal tensions within a *state, and as an attempt, in particular, to conciliate growing regional and sometimes nationalist pressures. Spain and France both adopted forms of devolved government in the 1970s and 1980s, and, in the UK, the Scottish Parliament, the Welsh Assembly and the Northern Ireland Assembly assumed their powers in 1999. Despite their lack of entrenched powers, once devolved institutions have acquired a political identity of their own, and possess a measure of democratic *legitimacy, they are very difficult to weaken and, in normal circumstances, impossible to abolish. Northern Ireland's Stormont Parliament was suspended in 1972, but only when it became apparent that its domination by the predominantly Protestant Unionist parties prevented it from stemming the rising tide of communal violence in the province. The newly created Northern Ireland Assembly was also temporarily suspended in early 2000.

The central issue in evaluating devolution is its impact upon the integrity of the state and the strength of centrifugal pressures. Its supporters argue that devolution satisfies the desire of regional or ethnic groups or constituent nations for a distinctive political identity whilst (unlike federalism) upholding the larger unity of the state by maintaining a single source of sovereignty. Critics, however, warn that devolution may fuel centrifugal pressures by strengthening regional, ethnic and national identities, leading to federalism or even state breakdown. What is clear is that devolution is a process and not an event, in the sense that it sets in train a re-working of political identities and relationships whose ultimate shape may not emerge for several years or maybe generations. A further factor is the potential for institutionalised conflict between national government and devolved bodies. Although the constitutional supremacy of the centre ultimately enables it to resolve disputes in its favour, the fact that devolved bodies may exercise significant legislative and fiscal powers and enjoy political entrenchment through their democratic legitimacy means that the system as a whole may acquire a quasi-federal character, requiring the development of linking institutions to foster cooperation between the two levels.

FEDERALISM

Federalism (from the Latin *foedus*, meaning 'pact', or 'covenant') usually refers to the legal and political structures that distribute power territorially within a *state. Nevertheless, in accordance with its original meaning, it has been taken to imply reciprocity or mutuality (as in the anarchist ideas of Pierre-Joseph Proudhon (1809–65)) or, in the writings of Alexander Hamilton (1755–1805) and James Madison (1751–1836), to be part of a broader *ideology of *pluralism. As a political form, however, federalism requires the existence of two distinct levels of government, neither of which is legally or politically subordinate to the other. Its central feature is therefore the notion of shared *sovereignty. On the basis of this definition, 'classical' federations are few in number: the USA, Switzerland, Belgium, Canada and Australia. However, many more states have federal-type features. Federalism differs from *devolution in that devolved bodies have no share in sovereignty, and it differs from confederations in that the latter are qualified unions of states in which each state retains its independence, which is typically guaranteed by the requirement of unanimous decision-making.

There are differences within federalism, between federal states that operate a *separation of powers between the executive and legislative branches of government (typified by the US *presidential system), and *parliamentary systems in which executive and legislative power is 'fused'. The former tend to ensure that government power is diffused both territorially and functionally, meaning that there are multiple points of contact between the two levels of government. Parliamentary systems, however, often produce what is called *executive federalism* (notably in Canada and Australia) in which the federal balance is largely determined by the relationship between the executives of each level of government. In states such as Germany and Austria so-called *administrative federalism* operates in which central government is the key policy-maker and provincial government is charged with the responsibility for the details of policy implementation.

Nevertheless, certain features are common to most, if not all, federal systems:

- both central government (the federal level) and regional government (the state level) possess a range of powers which the other cannot encroach upon; these include at least a measure of legislative and executive authority and the capacity to raise revenue and thus enjoy a degree of fiscal independence;
- the responsibilities and powers of each level of government are defined in a codified or written *constitution, meaning that the relationship between the centre and the periphery is conducted within a formal legal framework that neither level can alter unilaterally;
- the formal provisions of the constitution are interpreted by a supreme court, which thereby arbitrates in the case of disputes between the federal and state levels of government;
- linking institutions foster cooperation and understanding between federal and state levels of government, giving the regions and provinces a voice in the processes of central policy-making (this is usually achieved through the second chamber of the bicameral national legislature).

Significance

It is widely argued that the federal principle is more applicable to some states than to others. In the first place, federations have often been formed by the coming together of a number of established political communities which nevertheless wish to preserve their separate identities and, to some extent, their *autonomy. This clearly applies in the case of the world's first federal state, the USA, which was formed by former colonies that each possessed a distinctive political identity but jointly recognised their need for a new, more centralised, constitutional framework. A second factor influencing the formation of federations is the existence of an external threat or a desire to play a more effective role in international affairs. Small, strategically vulnerable states, for instance, have a powerful incentive to enter broader political unions. The drift towards the construction of a 'federal Europe' was thus, in part, brought about by a fear of Soviet aggression and by a perceived loss of European influence in the emerging bipolar world order. A third factor is geographical size. It is no coincidence that many of the territorially larger states in the world – USA, Canada, Brazil, Australia, Mexico and India – have opted to introduce federal systems. The final factor encouraging the adoption of federalism is cultural and ethnic heterogeneity. Federalism, in short, has often been seen as an institutional response to societal divisions and diversity.

One of the chief strengths of federal systems is that, unlike unitary systems in which sovereignty is concentrated in a single, central body, they give regional and local interests a constitutionally guaranteed political voice. The states and provinces exercise a range of autonomous powers and enjoy some measure of representation in central government, usually, as pointed out above, through the second chamber of the federal legislature. The second advantage of federalism is that, in diffusing government power, it creates a network of checks and balances that help to protect individual liberty. Third, federalism has provided an institutional mechanism through which fractured societies maintain unity and coherence. In this respect the federal solution may be appropriate only to a limited number of ethnically diverse and regionally divided societies; but in these cases it may be absolutely vital.

On the other hand, federalism has not been able to stem the general twentieth-century tendency towards *centralisation. Since the mid-1960s, for instance, the US system has been described as one of 'coercive federalism', in that the federal government has increasingly brought about the compliance of the states by passing laws that pre-empt their powers, and imposing restrictions on the states and localities in the form of mandates. Moreover, structures intended to create healthy tension within a system of government may also generate frustration and paralysis. One of the weaknesses of federal systems is that, by constraining central authority, they make the imposition of bold economic or social programmes more difficult. Finally, federalism may breed governmental division and strengthen centrifugal pressures within the state. Some have argued, as a result, that federal systems are inherently unstable, tending either towards the guaranteed unity which only a unitary system can offer, or towards greater *decentralisation and ultimate collapse.

GLOBALISATION

Globalisation is the emergence of a complex web of interconnectedness that means that our lives are increasingly shaped by events that occur, and decisions that are made, at a great distance from us. The central feature of globalisation is therefore that geographical distance is of declining relevance and that territorial boundaries, such as those between *nation-states, are becoming less significant. By no means, however, does globalisation imply that 'the local' and 'the national' are subordinate to 'the global'. Rather, it highlights the deepening as well as the broadening of the political process, in the sense that local, national and global events (or perhaps local, regional, national, international and global events) constantly interact, as indicated in Figure 8.1. *Economic globalisation* refers to the integration of national economies into a larger global economy, reflected in the growing importance of international trade and capital movement and the prominence of transnational corporations, sometimes portrayed as 'Macdonaldisation'.

Significance

The term globalisation is used to draw attention to a set of complex and multi-faceted changes that started to take place in the second half of the twentieth century. In the first place, global interdependence was one of the results of the superpower rivalry that characterised the Cold War period. The capabilities and resources of the post-1945 superpowers (the USA and the USSR) were so overwhelming that they were able to extend their influence into virtually

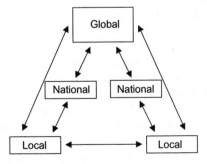

Figure 8.1   Global interdependencies

every region of the world. Second, the spread of international trade and the transnational character of modern business organisations brought a global economy into existence. In particular, the collapse of *communism gave impetus to the emergence of a global capitalist system. Third, globalisation has been fuelled by technological innovation. This has affected almost every realm of existence, ranging from the development of nuclear weapons and the emergence of global pollution problems such as acid rain and ozone depletion to the introduction of international telephone links, satellite television and the internet. Fourth, globalisation has an important politico-ideological dimension. One aspect of this has been the spread of Western liberal political values, sometimes portrayed as the worldwide triumph of *liberal democracy, but it is also linked to the growth of Islam as a transnational political creed and to burgeoning interest in green ideas and philosophies.

Much of the debate about globalisation focuses upon its impact upon the *state and its implication for national politics. Some have argued that globalisation implies the 'death of politics' and the irrelevance of the state. If national economies have effectively been absorbed into a larger global economy, and if information and cultural exchanges are now routinely transnational, national *government is perhaps an anachronism, even though effective supranational bodies have yet to emerge. The alternative interpretation is not that the state has become irrelevant but that its functions have changed. In this view, economic globalisation has fostered the emergence of 'competition states', states whose role is primarily to develop strategies for national prosperity in a context of intensifying transnational competition. Globalisation is also significant because it has unleashed countervailing forces, in the form of ethnic politics and particularist *nationalism. In an increasingly globalised world, *ethnicity may replace nationality as the principal source of social integration, its virtue being that, whereas *nations are bound together by 'civic' loyalties, ethnic and regional groups are able to generate a deeper sense of 'organic' identity.

Finally, there is debate about whether globalisation should be embraced or resisted. Its supporters highlight the prospect of rising prosperity and technological advance; its opponents warn against the spread of capitalist values, the deepening of inequality and loss of identity. Some, indeed, suggest that globalisation is largely a myth, exaggerated by politicians who wish to portray market-driven shifts in economic policy as necessary or inevitable.

IMPERIALISM

Imperialism is the policy of extending the *power or rule of a *state beyond its boundaries. In its earliest usage, imperialism was an *ideology that supported military expansion and imperial acquisition, usually by drawing upon nationalist or racialist doctrines. The term is now more commonly used to describe the system of political domination or economic exploitation that the pursuit of such goals helps to establish. The key feature of imperialism is therefore the asymmetrical relationship between the imperial power and its client territory or peoples. A distinction is often drawn between imperialism and colonialism. Some treat colonialism as a distinctive form of imperialism, in that colonies are territorially ruled directly by the imperial power whereas empires may allow client rulers to continue in power and enjoy significant discretion; others point out that imperial territories may be inhabited by members of the same ethnic group whereas the inhabitants of colonies are typically ethnically distinct from their colonial rulers; and others emphasise that colonies have been settled or 'colonised' and have not merely been subject to imperial conquest. What is called *neo-imperialism* or 'neo-colonialism' refers to the process through which industrially developed powers control foreign territory by economic or cultural domination while respecting the territory's formal political independence.

Significance

The phenomenon of imperialism has been ever-present in politics. Empires have, in fact, been the most common supranational bodies, ranging from the ancient empires of Egypt, China, Persia and Rome to the modern European empires of Britain, France, Portugal and the Netherlands. Although colonies continue to exist – for example, Tibet's subordination to China – the collapse of the USSR in 1991 brought to an end the last of the major empires, the Russian empire. Modern imperialism therefore usually takes the form of neo-colonialism and operates through structures of economic and cultural domination rather than overt political control. Debates about the merits of imperialism have also largely been abandoned. Nineteenth-century justifications for imperialism, in terms of the capacity of European colonisers to bring about moral and social development in Africa and Asia in particular, are now exposed as crass self-justification. Quite simply, the acceptance of modern ideas such as *democracy and national *sovereignty means that imperialism is universally condemned as a form of oppression or exploitation.

The major debates about imperialism centre upon its causes and the forms it takes. In the Marxist tradition, imperialism is seen as an economic phenomenon that typically results from the pressure to export capital. Lenin (1870–1924) was the principal exponent of this view, arguing that imperialism is the 'highest' (that is, the final) stage of capitalism. However, rival views suggest that imperialism is often fuelled by political rather than economic factors and is more commonly linked to popular *nationalism than to the desire for profit; that imperialism is not confined to capitalist states but has been practised by pre-capitalist as well as socialist ones; and that imperialism may prove to be an economic burden to imperial powers and not a boon, most commonly in the form of 'imperial overreach' (the tendency of expansionism to impose increases in military expenditure that outstrip the growth of the domestic economy). Debates about modern imperialism are dominated by the neo-Marxist emphasis upon the structure of global capitalism and the growing power of transnational corporations. In this view the global structure of production and exchange has divided the world into 'core' and 'peripheral' areas. Core areas in the industrialised North are technologically advanced and better integrated into the global economy, while peripheral areas, such as the less developed South, provide a source of cheap labour and are characterised by underdevelopment and a simple product mix.

INTERGOVERNMENTALISM

Intergovernmentalism is any form of interaction between *states which takes place on the basis of sovereign independence. Intergovernmentalism is therefore usually distinguished from *supranationalism, in which there is an authority that is 'higher' than that of the *nation-state. The most common form of intergovernmentalism is treaties or alliances, the simplest of which involve bilateral agreements between states. The intergovernmental aspect of treaties is embodied in the fact that they are voluntary agreements based upon the consent of all relevant parties. The other main form of intergovernmentalism is leagues or confederations, such as the League of Nations, the Organisation of Petroleum Exporting Countries (OPEC), the Organisation for Economic Cooperation and Development (OECD) and the Commonwealth of Nations. These are transnational or international organisations of states, in which *sovereignty is preserved through a process of unanimous decision-making that gives each state a veto, at least over matters of vital national importance.

Significance

Intergovernmentalism has been the most common form of international cooperation between states. Its growing significance in the twentieth century reflects both a recognition of the greater independence of states, which has spread from strategic and economic matters into political, social and cultural spheres of life, and the fact that intergovernmental bodies are easy to form. Treaties, alliances, leagues and confederations have the virtue that they allow states to work together and perhaps undertake concerted action but without sacrificing national independence. In cases such as OPEC's ability to regulate oil prices, particularly in the 1970s and 1980s, coordinated action through intergovernmental cooperation has been very effective.

However, the preservation of state sovereignty is also the central weakness of intergovernmentalism. In short, it restricts the scope of international cooperation to those areas where mutual trust exists and where national interests clearly coincide. International treaties, for instance, may be broken with impunity and, in cases such as arms control, they are very difficult to negotiate. Similarly, as member states retain their independence and are very reluctant to be bound by majority decisions, confederations have rarely been able to undertake united and effective action, sometimes being reduced to mere talking shops. This is why some confederations, such as the Confederation of Independent States (CIS), formed in 1991 by the former Soviet republics, have become entirely irrelevant, while others, such as the EEC, have gradually given way to supranational cooperation based upon the principle of *federalism.

INTERNATIONALISM

Internationalism is the theory or practice of politics based upon transnational or global cooperation. As a political ideal it is based upon the belief that political *nationalism should be transcended because the ties that bind the peoples of the world are stronger than those that separate them. The goal of internationalism is thus to construct political structures that can command the allegiance of all the peoples of the world, regardless of religious, racial, social and national differences. The major internationalist traditions are drawn from *liberalism and *socialism. *Liberal internationalism* is based upon individualism. This is reflected, for example, in the belief that universal *human rights ultimately have a 'higher' status than the sovereign authority of the *nation. *Socialist internationalism* is grounded in a belief in international class solidarity (proletarian internationalism), underpinned by assumptions about a common humanity. *Feminism, *racialism and *religious fundamentalism may be seen to support weak forms of internationalism, in that they highlight gender, racial and religious cleavages that cut across national boundaries.

Significance

The radical edge of internationalism is associated with its condemnation of nationalism as unnecessary and wrong. Internationalists deny the basic nationalist assertion that the nation is the sole legitimate unit of political rule, often arguing that nations are political constructs manufactured by rulers and elite groups to maintain social cohesion and political passivity. The moral force of internationalism is evident in its association with the ideas of global peace and cooperation. Such 'one-worldism' has, for example, provided the basis for the idealist tradition in international relations, which is characterised by a belief in universal morality. Immanuel Kant (1724–1804) is often seen as the father of this tradition, having envisaged a kind of 'league of nations' based upon the assertion that reason and morality combine to dictate that 'There should be no war.'

The weakness of internationalism is that it has generally underestimated the potency of nationalism and failed to establish international structures that can rival the nation's capacity to stimulate political allegiance. The dominant tradition in international relations has thus not been *idealism but *realism, which highlights the role of power politics and the *nation-state. Liberal internationalism has drawn particular criticism from conservatives and developing-world nationalists. The former allege that the idea of universal human rights simply fails to take account of distinctive national traditions and cultures, while the latter go further and argue that, as human rights are essentially a manifestation of Western liberalism, their spread amounts to a covert form of *imperialism. Socialist internationalism has been criticised on two grounds. The first is that the various Internationals that socialists have set up have either been mere talking shops or, in the case of the Communist International or Comintern, have been tools of Soviet imperialism. The second is that socialists have often overestimated the appeal of the internationalist ideal and have so missed the opportunity to link socialist goals and principles to national symbols and national culture.

LOCAL GOVERNMENT

Local government, in its simplest sense, is government that is specific to a particular locality, for example a village, district, town, city or county. More particularly it is a form of government that has no share in *sovereignty, and is thus entirely subordinate to central *authority or, in a federal system, to state or regional authority. Although the functions of and services provided by local authorities or councils vary from *state to state and over time, they usually include some responsibility for education, planning, refuse collection, local trade and perhaps transport, leisure and recreation, and personal social services. The term local government is sometimes used to refer to all political institutions whose authority or jurisdiction is confined to a territorial portion of a state. In this case three levels of local government can be identified: a basic level (district councils in England and Wales, municipalities or towns in the USA and communes in France); an intermediate level (counties in England and Wales and in the USA, and *départements* in France); a state or regional level (states in the USA, *Länder* in Germany and *régions* in France).

Significance

It would be a mistake to assume that the constitutional subordination of local government means that it is politically irrelevant. In the first place all political systems feature some form of local government. This reflects the fact that it is both administratively necessary – *centralisation ultimately involves unacceptable diseconomies of scale – and, because it is 'close' to the people, it is easily intelligible. Central–local relationships are usually conducted through some form of bargaining and negotiation rather than by diktat from above. The balance between central government and local government is affected by a number of factors. These include the following:

- whether local politicians are appointed or elected; the latter possess an independent power base and exercise a measure of democratic *legitimacy;
- the range and importance of locally provided services and the discretion available to local authorities;
- the number and size of local authorities and the structure of authority within them;
- local government's tax-raising powers and its degree of fiscal autonomy;
- the extent to which local politics is 'politicised', in the sense that national parties operate in and through local politics.

The defence of local government goes well beyond its capacity to provide a convenient, and perhaps indispensable, method of delivering public services. Following J. S. Mill (1806–73), local government has been praised both as a means of guaranteeing liberty by checking the exercise of central power and as a mechanism through which popular participation, and thus political education, can be broadened. This is to defend local government in terms of its capacity to deliver local democracy, a principle that combines the idea of local autonomy with the goal of popular responsiveness. From a more radical perspective, anarchists and council communists have favoured communes as a model of local self-government, on the grounds that they constitute 'human-scale' communities which allow people to manage their own affairs through face-to-face interaction, rather than through depersonalised and bureaucratic processes. On the other hand, local government has been criticised for entrenching a concern with parochial issues and local interests rather than matters of broader public importance; for promoting disunity and divisions within states; and for challenging the democratic legitimacy of national politicians.

NATION

Nations (from the Latin *nasci*, meaning 'to be born') are complex phenomena that are shaped by a collection of cultural, political and psychological factors. Culturally, a nation is a group of people bound together by a common language, religion, history and traditions. There is, however, no objective blueprint for the nation because all nations exhibit some degree of cultural heterogeneity. Politically, a nation is a group of people who regard themselves as a natural political community. Although this is classically expressed in the form of a desire to establish or maintain statehood, it also takes the form of civic consciousness. Psychologically, a nation is a group of people distinguished by a shared loyalty or affection in the form of *patriotism. Nevertheless, such an attachment is not a necessary condition for membership of a nation; even those who lack national pride may still recognise that they 'belong' to the nation.

However, such complexity has allowed quite different models of the nation to develop. Historians have sometimes distinguished between cultural nations and political nations. A *cultural nation* (such as the Greeks, the Germans, the Russians, the English and the Irish) has a national identity that is rooted in a common cultural heritage and language that may long pre-date the achievement of statehood or even the quest for national independence. A *political nation* (such as the British, the Americans and the South Africans) is bound together primarily by shared citizenship and may encompass significant cultural and ethnic divisions. Similarly, political thinkers may advance rival civic and organic views of the nation. The 'civic' concept of nationhood, supported, for instance, by liberals and socialists, is inclusive in the sense that it places heavier emphasis upon political allegiance than upon cultural unity, and stresses that the nation is forged by shared values and expectations. The 'organic' concept of nationhood (advanced by conservatives and, more radically, by fascists) is exclusive in that it gives priority to a common ethnic identity and, above all, a shared history. Inclusive concepts of the nation tend to blur the distinction between the nation and the *state, between nationality and *citizenship. Exclusive concepts of the nation tend to blur the distinction between the nation and the *race, between nationality and *ethnicity.

Significance

For over two hundred years the nation has been regarded as the most appropriate (and perhaps the only proper) unit of political rule. Indeed, international *law is largely based upon the assumption that nations, like individuals, have inviolable rights, notably the right to political independence and self-determination. The importance of the nation to *politics is most dramatically demonstrated by the enduring potency of *nationalism and by the fact that the world is largely divided into *nation-states. However, there is considerable disagreement about whether the nation plays a necessary or desirable role in political life. Supporters of the national principle portray nations as organic communities. In this light humankind is naturally divided into a collection of nations, each possessing a distinctive character and separate identity. This, nationalists argue, is why a 'higher' loyalty and deeper political significance attaches to the nation than to any other social group or collective body. National ties and loyalties are thus found in all societies, they endure over time, and they operate at an instinctual, even primordial, level. On the other hand, critics of the national principle argue that nations are political constructs, 'imagined' or 'invented' communities whose purpose is to prop up the established order in the interests of rulers and elite groups. In this view nationalism creates nations, not the other way round. Those who adopt this view have typically looked beyond the nation and supported forms of *internationalism.

NATION-STATE

The nation-state is a form of political organisation and a political ideal. In the first case it is an autonomous political community bound together by the overlapping bonds of *citizenship and nationality. It is thus an alternative to multinational empires and city-states. In the latter case the nation-state is a principle, reflected in Mazzini's (1805–72) goal: 'Every nation a state, only one state for the entire nation.' In practice, however, the nation-state is an ideal type and has probably never existed in perfect form anywhere in the world. No *state is culturally homogeneous; all contain some kind of cultural or ethnic mix. There are two contrasting views of the nation-state. For liberals and most socialists the nation-state is largely fashioned out of civic loyalties and allegiances; for conservatives and nationalists it is based upon ethnic or organic unity.

Significance

The nation-state is widely considered to be the only viable unit of political rule and is generally accepted to be the basic element in international politics. The vast majority of modern states are, or claim to be, nation-states. The great strength of the nation-state is that it offers the prospect of both cultural cohesion and political unity. When a people who share a common cultural or ethnic identity gain the right to self-government, community and citizenship coincide. This is why nationalists believe that the forces that have created a world of independent nation-states are natural and irresistible, and that no other social group could constitute a meaningful political community. This view also implies that supranational bodies such as the European Union will never be able to rival the capacity of national governments to establish legitimacy and command popular allegiance. Clear limits should therefore be placed upon, in this case, the process of European integration because people with different languages, cultures and histories will never come to think of themselves as members of a united political community.

Nevertheless, powerful forces have emerged that threaten to make the nation-state redundant, and there are those who argue that the nation-state ideal has always been a regressive one. A combination of internal pressures and external threats has produced what is commonly referred to as a 'crisis of the nation-state'. Internally, nation-states have been subject to centrifugal pressures, generated by an upsurge in ethnic and regional politics. This has meant that *ethnicity or religion have sometimes displaced nationality as the central organising principle of political life. Externally, nation-states have arguably been rendered redundant by the advent of *globalisation. This has meant that major decisions in the economic, cultural and diplomatic spheres are increasingly made by supranational bodies and transnational corporations which nation-states have only a limited capacity to influence. Those who criticise the nation-state ideal point out either that a 'true' nation-state can be achieved only through a process of 'ethnic cleansing' – as Hitler and the Nazis recognised – or that nation-states are always primarily concerned with their own strategic and economic interests, and are therefore an inevitable source of conflict or tension in international affairs.

NATIONALISM

Nationalism can broadly be defined as the belief that the *nation is the central principle of political organisation. As such, it is based upon two core assumptions: first, humankind is naturally divided into distinct nations, and second, the nation is a political community in the sense that it is the most appropriate, and perhaps only legitimate, unit of political rule. There is, nevertheless, disagreement about whether nationalism is a doctrine or an *ideology. The doctrine of nationalism, or what is seen as 'classical' political nationalism, is the belief that all nations are entitled to independent statehood, suggesting that the world should consist of a collection of *nation-states. This doctrine may, in turn, be reworked or reinterpreted when it is absorbed into one of a number of political ideologies. However, if nationalism is regarded as an ideology in its own right, it is seen to encompass a diverse range of forms, political, cultural and ethnic. *Political nationalism* includes any attempt to use the nation ideal to further specifically political ends, which may be highly diverse, as explained below. *Cultural nationalism* emphasises the regeneration of the nation as a distinctive civilisation, and thus stresses the need to defend or strengthen a national language, religion, or way of life rather than achieve overt political ends. *Ethnic nationalism* overlaps with cultural nationalism, but as ethnic groups are seen, correctly or incorrectly, to have descended from common ancestors, it implies a stronger and perhaps more intense sense of distinctiveness and exclusivity.

Political nationalism is a complex and diverse phenomenon. Its major forms are liberal nationalism, conservative nationalism, expansionist nationalism and anticolonial nationalism. *Liberal nationalism* assigns to the nation a moral status similar to that of the individual, meaning that nations have rights, in particular the right to self-determination. As liberal nationalism holds that all nations are equal, it proclaims that the nation-state ideal is universally applicable. *Conservative nationalism* is concerned less with the principled nationalism of self-determination and more with the promise of social cohesion and public order embodied in the sentiment of national *patriotism. From this perspective patriotic loyalty and a consciousness of nationhood is largely rooted in the idea of a shared past, turning nationalism into a defence of traditional values and institutions that have been endorsed by history. *Expansionist nationalism* is an aggressive and militaristic form of nationalism that is invariably associated with chauvinistic beliefs and doctrines, which tends to blur the distinction between nationalism and *racialism. In its extreme form, sometimes referred to as 'integral' nationalism, it arises from a sentiment of intense, even hysterical, nationalist enthusiasm. *Anticolonial nationalism* linked the struggle for 'national liberation' in Africa, Asia and Latin America to the desire for social development, and was typically expressed through socialist doctrines, most commonly through the vehicle of revolutionary *Marxism. However, developing-world nationalism has since the 1970s assumed a postcolonial character, which has been expressed most clearly through *religious fundamentalism.

Significance

It would be difficult to overestimate the significance of nationalism to modern *politics. For over two hundred years nationalism has helped to shape and re-shape history in all parts of the world, making it perhaps the most successful of political creeds. The rising tide of nationalism re-drew the map of Europe in the nineteenth century as autocratic and multinational empires crumbled in the face of liberal and nationalist pressures. This process was continued in the twentieth century through the Treaty of Versailles (1919) and culminated in 1991 with the collapse of the political successor to the Russian empire, the USSR. Both the First and Second World Wars were arguably the result of an upsurge in aggressive nationalism, and most regional and international conflicts are to some extent fuelled by nationalism. The political face of the developing world has been transformed since 1945 by the rise of anticolonialism and a subsequent postcolonial process of 'nation building', both of which are essentially manifestations of nationalism. On the other hand, there have been claims since the late twentieth century that nationalism has become an anachronism. These claims are variously based upon the fact that nationalism has achieved its aim in that the world is now mainly composed of nation-states; that nation-states are themselves losing authority as a result of *globalisation and the growth of *supranationalism; and that ethnic and regional political identities are displacing national ones.

The normative character of nationalism is notoriously difficult to judge. This is because nationalism has a schizophrenic political character. At different times nationalism has been progressive and reactionary, democratic and authoritarian, rational and irrational, and left-wing and right-wing. Nationalists argue that a 'higher' loyalty and deeper political significance attaches to the nation than to any other social group or collective body because nations are natural political communities. Nationalism is merely the recognition of this fact given ideological form. Supporters of nationalism, moreover, view nationalism as a means of enlarging *freedom and defending *democracy, since it is grounded in the idea of self-government. Such a defence of nationalism is most easily developed in relation to liberal nationalism and anticolonial nationalism. However, opponents of nationalism argue that it is implicitly and sometimes explicitly oppressive, and that it is invariably linked to intolerance, suspicion and conflict. Nationalism is oppressive both in the sense that it submerges individual identity and conscience within that of the national whole, and because of the potential it gives political leaders and elites to manipulate and control the masses. The argument that nationalism is inherently divisive stems from the fact that it highlights difference amongst humankind and legitimises an identification with, and preference for, one's own people or nation; in short, it breeds tribalism. This may be implicit in conservative nationalism and explicit in expansionist nationalism, but all forms of nationalism may harbour a darker face that is essentially chauvinistic and potentially aggressive.

PATRIOTISM

Patriotism (from the Latin *patria*, meaning 'fatherland') is a sentiment, a psychological attachment to one's *nation, literally a 'love of one's country'. The terms patriotism and *nationalism are often confused. Nationalism has a doctrinal character and embodies the belief that the nation is in some way the central principle of political organisation. Patriotism provides the affective basis for that belief, and thus underpins all forms of nationalism. It is difficult to conceive of a national group demanding, say, political independence without possessing at least a measure of patriotic loyalty and national consciousness. In that sense patriotism is sometimes considered to be a weak form of nationalism. However, not all patriots are nationalists. Not all of those who identify with or even love their nation see it as a means through which political demands can be articulated. For instance, to support one's national team in sporting events does not necessarily imply support for national self-determination.

Significance

Patriotism is widely considered to be natural and healthy. It is natural, as sociobiologists have argued, for people to seek security through group membership and to identify with others who share similar characteristics to themselves. It is desirable both because it is a means of generating national unity and solidarity and because it builds in individuals a sense of rootedness and belonging. Conservatives, and in a more extreme sense fascists, have therefore seen patriotic loyalty as the basis of national identity, and linked patriotism to *citizenship. However, patriotism has by no means been universally accepted. Opponents of patriotism, who tend to espouse forms of *liberalism and *socialism, view it as an irrational herd instinct that harbours chauvinism and breeds bigotry. In this light patriotism operates through a distinction between 'them' and 'us': there has to be a 'them' to fear or hate in order to give 'us' a stronger sense of loyalty and identity.

REGIONALISM

Regionalism is the transfer of decision-making authority from central government to intermediate bodies which stand between the centre and *local government and have territorial jurisdiction over a region or portion of a *state. Regionalism thus implies *decentralisation but without calling the integrity of the state and the final *authority of national *government into question. However, regionalism is an ambiguous and contested concept.

Regionalism, for instance, may take the form of *devolution, in either its administrative or legislative guise, or it may involve *federalism, in which case regional or provincial bodies are constitutionally entrenched and exercise a share of *sovereignty. The term is also sometimes applied to cooperation between and amongst *states in particular regions of the world, through the idea of regional integration. Regionalism at an international level may thus take the form of *intergovernmentalism or *supranationalism.

Significance

Regionalism has generally become more respectable and has, in states ranging from the UK, France and Spain to Canada and India, become a more powerful political movement since the 1960s. The forces supporting regionalism include the growth of ethnic and cultural *nationalism, and the declining capacity of the *nation-state to maintain a high level of political allegiance in an increasingly globalised world. In that sense regionalism may be a counterpart to *globalisation. However, it is sometimes argued that regionalism is only appropriate to certain states, notably to relatively large and culturally diverse states in which there are strong and meaningful traditions of regional political loyalty. Criticisms of regionalism fall into one of two categories. They either warn that regionalism threatens the *nation's territorial integrity by strengthening regional loyalties and identities at the expense of national ones or, from a separatist perspective, they argue that regionalism is a device employed by central government to contain and control centrifugal pressures within the state. This latter view implies that regionalism may take the form of 'regionalisation', the process by which central authorities respond to regional demand without redistributing policy-making power.

SUBSIDIARITY

Subsidiarity (from the Latin *subsidiarii*, meaning a contingent of supplementary troops) is, broadly, the *devolution of decision-making from the centre to lower levels. However, it is understood in two crucially different ways. In federal states such as Germany, subsidiarity is understood as a political principle that implies *decentralisation and popular participation, benefiting local and provincial institutions often at the expense of national ones. This is expressed in the idea that decisions should be 'taken as closely as possible to the citizen'. However, subsidiarity is also interpreted as a constitutional principle that defends national *sovereignty against the encroachment of supranational bodies. This is expressed in the commitment that the competence of supranational bodies should be restricted to those actions that cannot be sufficiently achieved by *nation-states.

Significance

The principle of subsidiarity is important because it addresses the question of the most appropriate level within a political system at which decisions should be made. In advocating that political decisions should always be made at the lowest possible level of government, it clearly endorses *decentralisation. However, it is better thought of as providing a test of appropriateness: if a governmental function can be carried out as efficiently or effectively by smaller or lower bodies, then it should be devolved, otherwise larger or higher bodies should take responsibility. The notion of subsidiarity is most firmly established in federal systems such as those in Germany and Switzerland, where it has been used in its political sense in allocating powers appropriately between federal government and provincial bodies, and sometimes between provincial bodies and *local government. The term has gained a wider currency, however, since its use in the Treaty of the European Union (Maastricht Treaty) of 1993. Opponents of Euro-federalism have used subsidiarity in a narrow constitutional sense as an embodiment of the rights of member states, and as a defence against the growth of a European 'super-state'.

SUPRANATIONALISM

Supranationalism is the existence of an authority that is 'higher' than that of the *nation-state and capable of imposing its will upon it. Supranationalism thus differs from *intergovernmentalism in that the latter allows for international co-operation only on the basis of the sovereign independence of individual *states. Although, strictly speaking, empires are supranational bodies, being structures of political domination that comprise a diverse collection of cultures, ethnic groups and nationalities, supranationalism usually refers to international bodies that have been established by voluntary agreement amongst states, and which serve limited and specific functions. The best examples of supranational bodies are therefore international federations, such as the European Union (EU), in which *sovereignty is shared between central and peripheral bodies. However, the EU is a difficult body to categorise as it encompasses a mixture of intergovernmental and supranational elements and is thus more accurately described as a federalising than a federal body.

Significance

The advance of supranationalism has been one of the most prominent features of post-1945 world politics. It reflects the growing interdependence of states, particularly in relation to economic and security decision-making, but also in matters such as environmental protection, and the recognition that *globalisation has perhaps made the notion of state sovereignty irrelevant. From this point of view the shift from intergovernmentalism to supranationalism is likely to be a continuing trend, as intergovernmental action requires unanimous agreement and does not allow for action to be taken against recalcitrant states. For instance, the United Nations, strictly speaking an intergovernmental body, acted in a supranational capacity during the Gulf War of 1991 by sanctioning military action against one of its member states, Iraq. This drift towards supranationalism is supported by those who warn that respect for state sovereignty is simply misguided, or that it is dangerous in that it allows states to treat their citizens however they wish, and produces an anarchical international order that is prone to conflict and war. Supranationalism is therefore one of the faces of *internationalism. Opponents of supranationalism continue, on the other hand, to stand by the principle of the nation-state, and argue that supranational bodies have not, and can never, rival the nation-state's capacity to generate political allegiance and ensure democratic accountability.

FURTHER READING

Anderson, B., *Imagine the Communities: Reflections on the Origins and Spread of Nationalism* (London: Verso, 1991).

Axford, B., *The Global System: Economics, Politics and Culture* (Cambridge: Polity Press, 1995).

Batley, R. and Stoker, G. (eds), *Local Government in Europe: Trends and Developments* (London: Macmillan, 1991).

Bogdanor, V., *Devolution* (Oxford: Oxford University Press, 1979).

Camilleri, J. and Falk, P., *The End of Sovereignty? The Politics of a Shrinking and Fragmented World* (Aldershot: Edward Elgar, 1992).

Gellner, E., *Nations and Nationalism* (Oxford: Basil Blackwell, 1983).

Hindley, F.H., *Sovereignty* (New York: Basic Books, 1986).

Hirst, P. and Thompson, G., *Globalisation in Question* (Cambridge: Polity Press, 1995).

Kegley, C. and Wittkopf, E., *World Politics: Trend and Transformation* (New York: St Martin's Press, 1995).

King, P., *Federalism and Federation* (London: Croom Helm, 1982).

Meny, Y. and Wright, V. (eds), *Centre–Periphery Relations in Western Europe* (London: Croom Helm, 1995).

Reynolds, C., *Modes of Imperialism* (Oxford: Martin Robertson, 1981).

Smith, A.D., *Theories of Nationalism* (London: Duckworth, 1991).

Taylor, P. and Groom, A. J. R. (eds), *International Organisations: A Conceptual Approach* (London: Pinter, 1978).

Tivey, L. (ed.), *The Nation-State* (Oxford: Martin Robertson, 1980).

Wilson, D. and Game, C., *Local Government in the United Kingdom* (London: Macmillan, 1994).

GLOSSARY OF KEY POLITICAL THINKERS

Theodor Adorno (1903–69) A German philosopher, sociologist and musicologist, Adorno was a leading member of the Frankfurt School of critical theory. His best-known works include *The Authoritarian Personality* (1950), and *Minima Moralia* (1951).

Thomas Aquinas (1224–74) An Italian Dominican monk, theologian and philosopher, Aquinas argued that reason and faith are compatible and explored the relationship between human law and God's natural law. His best-known work is *Summa Theologiae*, begun in 1265.

Hannah Arendt (1906–75) A German political theorist and philosopher, Arendt wrote widely on issues such as the nature of modern mass society and the importance of political action in human life. Her best-known works include *The Origins of Totalitarianism* (1951) and *The Human Condition* (1958).

Aristotle (384–22 BCE) A Greek philosopher, Aristotle's work ranged over physics, metaphysics, astronomy, meteorology, biology, ethics and politics; it became the foundation of Islamic philosophy and was later incorporated into Christian theology. His best known political work is *Politics*.

Augustine of Hippo (354–430) A theologian and political philosopher, Augustine developed a defence of Christianity that drew upon neo-Platonic philosophy, Christian doctrine and biblical history. His major work is *City of God* (413–25).

Michael Bakunin (1814–76) A Russian propagandist and revolutionary, Bakunin supported a collectivist form of anarchism that was based upon a belief in human sociability, expressed in the desire for freedom within a community of equals.

Jeremy Bentham (1748–1832) A British philosopher and legal reformer, Bentham was the founder of utilitarianism and a major influence upon the reform of social administration, government and economics in nineteenth-century Britain. His major works include *Fragments on Government* (1776) and *Principles of Morals and Legislation* (1789).

Jean Bodin (1530–96) A French political philosopher, Bodin was the first important theorist of sovereignty, which he defined as 'the absolute and perpetual power of a commonwealth'. His most important work is *The Six Books of the Commonweal* (1576).

Edmund Burke (1729–97) A Dublin-born British statesman and political theorist, Burke was the father of the Anglo-American conservative tradition that accepts the principle of 'change in order to conserve'. His most important work is *Reflections on the Revolution in France* (1790).

Friedrich Engels (1820–95) A German socialist theorist and life-long friend and collaborator of Marx, Engels elaborated Marx's ideas and theories for the benefit of the growing socialist movement in the late nineteenth century. His major works include *The Origins of the Family, Private Property and the State* (1884) and *Dialectics of Nature* (1925)

Michel Foucault (1926–84) A French philosopher, Foucault was a major influence upon poststructuralism and was concerned with forms of knowledge and the construction of the human subject. His most important works include *Madness and Civilisation* (1961), *The Archaeology of Knowledge* (1969) and *History of Sexuality* (1976–84).

Erich Fromm (1900–80) A German-born psychoanalyst and social philosopher, Fromm developed a critique of modern society that blended the ideas of Freud, Marx and, in later life, Buddhism. His best-known works include *Fear of Freedom* (1941), *The Sane Society* (1955) and *To Have or To Be?* (1976).

Francis Fukuyama (1952–) A US social analyst and political commentator, Fukuyama has advanced a strong defence of US-style market capitalism and liberal-democratic political structures. His works include *The End of History and the Last Man* (1992) and *Trust* (1996).

Antonio Gramsci (1891–1937) An Italian Marxist and social theorist, Gramsci rejected 'scientific' determinism by stressing, through the theory of hegemony, the importance of the political and intellectual struggle. His major work is *Prison Notebooks* (1929–35).

Jürgen Habermas (1929–) A German philosopher and social theorist, Habermas is the leading exponent of the 'second generation' of the Frankfurt School of critical theory. His main works include *Towards a Rational Society* (1970), *Legitimation Crisis* (1973) and *The Theory of Communicative Competence* (1984).

Georg Wilhem Friedrich Hegel (1770–1831) A German philosopher, Hegel was the founder of modern idealism and advanced an organic theory of the state that portrayed it as the highest expression of human freedom. His main works include *Phenomenology of Spirit* (1807) and *Philosophy of Right* (1821).

Thomas Hobbes (1588–1679) An English political philosopher, Hobbes developed the first comprehensive theory of nature and human behaviour since Aristotle and advanced a rationalist defence of absolutism. His major work is *Leviathan* (1651).

Immanuel Kant (1724–1804) A German philosopher, Kant advanced an ethical individualism that stressed the importance of morality in politics and has had considerable impact upon liberal thought. His most important works include *Critique of Pure Reason* (1781), *Critique of Practical Reason* (1788) and *Critique of Judgement* (1790).

John Maynard Keynes (1883–1946) A British economist, Keynes developed a critique of neoclassical economics that underlined the need for 'demand management' by government. His major work is *The General Theory of Employment, Interest and Money* (1936).

Peter Kropotkin (1842–1921) A Russian geographer and anarchist theorist, Kropotkin drew attention to the human propensity for freedom and equality, based upon the idea of mutual aid. His major works include *Mutual Aid* (1897), *Fields, Factories and Workshops* (1901) and *The Conquest of Bread* (1906).

Vladimir Ilich Lenin (1870–1924)   A Russian Marxist theorist and revolutionary, Lenin built upon the theories of Marx by emphasising the issues of organisation and revolution. His most important works include *What is to be Done?* (1902), *Imperialism, the Highest Stage of Capitalism* (1916) and *State and Revolution* (1917).

John Locke (1632–1704)   An English philosopher and politician, Locke was a key thinker of early liberalism and a powerful advocate of consent and constitutionalism. His most important political works are *A Letter Concerning Toleration* (1689) and *Two Treatises of Government* (1690).

Niccolò Machiavelli (1469–1527)   An Italian politician and author, Machiavelli portrayed politics in strictly realistic terms and highlighted the use by political leaders of cunning, cruelty and manipulation. His major work is *The Prince* (1513).

James Madison (1751–1836)   A US statesman and political theorist, Madison was a leading proponent of pluralism and divided government, urging the adoption of federalism, bi-cameralism and the separation of powers as the basis of US government. His best-known political writings are his contributions to *The Federalist* (1787–8).

Joseph de Maistre (1753–1821)   A French aristocrat and political thinker, de Maistre was a fierce critic of the French Revolution and an implacable supporter of monarchical absolutism. His chief political work is *Du pape* (1817).

Herbert Marcuse (1898–1979)   A German political philosopher and social theorist, Marcuse developed a radical critique of advanced industrial society but emphasised both its repressive character and the potential for liberation. His most important works include *Reason and Revolution* (1941), *Eros and Civilisation* (1958) and *One Dimensional Man* (1964).

Karl Marx (1818–83)   A German philosopher, economist and political thinker, Marx advanced a teleological theory of history that held that social development would eventually culminate with the establishment of communism. His classic work is *Capital* (1867, 1885 and 1894); his best-known work is *Communist Manifesto* (1848).

Giuseppe Mazzini (1805–72)   An Italian nationalist and apostle of liberal republicanism, Mazzini was an early advocate of the universal right to national self-determination, viewed as the key to freedom and international harmony.

Robert Michels (1876–1936)   A German politician and social theorist, Michels drew attention to elite tendencies within all organisations, summed up in the 'iron law of oligarchy'. His major work is *Political Parties* (1911).

James Mill (1773–1836)   A Scottish philosopher, historian and economist, Mill helped to turn utilitarianism into a radical reform movement. His best-known work is *Essay on Government* (1820).

John Stuart Mill (1806–73)   A British philosopher, economist and politician, Mill was an important liberal thinker who opposed collectivist tendencies and tradition and upheld the importance of individual freedom, based upon a commitment to individuality. His major writings include *On Liberty* (1859), *Considerations on Representative Government* (1861) and *The Subjection of Women* (1869).

Kate Millett (1934–   )   A US writer and sculptor, Millett developed radical feminism into a systematic theory that clearly stood apart from established liberal and socialist traditions. Her major work is *Sexual Politics* (1970).

Charles-Louis de Secondat Montesquieu (1689–1775)   A French political philosopher, Montesquieu emphasised the need to resist tyranny by fragmenting government power, particularly through the device of the separation of powers. His major work is *The Spirit of the Laws* (1748).

Gaetano Mosca (1857–1941)   An Italian elite theorist, Mosca argued that a cohesive minority will always be able to manipulate and control the masses, even in a parliamentary democracy. His major work is *The Ruling Class* (1896).

Friedrich Nietzsche (1844–1900)   A German philosopher, Nietzsche's complex and ambitious work stressed the importance of will, especially the 'will to power', and anticipated modern existentialism in emphasising that people create their own world and make their own values. His best-known writings include *Thus Spoke Zarathustra* (1883–84), *Beyond Good and Evil* (1886) and *On the Genealogy of Morals* (1887).

Robert Nozick (1938–)   A US academic and political philosopher, Nozick developed a form of libertarianism that was close to Locke's and has had considerable impact upon the New Right. His major works include *Anarchy, State and Utopia* (1974) and *Philosophical Explanations* (1981).

Michael Oakeshott (1901–90)   A British political philosopher, Oakeshott was a leading proponent of conservative traditionalism and an advocate of a non-ideological style of politics. His best-known works include *Rationalism in Politics and Other Essays* (1962) and *On Human Conduct* (1975).

Robert Owen (1771–1858)   A British industrialist and pioneer trade unionist, Owen developed a utopian form of socialism that emphasised the capacity of the social environment to influence character. His best-known work is *A New View of Society* (1812).

Vilfredo Pareto (1848–1923)   An Italian economist and social theorist, Pareto developed a form of elitism that is based largely upon the different psychological propensities of leaders and followers. His major work is *The Mind and Society* (1917–18).

Plato (427–347 BCE)   A Greek philosopher, Plato taught that the material world consists of imperfect copies of abstract and eternal 'ideas', and described the 'ideal state' in terms of a theory of justice. His major writings include *The Republic* and *The Laws*.

Karl Popper (1902–94)   An Austrian-born British philosopher, Popper's political writings upheld liberalism and the free society and condemned authoritarian and totalitarian tendencies. His main political work is *The Open Society and its Enemies* (1945).

Pierre-Joseph Proudhon (1809–65)   A French anarchist, Proudhon attacked both traditional property rights and communism, arguing instead for mutualism, a cooperative productive system geared towards need rather than profit. His best-known work is *What is Property?* (1840).

John Rawls (1921–)   A US academic and political philosopher, Rawls used a form of social contract theory to reconcile liberal individualism with the principles of redistribution and social justice. His major works include *A Theory of Justice* (1971) and *Political Liberalism* (1993).

Jean-Jacques Rousseau (1712–78)   A Geneva-born French moral and political philosopher, Rousseau developed a philosophy that reflects a deep belief in the goodness of 'natural man' and the corruption of 'social man'. His best-known political work is *The Social Contract* (1762).

Adam Smith (1723–90)   A Scottish economist and philosopher, Smith developed the first systematic analysis of the workings of the economy in market terms, crucially influencing emergent classical liberalism. His most famous work is *The Wealth of Nations* (1776).

Richard Henry Tawney (1880–1962)   A British social philosopher and historian, Tawney advocated a form of socialism that was firmly rooted in a Christian social moralism unconnected with Marxist class analysis. His major works include *The Acquisitive Society* (1921), *Equality* (1931) and *The Radical Tradition* (1964).

Max Weber (1864–1920)   A German political economist and sociologist, Weber was one of the founders of modern sociology and championed a scientific and value-free approach to scholarship. His most influential works include *The Protestant Ethic and the Spirit of Capitalism* (1902), *The Sociology of Religion* (1920) and *Economy and Society* (1922).

BIBLIOGRAPHY

Adorno, T. *et al*. (1950) *The Authoritarian Personality* (New York: Hooper).

Almond, G. A. and Verba, S. (1963) *The Civic Culture: Political Attitudes and Democracy in Five Nations* (Princeton, NJ: Princeton University Press).

Almond, G. A. and Verba, S. (1980) *The Civic Culture Revisited* (Boston, MA: Little, Brown).

Anderson, B. (1991) *Imagined Communities: Reflections on the Origins and Spread of Nationalism* (London: Verso).

Arblaster, A. (1994) *Democracy* (Milton Keynes: Open University Press).

Axford, B. (1995) *The Global System: Economics, Politics and Culture* (Cambridge: Polity Press).

Baggott, R. (1995) *Pressure Groups Today* (Manchester and New York: Manchester University Press).

Ball, A. and Millward, F. (1986) *Pressure Politics in Industrial Societies* (London: Macmillan).

Ball, T. (1997) 'Political Theory and Conceptual Change', in A. Vincent (ed.), *Political Theory: Tradition and Diversity* (Cambridge: Cambridge University Press).

Ball, T. (1988) *Transforming Political Discourse: Political Theory and Critical Conceptual History* (Oxford: Blackwell).

Ball, T., Farr, J. and Hanson, R. L. (eds) (1989) *Political Innovation and Conceptual Change* (Cambridge: Cambridge University Press).

Barbalet, J. M. (1988) *Citizenship* (Milton Keynes: Open University Press).

Barker, J. (1987) *Arguing for Equality* (London and New York: Verso).

Barry, B. and Hardin, R. (eds) (1982) *Rational Man and Irrational Society?* (Beverly Hills, CA: Sage).

Barry, N. (1987) *The New Right* (London: Croom Helm).

Barry, N. (1990) *Welfare* (Milton Keynes: Open University Press).

Batley, R. and Stoker, G. (eds) (1991) *Local Government in Europe: Trends and Developments* (London: Macmillan).

Baxter, B. (2000) *Ecologism: An Introduction* (Edinburgh: Edinburgh University Press).

Beetham, D. (1991) *The Legitimation of Power* (London: Macmillan).

Beetham, D. (ed.) (1994) *Defining and Measuring Democracy* (London: Sage).

Bell, D. (1960) *The End of Ideology* (Glencoe, IL: Free Press).

Bellamy, R. (ed.) (1993) *Theories and Concepts of Politics: An Introduction* (Manchester and New York: Manchester University Press).

Berlin, I. (1958) *Four Essays on Liberty* (Oxford: Oxford University Press).

Berry, C. (1986) *Human Nature* (London: Macmillan).

Birch, A. H. (1964) *Representative and Responsible Government: An Essay on the British Constitution* (London: Allen and Unwin).

Birch, A. H. (1972) *Representation* (London: Macmillan).

Birch, A. H. (1993) *The Concepts and Theories of Modern Democracy* (London and New York: Routledge).

Blau, P. and Meyer, M. (eds) (1987) *Bureaucracy in Modern Society* (New York: Random House).

Bobbio, N. (1996) *Left and Right* (Cambridge: Polity Press).

Bogdanor, V. (1979) *Devolution* (Oxford: Oxford University Press).

Bogdanor, V. (ed.) (1988) *Constitutions in Democratic Politics* (Aldershot: Gower).

Bottomore, T. (1985) *Theories of Modern Capitalism* (London: Allen and Unwin).

Bottomore, T. (1993) *Elites and Society* (London: Routledge).

Boulding, K. (1989) *Three Faces of Power* (Newbury Park, CA: Sage).

Bryson, V. (1995) *Feminist Political Theory: An Introduction* (London: Macmillan).

Buchanan, J. and Tulloch, G. (1962) *The Calculus of Consent* (Ann Arbor, MI: Michigan University Press).

Bull, H. (1977) *The Anarchical Society* (London: Macmillan).

Burchill, S. and Linklater, A. (1996) *Theories of International Relations* (London: Macmillan).

Calvert, P. (1990) *Revolution and Counter-Revolution* (Buckingham: Open University Press).

Camilleri, J. and Falk, P. (1992) *The End of Sovereignty? The Politics of a Shrinking and Fragmented World* (Aldershot: Edward Elgar).

Chalmers, A. F. (1986) *What Is This Thing Called Science?* (Milton Keynes: Open University Press).

Clarke, P. (1979) *Liberals and Social Democrats* (Cambridge: Cambridge University Press).

Cohen, G. A. (1978) *Karl Marx's Theory of History: A Defence* (Oxford: Clarendon Press).

Dahl, R. (1956) *A Preface to Democratic Theory* (Chicago, IL: University of Chicago Press).

Dallmayr, F. and McCarthy, T. (eds) (1997) *Understanding and Social Inquiry* (Notre Dame, IN: University of Notre Dame Press).

Devlin, P. (1968) *The Enforcement of Morals* (Oxford: Oxford University Press).

Dunleavy, P. (1991) *Democracy, Bureaucracy and Public Choice: Economic Explanations in Political Science* (Hemel Hempstead: Harvester Wheatsheaf).

Dunleavy, P. and O'Leary, B. (1987) *Theories of the State: The Politics of Liberal Democracy* (London: Macmillan).

Easton, D. (1979) *A Framework for Political Analysis* (Chicago, IL: University of Chicago Press).

Easton, D. (1981) *The Political System* (Chicago, IL: University of Chicago Press).

Eatwell, R. and O'Sullivan, N. (eds) (1989) *The Nature of the Right: European and American Politics and Political Thought since 1789* (London: Pinter).

Elgie, R. (1995) *Political Leadership in Liberal Democracies* (London: Macmillan).

Esping-Andersen, G. (1990) *The Three Worlds of Welfare Capitalism* (Cambridge: Polity Press).

Etzioni, A. (1995) *The Spirit of Community: Rights, Responsibilities and the Communitarian Agenda* (London: Fontana).

Finifter, A. (ed.) (1993) *Political Science: The State of the Discipline* (Washington, DC: American Political Science Association).

Flatham, R. (1980) *The Practice of Political Authority* (Chicago, IL: Chicago University Press).

Freeden, M. (1991) *Rights* (Minneapolis, MN: University of Minnesota Press).

Freeden, M. (1996) *Ideologies and Political Theory: A Conceptual Approach* (Oxford: Clarendon Press).

Friedrich, C. J. and Brzezinski, Z. (eds) (1966) *Totalitarian Dictatorship and Autocracy* (Cambridge, MA: Harvard University Press).

Fromm, E. (1984) *The Fear of Freedom* (London: Ark).

Fukuyama, F. (1989) 'The End of History?', *National Interest*, Summer.

Fukuyama. F. (1992) *The End of History and the Last Man* (Harmondsworth: Penguin).

Gallie, W. B. (1955–6) 'Essentially Contested Concepts', *Proceedings of the Aristotelian Society*, **56**, pp. 157–97).

Gellner, E. (1983) *Nations and Nationalism* (Oxford: Basil Blackwell).

Gibbins, J. (ed.) (1989) *Contemporary Political Culture: Politics in a Post-modern Age* (London: Sage).

Giddens, A. (1998) *The Third Way: The Renewal of Social Democracy* (Cambridge: Polity Press).

Goodin, R. (1995) *Utilitarianism as a Public Philosophy* (Cambridge: Cambridge University Press).

Goodin, R. E. and Pettit, P. (1995) *A Companion to Contemporary Political Philosophy* (Oxford: Blackwell).

Graham, B. D. (1993) *Representation and Party Politics: A Comparative Perspective* (Oxford: Blackwell).

Gramsci, A. (1971) *Selections from the Prison Notebooks* (London: Lawrence and Wishart).

Gray, J. (1995) *Liberalism* (Milton Keynes: Open University Press).

Gray, T. (1990) *Freedom* (London: Macmillan).

Green, L. (1988) *The Authority of the State* (Oxford: Clarendon Press).

Griffin, R. (ed.) (1995) *Fascism* (Oxford and New York: Oxford University Press).

Habbermas, J. (1973) *Legitimation Crisis* (Boston, MA: Beacon).

Hague, R., Harrop, M. and Breslin, S. (1992) *Comparative Government and Politics: An Introduction* (London: Macmillan).

Hailsham, Lord (1976) *Elected Dictatorship* (London: BBC Publications).

Hall, S. and Jacques, M. (eds) (1983) *The Politics of Thatcherism* (London: Lawrence and Wishart).

Hart, H. L. A. (1961) *The Concept of Law* (Oxford: Oxford University Press).

Harvey, D. (1989) *The Condition of Post Modernity* (London: Basil Blackwell).

Held, D. (1990) *Political Theory and the Modern State* (Cambridge: Polity Press).

Held, D. (ed.) (1991) *Political Theory Today* (Cambridge: Polity Press).
Hennessy, P. (1986) *Cabinet* (Oxford: Blackwell).
Heywood, A. (1998) *Political Ideologies: An Introduction* (London: Macmillan).
Heywood, A. (1999) *Political Theory: An Introduction* (London: Macmillan).
Hindley, F. H. (1986) *Sovereignty* (New York: Basic Books).
Hirst, P. and Thompson, G. (1995) *Globalisation in Question* (Cambridge: Polity Press).
Hitler, A. (1969) *Mein Kampf*, trans. R. Mannheim (London: Hutchinson).
Holden, B. (1993) *Understanding Liberal Democracy* (Hemel Hempstead: Harvester Wheatsheaf).
Horton, J. (1992) *Political Obligation* (London: Macmillan).
Hutcheon, L. (1989) *The Politics of Post Modernism* (New York: Routledge).
Johnson, N. (1989) *The Limits of Political Science* (Oxford: Clarendon).
Kegley, C. (ed.) (1995) *Controversies in International Relations Theory: Realism and the Neoliberal Challenge* (New York: St Martin's Press).
Kegley, C. and Wittkopf, E. (1995) *World Politics: Trend and Transformation* (New York: St Martin's Press).
Kenny, M. (1995) *The First New Left: British Intellectuals after Stalin* (London: Lawrence and Wishart).
King, P. (1982) *Federalism and Federation* (London: Croom Helm).
Kingdom, J. (1992) *No Such Thing as Society? Individualism and Community* (Buckingham: Open University Press).
Kirchheimer, O. (1966) 'The Transformation of the Western European Party Systems', in J. la Palombara and M. Weiner (eds), *Political Parties and Political Development* (Princeton, NJ: Princeton University Press).
Kolakowski, L. (1979) *Main Currents of Marxism*, 3 vols (Oxford: Oxford University Press).
Kuhn, T. (1962) *The Structure of Scientific Revolutions* (Chicago, IL: Chicago University Press).
Kumar, K. (1991) *Utopianism* (Milton Keynes: Open University Press).
Kymlika, W. (1990) *Contemporary Political Philosophy: An Introduction* (Oxford and New York: Oxford University Press).
Laclau, E. and Mouffe, C. (1985) *Hegemony and Socialist Strategy* (London: Verso).
LeDuc, L., Niemi, R. and Norris, P. (eds) (1996) *Comparing Democracies: Elections and Voting in Global Perspective* (London: Sage).
Leftwich, A. (ed.) (1984) *What Is Politics? The Activity and Its Study* (Oxford and New York: Blackwell).
Lenin, V. I. (1968) *What is to be Done?* (Harmondsworth and New York: Penguin).
Lijphart, A. (1977) *Democracy in Plural Societies: A Comparative Exploration* (New Haven, CT: Yale University Press).
Lijphart, A. (ed.) (1992) *Parliamentary Versus Presidential Government* (Oxford: Oxford University Press).
Lindblom, C. (1959) 'The Science of Muddling Through', *Public Administration Review*, **19**, pp. 79–88.
Lukes, S. (1974) *Power: A Radical View* (London: Macmillan).
Lyotard, J.-F. (1984) *The Postmodern Condition: The Power of Knowledge* (Minneapolis, MN: University of Minnesota Press).

MacCallum, G. (1991) 'Negative and Positive Freedom', in D. Miller (ed.), *Liberty* (Oxford: Oxford University Press).

MacIntyre, A. (1981) *After Virtue* (Notre Dame, IL: University of Notre Dame Press).

Marcuse, H. (1964) *One-Dimensional Man: Studies in the Ideology of Advanced Industrial Society* (Boston, MA: Beacon).

Marsh, D. and Stoker, G. (eds) (1995) *Theory and Methods in Political Science* (London: Macmillan).

Marty, M. E. and Appleby, R. S. (eds) (1993) *Fundamentalisms and the State: Re-making Polities, Economies, and Militance* (Chicago, IL, and London: University of Chicago Press).

Marx, K. and Engels, F. (1967) *The Communist Manifesto* (Harmondsworth: Penguin).

Matchan, T. R. (ed.) (1982) *The Libertarian Reader* (Totowa, NJ: Rowan and Littlefield).

McDowell, L. and Pringle, R. (eds) (1992) *Defining Women: Social Institutions and Gender Divisions* (Cambridge: Polity Press).

McLellan, D. (1986) *Ideology* (Milton Keynes: Open University Press).

McLennan, G. (1995) *Pluralism* (Buckingham: Open University Press).

Mendus, S. (1989) *Toleration and the Limits of Liberalism* (London: Macmillan).

Meny, Y. and Wright, V. (eds) (1995) *Centre–Periphery Relations in Western Europe* (London: Croom Helm).

Merleau-Ponty, M. (1993) *Adventures of the Dialectic* (London: Heinemann).

Michels, R. (1962) *Political Parties: A Sociological Study of the Oligarchal Tendencies of Modern Democracy* (New York: Collier).

Miller, D. (1984) *Anarchism* (London: Dent).

Millett, K. (1970) *Sexual Politics* (London: Virago).

Mills, C. W. (1956) *The Power Elite* (New York: Oxford University Press).

Move, T. (1965) *Utopia*, trans. P. Turner (Harmondworth: Penguin).

Nairn, T. (1988) *The Enchanted Glass: Britain and its Monarchy* (London: Picador).

Negrine, R. (1996) *The Communication of Politics* (London: Sage).

Neumann, S. (1956) *Modern Political Parties* (Chicago, IL: University of Chicago Press).

Neustadt, R. (1980) *Presidential Power: The Politics of Leadership from FDR to Carter* (New York: John Wiley).

Norton, P. (ed.) (1990) *Legislatures* (Oxford: Oxford University Press).

Norton, P. (ed.) (1990) *Parliaments in Western Europe* (London: Frank Cass).

Nozick, R. (1974) *Anarchy, State and Utopia* (Oxford: Blackwell).

Ollman, B. (1993) *Dialectical Investigations* (London: Routledge).

O'Neill, J. (ed.) (1993) *Modes of Individualism and Collectivism* (London: Gregg Revivals).

Pakulski, J. (1990) *Social Movements: The Politics of Protest* (Melbourne: Longman).

Parsons, W. (1995) *Public Policy: Introduction to the Theory and Practice of Policy Analysis* (Aldershot: Edward Elgar).

Pettit, P. (1997) *Republicanism: A Theory of Freedom and Government* (Oxford: Oxford University Press).

Pinkney, R. (1990) *Right-Wing Military Government* (London: Pinter).

Rawls, J. (1971) *A Theory of Justice* (London: Oxford University Press).

Raz, J. (1986) *The Authority of Law* (Oxford: Clarendon Press).

Rex, J. and Mason, D. (eds) (1992) *Theories of Race and Ethnic Relations* (Cambridge: Cambridge University Press).

Reynolds, C. (1981) *Modes of Imperialism* (Oxford: Martin Robertson).

Rorty, R. (ed.) (1967) *The Linguistic Turn* (Chicago, IL: University of Chicago Press).

Rose, R. (1991) *The Postmodern Presidency: The White House Meets the World* (New York: Chartham House).

Rose, R. and Suleiman, E. N. (eds) (1980) *Presidents and Prime Ministers* (Washington, DC: American Enterprise Institute).

Ryan, A. (1987) *Property* (Milton Keynes: Open University Press).

Sandel, M. (1982) *Liberalism and the Limits of Justice* (Cambridge: Cambridge University Press).

Sartori, G. (1976) *Parties and Party Sytems: A Framework for Analysis* (Cambridge: Cambridge University Press).

Saunders, P. (1990) *Social Class Stratification* (London: Routledge).

Saunders, P. (1995) *Capitalism: A Social Audit* (Buckingham: Open University Press).

Schattschneider, E. E. (1960) *The Semisovereign People* (New York: Holt, Rinehart and Winston).

Schmitter, P. C. and Lehmbruch, G. (eds) (1979) *Trends towards Corporatist Intermediation* (London: Sage).

Scruton, R. (1984) *The Meaning of Conservatism* (London: Macmillan).

Simon, H. (1983) *Models of Bounded Rationality* (Cambridge, MA: MIT Press).

Smith, A. D. (1991) *Theories of Nationalism* (London: Duckworth).

Tam, H. (1998) *Communitarianism: A New Agenda for Politics and Citizenship* (London: Macmillan).

Taylor, P. and Groom, A. J. R. (eds) (1978) *International Organisations: A Conceptual Approach* (London: Pinter).

Thompson, G., Frances, J., Levacic, R. and Mitchell, J. (1991) *Markets, Hierarchies and Networks: The Coordination of Social Life* (London: Sage).

Tivey, L. (ed.) (1980) *The Nation-State* (Oxford: Martin Robertson).

Tormey, S. (1995) *Making Sense of Tyranny: Interpretations of Totalitarianism* (Manchester and New York: Manchester University Press).

Verney, D. V. (1959) *The Analysis of Political Systems* (London: Routledge & Kegan Paul).

Vincent, A. (1995) *Modern Political Ideologies* (Oxford: Blackwell).

Vincent, A. (1997) *Political Theory: Tradition and Diversity* (Cambridge: Cambridge University Press).

Waltman, J. and Holland, K. (eds) (1988) *The Political Role of Law Courts in Modern Democracies* (New York: St Martin's Press).

Weaver, R. K. and Rockman, B. A. (eds) (1993) *Do Institutions Matter?* (Washington, DC: Brookings Institution).

Weller, P. (1985) *First Among Equals: Prime Ministers in Westminster Systems* (Sydney: Allen and Unwin).

White, J. B. (1984) *When Words Lose Their Meaning* (Chicago, IL: University of Chicago Press).

Williams, P. (1989) *Mahayana Buddhism* (London and New York: Rout-
ledge).
Wilson, D. and Game, C. (1994) *Local Government in the United Kingdom*
(London: Macmillan).
Wright, A. (1987) *Socialisms: Theories and Practices* (Oxford and New
York: Oxford University Press).

INDEX

Note: Numbers in **bold** refer to a full discussion of a concept, including definitions of any significant sub-categories (as indicated in the text by the use of *italics*), or biographical details of a key political thinker.

Abacha, General, 171
absolutism, 38, 61, **157–8**, 158, 183
accountability, 16, **117–18**, 138, 170, 200, 214, 260
Adorno, T., 159, **262**
adversary politics, 214
alienation, 49
Almond, G. A., 216–17
anarchism, 20, 27, 28, 31, 41, 42, **45–7**, 51, 55, 62, 111, 118, 250
anomie, 122
anti-Semitism, 57, 66–7, 70
Aquinas, T., 95, **262**
Arendt, H., 33, 232, **262**
Aristotle, 20, 25, 34, 52, 88, 94, 95, 122, 135, **262**
Aryanism, 66
August Caesar, 166
Augustine of Hippo, 95, **262**
Austin, J., 25, 38
authoritarianism, 16, 68, **158–9**, 184
authority, **15–16**, 27, 29, 30, 37, 39, 45, 53, 62, 68–9, 123, 145, 158, 192, 213, 221
autonomy, 45, 67, **118–19**, 162, 237, 241

Bakunin, M., 121, **262**
balance of power, 37, 106–7
Ball, T., 7
behaviouralism, **85–6**, 89, 94, 96, 97, 99, 101, 108, 217
Bell, D., 24
Bentham, J., 109, 134, **263**
Berlin, I., 129–30

bicameralism, 124, **189–90**, 240
bill of rights, 120, **190–1**, 198
Birch, A.-H., 7
Bismarck, O. von, 166
Blair, T., 78
Bloch, E., 112
Bodin, J., 37–8, 157, **263**
Bonapartism, 159
Boulding, K., 35
Brzezinski, Z., 184
Buchanan, J., 104
Buddhism, 8, 92
Bull, H., 107
bureaucracy, 19, 93, 118, 153, **191–3**, 201, 215
Burke, E., 17, 53, 144, 145, 151, **263**

cabinet, 173, 179, 180, **193–4**, 198, 201–2, 220, 221, 224–6
capitalism, 22, 26, 33, 48, 50, 52, 55, 61, 64, 67, 69, 75, 78–9, 111, 138, 142, 158, **159–61**, 170, 209–10, 231
centralisation, **237–8**, 242, 250
Chamberlain, H. S., 70
Christian democracy, **47–8**
Christianity, 47–8, 72
Churchill, R., 79
Cicero, 181
citizenship, **119–20**, 140, 182, 217, 252, 257
civic culture, 216–17
civil liberty, 25, **120–1**, 125, 147, 190, 198
civil society, **17–18**, 25, 39, 126, 134, 158, 162, 169, 184, 205, 224

Clinton, B., 78
coalition, 18, **194–5**, 213, 219, 225
cohabitation, 181
collective responsibility, 146, 193
collectivisation, 49, 79, 121, **162**
collectivism, 27, 76, **121–2**, 133, 136
colonialism, 70, 106, 226, 245
committee, 146, 193, **195–6**, 215
communism, 10, 24, 27, 28, 46,
   48–51, 64–5, 71, 76–7, 158, 167,
   185
communitarianism, 45, **51–2**, 62, 96,
   100, 119, 149
community, 24, 51, 75, 100, **122–3**,
   130, 134, 136, 143
Comte, A., 100
concept, 3–11, *passim*
confederation, 247
consensus, **18–19**, 34, 162, 195
consent, 16, 30, 60, 78, 123, 16l9
conservatism, 23, 27, 28, 45, 46, **52–4**,
   68–70, 69–80, 105, 130, 150–1,
   255
consociationalism, **162–3**
constitution, 20, 88, 93, 169, 190,
   196–9, 241
constitutionalism, 38, 54, 60, 75, 117,
   124–5, 158, 183, 189, 198, 230
corporatism, 78, **164–5**, 223, 224
coup d'état, 182
Cromwell, O., 166

Dahl, R., 177
Darwinism, 70
decentralisation, 67, 118, 124, **237–8**,
   239, 242, 257, 259
delegate, 144
democracy, 7, 10, 30, 38, 54, 67, 86,
   102, 117, 119, 124, **125–7**, 137,
   143–5, 167, 178–9, 185, 217, 224,
   228, 256
Destutt de Tarcy, A., 22
Devlin, P., 26
devolution, 21, 162, 176, 190,
   238–10, 258
dialectic, 86
dialectical materialism, 49, 64, 87, 91
dictatorship, 57, 157, **166–7**, 171,
   178, 185, 228

discourse, **87–8**, 102
Disraeli, B., 53, 54
Donne, J., 75
Durkheim, E., 122

Easton, D., 34, 85, 94, 108, 112
ecologism, 24, 28, **55–6**, 68, 100, 111
ecology, 55
election, 46, 93, 123, 144, 169,
   199–201, 227
elective dictatorship, 174
elitism, 10, 36, 94, **167–8**, 177
empiricism, **88–9**, 92, 104
Engels, F., 48, 64, 87, 90, **263**
environmentalism, 55
equality, 22, 27, 45, 51, 55, 57, 58, 60,
   61, 74, 76, 96, 99, 125, **128–9**, 132,
   135, 143, 148, 153, 170, 204
Esping-Andersen, G., 152
essentially contested concepts, 7
ethnicity, 175, **226–7**, 244, 252, 253
Etzioni, A., 51
executive, 19, **201–3**, 215, 229

fascism, 23, 27, 28, 51, 54, 55, **56–8**,
   65–9, 71, 78, 131, 164, 167, 185,
   227, 233
federalism, 21, 38, 124, 162, 176, 181,
   190, 238, **240–2**, 258
feminism, 24, 27, 42, 52, **58–60**, 62,
   68, 96, 99, 100, 111, 121, 170,
   174–5, 204–5, 248
Foucault, M., 87, **263**
foundationalism, 102
Franco, General, 159
freedom, 7, 16, 17, 21, 27, 39, 45,
   51, 57, 60–1, 62–3, 68–9, 74,
   77, 96, 99, 118, 120, 124, **129–31**,
   132, 152, 170, 175, 181, 198, 213,
   238, 256
Friedrich, C., 184
Fromm, E., 131, 232, **263**
Fukuyama, F., 61, 169, **263**
functionalism, **89–90**
fundamentalism, 71–3, 76

Gallie, W. D., 7
Gandhi, Mahatma, 92
Gemeinschaft, 122

gender, 58–60, 175, **204–5**
general will, 38, 166, 178
Gentile, G., 57
Gesellschaft, 122
globalisation, 39, 42, 55, 57, 72, 78,
    194, 204, 209, 227, **243–4**, 246,
    253, 260
Gobineau, J.-A., 70
Goodman, P., 112
governance, **19–21**, 93
government, 16, 18, **19–21**, 24, 29,
    30, 31, 37, 45, 68, 93, 195, 196
Gramsci, A., 24, 205, **264**

Habermas, J., 30, **264**
Hailsham, Lord, 174
Hall, S., 159
Hamilton, A., 240
Hart, H. L. A., 25, 42
Hegel, G. W. F., 17, 86, 87, 92, **264**
hegemony, 24, 30, 88, **205–6**, 211,
    217
hierarchy, 19, 27, 138
Hinduism, 72
historical materialism, 64, 89, **90–1**,
    92
Hitler, A., 40, 57–8, 66, 166, 171,
    254
Hobbes, T., 29, 31, 36, 38, 94, 95,
    134, 141, 157, 176, **264**
human nature, **21–2**, 26, 31, 41, 45,
    53, 98, 133
human rights, 25, 93, 110, 120,
    131–3, 147, 191, 248
Hume, D., 88

idealism, **91–3**, 106, 249
ideology, **22–4**, 43–80, 124, 148, 205,
    217, 218, 240, 245, 254
imperialism, 70, **245–6**, 249
incrementalism, 32
individual responsibility, 146
individualism, 22, 27, 46, 52, 58, 60,
    62, 68, 77, 79, 80, 101, 119, 121,
    133–4, 136, 148
individuality, 133
industrialism, 55
influence, 35
institutionalism, **93–4**

intergovernmentalism, **246–7**, 258,
    259, 260
internationalism, 27, 49, **248–9**, 252,
    259
Islam, 72, 136
issue, 31

Jacques, M., 159
Judaism, 72
judiciary, 26, 93, 139, **206–7**, 229
Julius Caesar, 166
justice, 7, 24, 60, 62, 92, 96, 99, 132,
    134–6, 138, 206

Kant, I., 92, 248, **264**
Kautsky, K., 64
Keynes, J. M., 47, 74, 161, **264**
Keynesianism, 47, 74, 78
King, M. L., 92, 227
Kropotkin, P., 31, 45, 52, **264**

laissez-faire, 52, 54, 61, 63, 161
law, **24–6**, 29, 30, 37, 39, 45, 72, 120,
    135, 190–1, 196–7, 206–7, 252
leadership, 57, **136–8**, 178, 194, 215,
    221–2, 224–6
left/right, **27–8**, 71, 128–9, 137
legislature *see* parliament
legitimacy, 15, **29–30**, 124, 203, 239,
    250
Lenin, V. I., 91, 137, 209, 246, **265**;
    see also Leninism
Leninism, 49, 65, 91, 137, 209, 246,
    265
liberal democracy, 17, 60, 62, 109,
    120, 124, 139, 149, 164, **169–70**,
    177, 197, 223, 230
liberalism, 23, 27, 28, 45, 53, 54, 59,
    60–2, 63, 65, 96, 100, 102, 104, 111,
    119, 123, 124–5, 133, 149, 248,
    254, 257
libertarianism, 26, 46, **62–3**, 118
liberty *see* freedom
Lijphart, A., 162–3, 186
Lincoln, 125
Lindblom, C., 32
local government, **249–51**, 257, 259
Locke, J., 26, 29, 88, 94, 95, 134, 141,
    142, 149, 176, **265**

Lukes, S., 7, 36
Lyotard, J.-F., 102

MacCallum, G. C., 130
Machiavelli, N., 88, 93, **265**
MacIntyre, A., 51
Madison, J., 176, 240, **265**
Maistre, J. de, 159–60, **265**
mandate, 126, 144, 174, 200, **208–9**
Marcuse, H., 112, 185, **265**
market, 19, 27, 47, 61, 63, 68–70, 78,
   111, 136, 160–1, 165, 169, **209–10**
Marx, K., 23, 24, 34, 48–50, 63–5,
   86, 90–1, 96, 99, 161, 205, 231, **265**;
   see also Marxism
Marxism, 36, 42, 48–51, 52, 55, 59,
   62, **63–5**, 67, 71, 76, 87, 94, 96, 102,
   111–12, 122, 148, 177, 182–3, 193,
   205, 211, 217, 224, 230–1, 246;
   see also Karl Marx
Marxism–Leninism, 49, 206; *see also*
   Leninism; Marxism
mass media, 184, 205, **210–11**, 215,
   221, 225, 228
Mazzini, G., 252–3, **266**
McLuhan, M., 211
meritocracy, 60, 80, 128, 136, **138–9**
Michels, R., 167, 168, 219, **266**
militarism, **170–2**
Mill, J. S., 26, 96, 110, 131, 150, 151,
   250, **266**
Millett, K., 35, 174, **266**
Mills, C. Wright, 167, 168
monarchy, 90, 157, 181, **211–13**
Montesquieu, C.-L., 88, 176, **266**
More, T., 50, 110–1
Mosca, G., 167, 168, **266**
Mussolini, B., 57–8, 164, 171

Napoleon Bonaparte, 166
Napoleon III, 159, 166
nation, 56, 68, 106, 121, 213, 238,
   244, 248, **251–2**, 252–7
nationalism, 27, 39, 42, 54, 56, 69, 71,
   72, 106, 122, 224, 227, 246, 248,
   254–6, 256–7, 258
nation-state, 227, 243, 246, 249,
   252–4, 254–5, 258, 259, 260
natural rights, 131, 147–8

Nazism, 55, 57–8, **65–7**, 70, 106, 123,
   227, 254
neo-conservatism, 68–9
neo-liberalism, 68, 69
neo-Marxism, 30, 64, 91
network, 19, 20
Neustadt, R., 230
neutrality, 98, **139–40**, 191, 206–7
New Left, 46, **67–8**, 99, 112, 233
New Right, 24, 28, 40, 41, 46, 48, 54,
   60, 63, **68–70**, 75, 80, 99, 120, 130,
   136, 148, 165, 177, 224
Nietzsche, F., 105, 137, **266–7**
Nozick, R., 99, **267**

Oakeshott, M., 23, **267**
obligation, 20, 29, 123, **140–1**
One Nation conservatism, 53, 54, 78
opposition, 185, **213–14**
order, 26, 27, **30–1**, 45, 53, 151
Owen, R., 52, **267**

Papadopoulis, Colonel, 171
Pareto, V., 167, 168, **267**
parliament, 93, 172–4, 178, 189–90,
   195, 197, 200–1, **214–16**
parliamentary government, **172–4**,
   179, 183, 189, 201–3, 213–14,
   214–16, 220, 224, 230, 240
parliamentary sovereignty, 38, 197
party systems, 219
paternalism, 51, 152
patriarchy, 26, 55, 59, 62, **174–5**,
   204
patriotism, 181, 251, **256–7**
permissiveness, 69, 149
Peron, J., 159
Peronism, 159
philosophical materialism, 92
philosophy, 94–5; *see also* political
   philosophy
Pinochet, General, 171
planning, 49, 51, 162
Plato, 50, 87, 92, 94, 95, 99, 135, 141,
   167, **267**
Plekanov, G., 64, 87
pluralism, 36, 58, 60, 72, 73, 94, 149,
   150, 168, 169, **175–6**, 211, 223–4,
   240

policy, **31–3**, 94, 117, 146, 207
polis, 33
political correctness, 6
political culture, 173, 201, **216–17**, 223
political party, 18, 25, 46, 55, 108, 195, 213, 215, **218–20**, 222, 232
political philosophy, 29, 30, **94–6**, 100
political science, 22, 29, 95, **96–8**, 98, 100
political spectrum, *see* left/right
political theory, 41, **98–100**, 101, 112, 141, 168, 175, 181
politics, 18, 19, 26, **33–5**, 36, 71–2, 94–100, 120, 207
Popper, K., 96, **267**
populism, **178–9**
positivism, 89, 97, 99, **100–1**
post-Fordism, 232
postmaterialism, 67, 232–3
postmodernism, 8, 59, 60, 87, 100, **101–2**
poststructuralism, 102
power, 7, 15, 29, 34, **35–7**, 37, 39, 57, 94, 176–7
pragmatism, 53, 88
president, 179–81, 202, **220–2**, 224
presidential government, 162, 172, **179–81**, 193, 201–3, 213, 215–16, 220–2, 230, 240
presidentialism, 221–2, 226
pressure group, 55, 56, 108, 164–5, 176, 215, 218, **222–4**, 232
prime minister, 180, 193–4, 202, 220, **224–6**
progress, 57, 150
property, 26, 45, 53, 132, **141–3**, 162
proportional representation, 200–1; *see also* representation
Proudhon, P.-J., 45, 240, **267**
public goods, 103
public/private divide, 17, 34, 39, 59, 111, 174, 184

race, 56, 121, 175, **226–7**, 252
racialism, 57, 65–7, **70–1**, 96, 122, 227, 248, 255
racism, **70–1**; *see also* racialism

rational choice theory, 32, 94, 99, **102–4**, 168, 193
rationalism, 57, 60, 103, **104–5**, 150, 151, 157
Rawls, J., 99, 138, **268**
reaction, 150
realism, 92, **105–7**, 249
referendum, 126, **227–9**
Reganism, 69, 78
regionalism, **257–8**
relativism, 102
religious fundamentalism, **71–3**, 131, 248
representation, 124, 126, **143–5**, 158, 173, 189, 200–1, 208–9, 224
republicanism, **181–2**
responsibility, 51, 63, 78, 117, 119, 121, 133, **145–7**, 172, 173, 193
revolution, 64, 76, **182–4**
rights, 25, 27, 55, 63, 69, 78, 96, 120, 131–3, 140, 141, **147–9**, 169, 190–1, 204
Rousseau, J.-J., 38, 94, 95, 141, 178, **268**

Saddam Hussein, 40, 166, 171
Saint-Simon, C.-H., 100
Salazar, A. de O., 164
Sandel, M., 51
Sartre, J. P., 22
Schattschneider, E. E., 36
Schumpeter, J., 168
science, 85, 96–8, 100–1, 102; *see also* political science
scientism, 96
secularism, 72, 73
separation of powers, 124, 172, 176, 179, 181, 207, 220, 224, **229–30**, 240
Simon, H., 32
Smith, A., 134, 161, **268**
social class, 49, 64, 67, 76, 80, 91, 98, 101, 121, 175, **230–2**
social contract, 134, 141, 148
social democracy, 28, 47, 51, 67, **73–5**, 76
social market, 47; *see also* market
social movement, 68, 218, 220, 222, **232–3**

socialism, 24, 27, 28, 45, 46, 48–51,
    54, 55, 63–5, 67–8, 71, 73–5, **75–7**,
    78–9, 104, 111, 122, 142, 209–10,
    248, 257
sovereignty, **37–9**, 39, 118, 145, 157,
    197, 198, 212, 238, 240, 247, 258,
    259, 260
Stalin, J., 40, 162, 166; *see also*
    Stalinism
Stalinism, 28, 40, 49, 65, 162, 166
state, 16, 17, 25, 29, 37, **39–42**, 45, 49,
    50, 61, 62, 68, 72, 74, 77, 90, 93, 97,
    106, 118, 121, 126, 139, 176,
    184–5, 237–65
subsidiarity, **258–9**
Sula, 166
supranationalism, 21, 57, 246, 258,
    259–60
systems theory, 20, 89, **107–9**, 183

Tawney, R. H., 131, 139, **268**
Thatcher, M., 68, 133; *see also*
    Thatcherism
Thatcherism, 69, 78, 133, 159

theocracy, 72
theory, 98; *see also* political theory
third way, 28, **78–9**
toleration, 58, 60, **149–50**, 177
Tönnies, F., 122
Toryism, 51, **79–80**
totalitarianism, 17, 28, 57, 157, 166,
    171, **184–5**, 232
tradition, 27, 53, 62, 79, 102, **150–1**
trusteeship, 145
Tulloch, G., 104

Übermensch, 137
utilitarianism, 32, 61, 96, 103,
    109–10, 148–9
utility, 109
utopianism, 46, 68, 92, **110–12**, 184

Verba, S., 216–17
Völksgemeinschaft, **123**

Weber, M., 8, 15, 28, **39–42**, 192, **268**
welfare, 53, 63, 119, 130, 147, **151–3**

Zen Buddhism, 8